# *Home Cooking*
## THE COSTCO WAY™

Pasta with Broccoli Rabe
can be found on page 89.

# Home Cooking
## THE COSTCO WAY™

*Fantastic recipes using Costco products*

Tim Talevich
*Editorial Director*

*With a foreword by*
Mary M. Ostyn

Issaquah, Washington

| | |
|---|---|
| Senior Vice President E-commerce and Publishing: | Ginnie Roeglin |
| Publisher: | David W. Fuller |
| Editorial Director: | Tim Talevich |
| Art Director: | Doris Winters |
| Associate Editorial Director: | Anita Thompson |
| Associate Art Director: | Lory Williams |
| Associate Editor: | Judy Gouldthorpe |
| Senior Designer: | Dawna Tessier |
| Photographers: | Darren Emmens Devin Seferos Kate Baldwin |
| Food Stylists: | Amy Muzyka-McGuire Christine Jackson |
| Kitchen Manager: | Linda Carey |
| Studio Assistant: | Melissa Fraser |
| Business Manager: | Jane Klein-Shucklin |
| Advertising Manager: | Steve Trump |
| Assistant Advertising Manager: | Kathi Tipper |
| Advertising Assistants: | Melanie Woods Toni Pinto |
| Advertising Copywriter: | Bill Urlevich |
| Online Editor: | David Wight |
| Production Manager: | Pam Sather |
| Assistant Production Manager: | Antolin Matsuda |
| Prepress Supervisor/ Color Specialist: | MaryAnne Robbers |
| Print Management: | James Letzel and Ayako Chang, GSSI |
| Distribution: | Rossie Cruz Dorothy Strakele |

All food photographs by Iridio Photography, Seattle, Washington, with the following exceptions:
Anna Allen, 7
Ed Oulette/© Sandra Lee Semi-Homemade®, 10, 11
Mark Bennington, 12 (author's photo)
Keller & Keller, 13 (Kimball photo)
California Pear Advisory Board, 27 (top right)
Citterio, 61
Evan Sung, 89 (chef photo)
Lis Parsons, 99 (chef photo)
McCormick, 147 (top right)
Folgers, 179 (top right)

FIRST EDITION
Printed by Daehan Printing & Publishing, (Mirae N Culture Co., Ltd.), Seoul, South Korea
ISBN-13: 978-0-9819003-1-5
ISBN-10: 0-9819003-1-3
Library of Congress Control Number: 2009932546

Cover photo recipe page 85

27

94

# Contents

110

203

# To Our Valued Members

We are delighted to offer this gift in time for the holidays—our eighth annual cookbook in our series of *Costco Way* cookbooks—to thank you for your business and loyal membership. This book has been made possible through the support of Costco's many food suppliers.

As in past years, we've asked our suppliers to develop recipes that showcase their products that we sell at Costco. We have also included recipes from many of our favorite celebrity chefs such as Nigella Lawson, Rocco DiSpirito and Mark Bittman in the "Chef's Choice" section in the center of the book. These top chefs have worked their magic to develop recipes and tips using their favorite ingredients from Costco. Most of the recipes throughout the book have a short list of affordable, readily available ingredients and are quick and easy to prepare.

This year, you'll find a new chapter, "Stretching Your Food Dollar," in the beginning of the book. We have asked leading experts, including Sandra Lee and Christopher Kimball of *Cook's Illustrated* magazine, to share tips on creating a food budget, buying in bulk, stretching meals, storing food and making the most of the leftovers—all relevant topics in these economic times. This chapter also includes advice from authors Kati Neville and Lindsay Tkacsik on their "fix, freeze and feast" method, and concludes with a couple dozen great ideas from Costco members, which I think you'll find particularly clever.

Again this year, some of the recipes have nutritional information listed with them. This is helpful for anybody watching calories and following a controlled, healthful diet.

Above everything else, the secret to all the great dishes featured in this book is top-quality ingredients. When you purchase your ingredients from Costco, you know that you are getting the best—and at a great price.

We hope you enjoy *Home Cooking The Costco Way* and try out our recipes with your family and friends. You can also find our past years' cookbooks online at Costco.com. Just type "Costco Cookbooks" in the search window on our home page.

Bon appétit from all of us at Costco!

*Ginnie Roeglin*

Ginnie Roeglin,
Senior Vice President,
E-commerce and Publishing

# Foreword

We all know the drill. You walk into the grocery store with a long list and a finite budget. The last thing you want to do is spend two weeks' worth of grocery money on one week of food. But prices these days make it ever more challenging to stay within a budget.

As the mother of 10 kids—most of them hungry teens and preteens—I believe in the power of a good grocery list. But saving money goes beyond list-making. And it doesn't doom you to endless beans and rice.

Think in terms of meals, not just ingredients. Before I head to the store, I sit down with a notebook and a heap of cookbooks and plan two weeks of dinners. Half the meals are family favorites. Pasta, Thai food and pizza are regulars at our house. Then I thumb through cookbooks and fill the rest of the two-week menu with new and interesting-sounding recipes.

When trying new recipes, I focus on taste, cost and ease of cooking. Don't overlook ethnic food. I've found Chinese, Mexican and Ethiopian food to be both affordable and delicious. Once I have each day's dinner figured out, I write down needed ingredients for each recipe. I then fill out the grocery list with pantry staples and easy breakfast and lunch items.

Shopping with a complete list means fewer trips to the store, which cuts back on impulse buying, a real budget-breaker. Where you shop is important too. I've been a Costco member almost as long as I've been a tightwad. Family-sized items make pantry-stocking a cinch. Affordable prices and unbeatable quality lets you buy with confidence.

If you are looking to expand your cooking repertoire, this year's Costco cookbook, *Home Cooking The Costco Way*, is a great place to start. All of these recipes can be made with products available at Costco. I think you'll love the convenience and the taste, and of course, the value.

Wishing you all the best on your own cooking adventure!

*Mary Ostyn is the author of* Family Feasts for $75 a Week *(available at* Costco.com*).*
*She blogs at* http://owlhaven.net.

*Mary M. Ostyn*

Mary M. Ostyn

# About This Book

This is the eighth year we have created a cookbook designed to showcase the exciting array of foods sold at Costco. As with the last five books, *Home Cooking The Costco Way* will be handed out to members on a first-come, first-served basis the weekend after Thanksgiving as a token of our appreciation for their membership.

As with Costco itself, the format of the book is simple and direct. In keeping with the tenor of the times, this year we have focused our special features at the front of the book on ways to get the best value out of dollars that may be more stretched than they have been in the past. We thank Food Network star Sandra Lee, authors Kati Neville and Lindsay Tkacsik, and *Cook's Illustrated* editor Chris Kimball for their articles in that section. And we thank the many members who sent us budget-stretching tips.

Our popular "Chef's Choice" chapter offers 26 pages of recipes developed by some of the country's most accomplished chefs. All of these chefs have achieved national or international renown with cookbooks of their own, television shows and/or exceptional restaurants. Thanks to all of them for helping to make this another exciting addition to *The Costco Way* cookbook series.

The rest of the book is arranged in a basic manner with sections for breakfasts, appetizers, salads and soups, side dishes, entrées, desserts and beverages. The index at the back of the book contains listings by recipe and food item. We also have included a "Supplier Listing" section with contact information for all of the participating food suppliers.

Every recipe has been identified with the supplier's name and logo. We want to thank each of these suppliers for their support of this book. (Please note that some branded products may not be sold in your part of the country. In such cases, you should substitute a similar product.)

I hope you will enjoy this offering of culinary delights and that some of these dishes become your own home cooking favorites.

David W. Fuller,
Publisher

# Home Cooking
## THE COSTCO WAY ™

# Stretching Your
# Food Dollar

I n these economic times, people are looking at stretching their dollars everywhere, and that includes their food budget. I have good news: It's not that hard to do! I firmly believe that you can save a little money here and there in your kitchen—and that when it all adds up, it means extra money for other needs in your life. This chapter of *Home Cooking The Costco Way* provides a variety of smart tips to help stretch your food dollar, from making meals in bulk in advance to smart storage ideas. I especially like the clever tidbits provided by Costco members. I'll start things off with my Top 15 money-saving tips. Remember, eating together at home is a beautiful way of sharing. And it makes sense in terms of the budget, too.—*Sandra Lee*

# Sandra's Top 15 money-saving tips

**Sandra Lee**
Costco member Sandra Lee is editor-in-chief of *Sandra Lee Semi-Homemade* magazine, the host of two highly rated Food Network television shows (the multi-Emmy-nominated *Semi-Homemade Cooking* and *Sandra's Money Saving Meals*), and a *New York Times* bestselling author. For more about Sandra, see her Web site, *www.SandraLee.com.*

## Don't go with your gut. Plan, make a list and stick to it.

Plan your meals out for the week and make a list that you stick to. This prevents impulse purchases.

## Measure ingredients accurately.

Be careful when measuring ingredients. For example, Pumpkin Pie Spice is one of my pantry items because it brings so much flavor to a dish. One teaspoon of an average brand costs about 71 cents. If you make that a heaping teaspoon, you are at a dollar.

## Buy staples in bulk.

Buying items in bulk, such as a 5-pound bag of onions, will save you money. Buying a whole chicken and cutting it yourself will save more than 50 percent. You can also save money with family packs of chicken and 3-pound bags of ground meat.

## Think about sensible substitutes.

Can you substitute a less expensive ingredient? For example, for my Slow Cooker Cheesecake I used ricotta, costing me $1.67, compared to cream cheese at $3.75. I save $2.08, or 55 percent.

## Eat your veggies.

Feel-good meals with healthy bases, such as black bean burgers, cost about 67 cents per person to make.

## Stock your pantry well.

Keeping a few key items on hand, such as seasonings, baking mix, condiments and lean protein, will ensure that a tasty meal is just a mixing spoon away.

## Invest in a slow cooker.

Slow cookers use just 100 watts of electricity, which means that if you use it once a week for eight hours at a time, it'll only cost you about 20 cents a month in electricity!

## Be clever with cookware.

Some products do double-duty as cooking and serving pieces, and more. For example, a three-in-one cake server can serve as a cake stand, chip and dip platter, and punch bowl.

## If it's out of season, go frozen.

The frozen section is where you can get an item that is out of season at a reasonable price. In season, four ears of corn will run you $1; out of season, one ear will cost you $1. You can get a bag of corn, frozen at the peak of freshness, for around $1.99, equaling about four ears.

## Do the prep work yourself.

One medium onion that you chop yourself will cost you 28 cents; the same amount of frozen prechopped onion will cost you double that, 56 cents. At the salad bar, it would cost $4.99 per pound. I now chop my own garlic, a bulb at a time. I pay 75 cents for the bulb; pre-chopped, it would be about $1.99.

## Be creative.

Inexpensive condiments such as mustard, hot sauce or soy sauce can make a meal sing.

## Encore, encore.

Still have meat on a main dish such as ham? It only takes 2 cups of ham to star in a Ham and Potato Casserole, Ham and Rice Casserole or Ham and Spinach Bake.

## Bottle it up.

A teaspoon of lemon juice from the bottle costs 15 cents versus fresh lemons at 25 cents—that's a 40 percent savings.

## Waste not, want not.

Freeze food in individual or meal-size portions.

## Eat, drink light, and be merry.

A cup of milk costs 24 cents, compared to 96 cents for a cup of light cream. And heavy cream costs $1.52 per cup.

# Fix, freeze and feast

**Kati Neville and Lindsay Tkacsik**
Kati Neville and Lindsay Tkacsik are Costco members, enthusiastic make-ahead cooks and founders of meal assembly businesses. Their mission: help busy parents put delicious meals on the table, at a low cost, and with minimal effort.

To pour sauce into a freezer bag, put the bag in a large plastic sour cream or cottage cheese tub. Fold the top of the bag over the rim of the container.

One smart way to prepare food is through the "fix, freeze, feast" method, advise Costco members Kati Neville and Lindsay Tkacsik. In fact, they wrote a cookbook with that name (Storey Publishing, 2007, *www.fixfreezefeast.com*). This approach is smart, they say, because it:

■ Saves money by using large, economical package sizes, like the ones found at Costco;

■ Saves time by having you prepare several meals in about the same time it takes to make a single one;

■ Helps you serve healthy meals rather than last-minute "make-do's" or fast food.

The method calls for setting up an assembly line of sorts to make several meals, freezing them, then pulling them out when the time is right. For example, you might make a large batch of Chicken Cordon Bleu using one package (about 7 pounds) of boneless, skinless chicken breasts from Costco. This recipe would yield three entrées, each serving four people. Here's a look at how it works.

## Fix

**Preparation is key.** Keep your pantry and fridge stocked with the essentials such as honey, soy sauce, olive oil, balsamic vinegar, onions, brown sugar, garlic, eggs, dry bread crumbs, oregano, ketchup, black pepper and butter. It's also important to start with a tidy kitchen with the sink empty and the countertops clear.

Doing the prep work is the next step. That means mincing and chopping all ingredients as instructed, and having it all ready before assembly.

There's one last step: Make labels for your meals. Get the freezer bags you'll need for your meals and label them—it's a lot easier to do this when they're flat. Including cooking directions on the labels is a smart idea.

## Freeze

After the meals are prepared, carefully packaging and freezing them help ensure quality. Follow these tips:

■ When making marinades, use a large, clear liquid measuring cup instead of a bowl. This will take the guesswork out of evenly dividing up the liquid among bags.

■ Use heavy-duty freezer bags. Quality storage containers also work well, but freezer bags can save space. Remove as much air as possible from any container you use to prevent ice crystals.

■ If you're packing meat with bones, double-bag the meal to help avoid leaks.

■ Keep a freezer inventory to know what you have stored.

## Feast

All the hard work is done. For safety, always thaw frozen meals in the fridge, not on the counter. Once an entrée has been thawed, you must cook it. Follow directions given in the original recipe.

**One last tip:** Consider swapping your frozen meals with friends. This adds variety to your meals and helps you expand your cooking repertoire.

Home Cooking The Costco Way

# Storing food right

**Christopher Kimball**

Christopher Kimball is the founder of America's Test Kitchen, home to *Cook's Illustrated* and *Cook's Country* magazines and the company's growing book publishing program. He is also the host of the hit public TV shows *America's Test Kitchen* and *Cook's Country*. He lives in Boston and Vermont with his wife and four children.

Buying food in large quantities can save you money, but not if the food goes bad. So what's the best way to store common kitchen staples and how long will they really last? *Cook's Illustrated* offers these tips:

## Butter

When stored in the refrigerator, **butter** (even when wrapped) can pick up odors and turn rancid within a few weeks. Keep butter in the freezer and transfer it, one stick at a time, to the fridge.

## Chocolate

Never put **chocolate** in the fridge or freezer. Wrap opened bars of chocolate tightly in plastic and store in a cool pantry. Milk and white chocolates will keep for up to six months; **semisweet**, **bittersweet** and **unsweetened** chocolate are fine for one year.

## Coffee

**Ground coffee** belongs in the freezer. If you have an extra 10 minutes, measure frozen ground coffee into the filter and let it warm to room temperature. It will make better-tasting coffee than super-cold grounds.

## Eggs

Do not store **eggs** in the egg tray in your refrigerator. The paper carton protects eggs from picking up odors. Keep the eggs on a shelf in the fridge, not on the door. Keeping eggs in their carton also lets you track their expiration or sell-by date.

## Flour

Humidity is the biggest enemy for **flour**. Transfer flour to an airtight container. Make sure to use a container that's wide enough to dip a dry measure into.

The natural oils in **whole-wheat flour** and **cornmeal** go rancid after just a few months. If you go through whole-grain flours slowly, slip packages into large zipper-lock bags and store them in the freezer.

## Nuts

Keep all **nuts** in the freezer; they'll stay fresh for at least 1 year.

## Oils

Avoid light and heat. Even when stored in a cool pantry, flavorful oils (like **olive** and **toasted sesame**) will become rancid after several months. Keep toasted sesame oil in the fridge. Keep olive oil in the pantry; don't buy more than you can use in a few months.

Don't keep neutral-tasting oils, such as **canola** and **vegetable**, for longer than 6 months. If in doubt, heat a little oil in a skillet. If the oil has an off smell, throw out the bottle. Also, over-the-hill oils become viscous with time and sticky under the cap.

## Spices and dried herbs

**Whole spices** will last about twice as long as ground spices. The flavor of **ground spices** will go downhill after a year, as will the flavor of **dried herbs**. Write the purchase date on stick-on dots to track the age of spices and herbs. To maximize the flavor from any dried herb, push the herb through a mesh sieve (or crush the herb between your fingers) to release flavorful oils.

## Sweeteners

**Granulated sugar** will keep indefinitely if stored in an airtight container. **Brown sugar** can become rock-hard after a few months. An airtight container slows down moisture loss, but once brown sugar gets hard, use this trick to revive it: Place the hardened sugar in a bowl, add a slice of sandwich bread, cover the bowl and microwave for 10 to 20 seconds.

**Honey and molasses** will last indefinitely. Keep **honey** out of the fridge, where it will crystallize. The biggest issue over time with these sweeteners is that the lids become stuck in place. Dip a paper towel in vegetable oil and wipe the threads of the jar with the oil. This keeps the lid from sticking.

Once opened, keep **maple syrup** in the fridge for up to 1 year. Unopened bottles are fine in the pantry for a few years.

*Reprinted with permission from Cook's Illustrated magazine. Selected articles and recipes are available online at www.cooksillustrated.com.*

# Food-smart tips from Costco members

For smart tips on stretching your food dollar at Costco, some of the best experts are Costco members themselves. We asked Costco members to submit their money-stretching tips and received hundreds of clever ideas. While some were a little extreme (we're not sure if reusing dental floss is a good idea), a selection of the best tips is included here.

How about you? If you have a great tip, submit it to *smarttips@costco.com*. We'll try to share it with other members, either in next year's cookbook or in *The Costco Connection*, our magazine that can be found online each month at Costco.com.

What a Costco rotisserie chicken is worth:
- Three enchiladas
- 23 English Cornish pasties (chicken-vegetable pies)
- 4 cups of chicken broth made from the bones

Would you say I'm stretching it?
—*Diana Sabel, Gig Harbor, Washington*

Save the mesh bags that produce comes in and reuse them. The big bags work great for sifting compost to sort out the large chunks. The small coarse bags can be turned into kitchen scrubbers. Cut off all metal bits, tie a knot in one end and fill it full of other mesh bags until it's a comfortable size for your hand. Scrunch it in and tie a knot to close. Last, use the bags for bath scrubs.

The large burlap rice bags work great for storing flower bulbs in the winter; they even have a handle already.
—*Rebecca Thelen, Saint Louis Park, Minnesota*

To use all the lemons in a large bag, squeeze some and freeze the juice in ice cube trays. (You can transfer the cubes to a freezer bag.) Use one cube in each glass of ice tea or lemonade for extra flavor without diluting the drink as ice cubes do.
—*Carol C. Godwin, Brighton, Michigan*

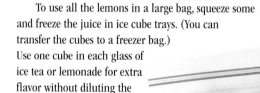

My family loves slices of fresh lemon in our drinks. To keep the lemons as fresh as possible, slice them and lay them on a small tray in the freezer for about 30 minutes. Then store the loose, frozen slices in a freezer bag in the freezer. Whenever you want some lemon for drinks, juicing or grating, pull out as many slices as needed.
—*Meredith Hilt, Bluemont, Virginia*

Save time and energy by using the clear plastic apple containers to store your holiday ornaments. The clear containers make items easy to see, and the shape keeps the items separated and safe.
—*Sandi Hill, Kirkland, Washington*

The wooden boxes that clementines come in have so many uses! At home, they are the perfect fit to hold the large-size seasonings and spices that Costco sells. One clementine box holds about 8 different spice containers, lots of gravy and mix packets, as well as many other small items in the pantry.
—*Patti Pitkin, Plainville, Connecticut*

14

Love Costco coffee both hot and cold? When you find you have extra coffee left over, instead of tossing it down the drain, freeze it in ice cube trays and store the cubes in a freezer bag. Next time you blend up Costco's Mocha Frappe Freeze, add some of your frozen coffee cubes to keep it cold without watering it down. You may love it so much you will find yourself making extra coffee on purpose.

—Denise Skyba, Snohomish, Washington

Strawberries … too many. Freeze them this easy way: Take a plastic deviled egg platter; place the largest strawberries in the oval sections; place the smaller strawberries in the center section of the platter; place the platter in the freezer; repeat when frozen solid; then place the berries in freezer bags (purchased at Costco), ready for berry recipes!

—Ann Holmberg, Post Falls, Idaho

Shopping in bulk at Costco is possible even for a family of two! Our regular purchases are:

**Almonds:** I grind up the entire bag in my food processor, then freeze in 2-cup plastic containers and use to sprinkle on oatmeal for breakfast, on vegetables and in baked goods.

**Oatmeal:** I place the entire 144-ounce package of Old-Fashioned Quaker Oats in the freezer until needed.

**Mozzarella:** I divide the bag into 2-cup containers, freeze and use as needed—in salads and open-faced broiled sandwiches, and on burgers and pizza.

—Deborah Sullivan, Chapel Hill, North Carolina

Even when there are only two people in the family, shopping at Costco works so well and saves money! When I cook I plan for at least two meals.

■ Roasted chicken appears the next day as Chinese chicken salad.

■ Ground beef makes meat loaf and also spaghetti sauce.

■ Fresh fruits and vegetables (remember, five a day!) are the most time consuming, so plan for at least two meals and also keep a batch ready for healthy snacks. Wash, peel and prep enough for an encore appearance. Store in an airtight container and do not add dressing until it is served.

—Gail Covitt,
Encinitas, California

When I buy the 5 pounds of spinach and large fresh mushrooms, I rinse them, put them into small zip-top bags and add a little olive oil and some garlic powder to each. I place each bag in the microwave for 1-2 minutes. They freeze beautifully and when I want spinach or mushrooms, I just defrost and they are as fresh as when I first bought them. I sauté them with fresh garlic and olive oil.

—Toni Jacobus, Naples, Florida

For those Costco customers in the rare situation of having leftover wine, small amounts can be frozen in ice cube trays; once frozen transferred to zip-top freezer bags; and used in soups, stews, etc., for enhancing flavor as needed/wanted.

—Karen Verdura, Farmington Hills, Michigan

I use ice cube trays to freeze onions, green peppers, green chilis, extra 505 green chile sauce, etc. Chop the veggies in a blender, pour into ice cube trays and freeze. Pop into gallon zip-top bags when frozen and return to the freezer.

—Debbie Vernell, Gypsum, Colorado

My 2- and 4-year-old sons love drinking yogurt. I buy plain yogurt at Costco and mix it with fresh fruit or juice to make drinking yogurt. They love the idea of making their own drinks and in the process they learn how colors when mixed together become some other color.

—Clara Yang, Placerville, California

When purchasing Costco-size quantities of yogurt cups, freeze several of them with a popsicle stick inserted into the top foil for a summer or anytime treat. Kids and adults alike love them.

—Linda Carey, Seattle, Washington

# Breakfasts

## Sausage and Rosemary Strata
### Panné Provincio

Cooking spray
1 pound breakfast sausage
8 large eggs
1 cup water
6 cups cubed (1/2 inch)
   Panné Provincio
   Roasted Garlic Bread
1 tablespoon chopped
   fresh rosemary
1 cup shredded
   Cheddar cheese

Preheat oven to 350°F. Coat 8 individual ramekins or an 8-by-8-inch baking dish with cooking spray.

Sauté sausage over medium heat until cooked through, breaking into small pieces; set aside.

In a large bowl, combine eggs and water and whisk until well blended. Add bread cubes, cooked sausage, rosemary and shredded cheese and mix well. Let the mixture stand for 10 minutes.

Pour into the prepared dishes and set in the oven. Bake individual ramekins for 25 minutes or the baking dish for 40 minutes, or until the mixture is completely set and the internal temperature is at least 165°F.

Let cool for 5 minutes and then serve warm or turn out onto a plate and serve family-style. Makes 8 servings.

**Tips:** Top with chopped green onions to add color and flavor. Ham can be substituted for the sausage. Sprinkle with extra cheese after baking for a more indulgent option.

## Croissant Scramble
### Vie de France

1 Vie de France butter
   croissant
Vegetable oil
2 tablespoons chopped
   green bell pepper
2 tablespoons chopped
   red bell pepper
1 tablespoon
   chopped onion
3 large eggs
1 tablespoon heavy cream
1 tablespoon chopped
   mushrooms
Salt and pepper
1 1/2 slices tomato
3 slices avocado
Prepared hollandaise
   sauce (optional)

Using a 3-inch round cookie cutter, cut a hole in the middle of the croissant. Set aside.

Heat a medium sauté pan over medium heat. Add enough oil to coat the pan. Add peppers and onion and cook until slightly tender, about 5 minutes.

Whisk eggs and cream until fully blended. Add eggs to the pan and cook, stirring often, until no longer runny. Just before the eggs are finished, add mushrooms and salt and pepper to taste.

Place the 3 half-moon slices of tomato, standing up, along the back of the hole in the croissant.

Place the 3 slices of avocado, standing up, in front of the tomato.

Fill the hole with the eggs. Drizzle with hollandaise sauce, if desired. Makes 1 serving.

## Vegetarian Frittata with Feta
The Oppenheimer Group/Michael Cutler Co.

3 eggs

6 egg whites

1/4 teaspoon ground black pepper

1 tablespoon minced fresh basil

2 teaspoons olive oil

1 garlic clove, minced

1/2 Cutler jumbo yellow onion, diced

1 Oppenheimer red, yellow or orange bell pepper, seeded and chopped

1 zucchini, sliced

2 cups spinach, torn into 1-inch pieces

1 ounce feta cheese, crumbled

1 cup chopped fresh tomatoes

Whisk eggs, egg whites, black pepper and basil in a medium bowl until frothy; set aside.

Preheat the oven broiler.

Heat olive oil in a medium ovenproof skillet over medium-high heat. Add garlic and onion and sauté until softened. Add bell pepper and zucchini and sauté until softened. Add spinach and fold until wilted.

Pour the eggs over the sauté and fold to combine. Cook over medium-low heat, without stirring, until the eggs are mostly set.

Sprinkle feta over the frittata and broil until the cheese melts. Garnish with tomatoes. Makes 4 servings.

expect the world from us™

## Smoked Salmon, Goat Cheese and Potato Frittata
Kirkland Signature/Michael Foods

2 cups (16 ounces) Kirkland Signature* Real Egg Product

2 tablespoons chopped fresh basil

1/4 teaspoon salt

1/8 teaspoon ground pepper

2 tablespoons canola oil

1 20-ounce package refrigerated homestyle sliced potatoes, or 3 cups frozen shredded hash browns

1 cup thinly sliced red onion

1 cup chopped red bell pepper

3 ounces sliced smoked salmon

3 ounces goat cheese

Stir together Real Egg Product, basil, salt and pepper; set aside.

Heat oil over medium-high heat in a 12-inch nonstick skillet. Place potatoes and onions in a single layer in the skillet. Cook for 5-6 minutes, or until potatoes are golden brown on the bottom. Flip potatoes; add bell pepper and continue cooking for 4-5 minutes, or until potatoes are tender.

Reduce heat to medium-low. Top potatoes with salmon and crumbled goat cheese. Spread into a thin layer. Pour egg mixture evenly over the potatoes. Cook for 10-12 minutes, or until almost set.

Preheat the broiler.

Wrap the skillet handle with aluminum foil. Broil the frittata 4-6 inches from the heat for about 2 minutes, or until the egg mixture is set. Makes 4 servings.

*Brands may vary by region; substitute a similar product.*

## Egg, Bacon and Arugula Open-Faced Sandwiches
La Brea Bakery

12 ounces bacon
4 slices La Brea Bakery* Whole Grain Loaf
7 large eggs
1/4 cup heavy cream

Salt and pepper
2 tablespoons unsalted butter
1 large tomato, sliced
12 arugula leaves, stems discarded

Cook bacon in a 12-inch nonstick skillet over medium heat until crisp. Transfer to paper towels to drain. Keep warm, covered. Pour off fat from the skillet and wipe clean with paper towels.

Lightly toast the bread.

Whisk together eggs and cream; season to taste with salt and pepper. Heat butter in the skillet over medium-low heat. Add the eggs and cook, stirring slowly, until just cooked through.

Place tomato slices on the toasted bread, followed by arugula and bacon. Top with the scrambled eggs and a few grindings of pepper. Makes 4 servings.

*Brands may vary by region; substitute a similar product.*

## Nook and Cranny Soufflé
Thomas'

- 1 3-ounce package cream cheese, softened
- 6 Thomas'* Original Flavor English Muffins, split
- 2 cups (8 ounces) shredded Cheddar or Colby cheese, divided
- 6 eggs
- 2 cups milk
- 2 tablespoons chopped green onions
- 1 teaspoon Worcestershire sauce
- 1/2 teaspoon dry mustard
- 1/2 teaspoon salt
- 1/8 teaspoon pepper

Spread cream cheese on each muffin half. Cut into 1/2-inch cubes. Place half the cubes in a greased 11 3/4-by-7 1/2-by-1 3/4-inch baking dish. Top with 1 1/2 cups shredded cheese. Repeat with the remaining muffin cubes and 1/2 cup cheese.

In a large bowl, beat eggs until light and fluffy. Stir in the remaining ingredients. Pour over the muffins. Let stand for 15 minutes.

Preheat oven to 300°F.

Bake for 45 minutes, or until puffed and browned. Let stand for 10 minutes before serving. Makes 6 servings.

*Brands may vary by region; substitute a similar product.*

## Breakfast Wraps with Mango and Tomato Salsa
El Monterey

El Monterey* Breakfast Wraps (10 per box)

*SALSA*

- 2 ripe, firm mangoes, peeled, pitted and cubed
- 3 cups peeled and finely chopped plum tomatoes
- 2 small white onions, finely chopped
- 4 garlic cloves, crushed
- 2-3 red chiles, finely chopped
- 10 tablespoons lemon juice
- Grated peel of 1 lemon
- 2-3 teaspoons sugar
- Salt to taste

Mix all salsa ingredients in a bowl. Cover and chill well before serving.

Prepare breakfast wraps according to package directions for the microwave. Top with the salsa. Makes 10 servings.

*Brands may vary by region; substitute a similar product.*

# Hearty Egg Casserole

Moark LLC/Nucal Foods/
Cal-Maine Foods/Zephyr Egg/Wilcox
Farms/Hillandale Farms/Oakdell Egg
Farms/Hickman's Family Farms

Cooking spray

1 28-ounce package frozen
  Southern-style hash brown
  potatoes (about 6 cups)

1 8-ounce package shredded sharp
  Cheddar cheese (2 cups)

10 eggs, well beaten

1 cup reduced-fat sour cream

1 cup skim or low-fat milk

2 tablespoons honey Dijon mustard
  (optional)

1 teaspoon salt

1/4 teaspoon ground pepper

Sliced red onion (optional)

Parsley sprig (optional)

Mixed greens (optional)

Preheat oven to 350°F. Evenly coat a 13-by-9-inch (3 quart) glass baking dish with cooking spray.

Evenly spread potatoes in the baking dish. Sprinkle with cheese.

In a large bowl, beat together eggs, sour cream, milk, mustard, salt and pepper until thoroughly blended. Pour over the potatoes.

Bake until puffed and browned and no visible liquid egg remains, about 45 minutes.

Garnish with onion and parsley. Serve with mixed greens. Makes 8 servings.

# Breakfast Burritos
## Kirkland Signature/Orleans International

1 pound Kirkland Signature
   ground beef
1 sweet onion, chopped, divided
2-3 garlic cloves, chopped, divided
1 packet taco seasoning mix
2 tablespoons butter
2  4-ounce cans diced green chiles,
   or to taste

12 eggs
3-6 tablespoons milk
25 cherry tomatoes, cut into
   small pieces
Salt and pepper
12 large flour tortillas
Shredded cheese

Preheat oven to 175°F.

Cook ground beef and half of the onions and garlic in a skillet over medium heat, stirring to crumble. When the beef is browned, stir in taco seasoning mix. Drain liquid from the pan.

Melt butter over medium heat in a large skillet. Add chiles and remaining onions and garlic and sauté until the onion is translucent.

Beat eggs with milk in a bowl.

Add eggs to the large skillet, then the seasoned ground beef mixture, tomatoes, and salt and pepper to taste. Cook, stirring, until the eggs are done.

Spoon the egg mixture into tortillas. Top with shredded cheese and roll into burritos.

Wrap each burrito in foil. Keep warm in the oven until ready to serve.
Makes 8-12 servings.

## Peach Potato Pancakes
Trinity Fruit

3 russet potatoes
2 eggs
1 teaspoon seasoning salt
1/2 teaspoon baking powder
1/2 cup vegetable oil
8 Trinity peaches, divided
2 tablespoons butter
1 teaspoon brown sugar
1/2 teaspoon flour

Peel and grate potatoes; place in a bowl.

In another bowl, mix eggs, seasoning salt and baking powder. Blend half of the mixture into the potatoes, then pour back into the bowl and mix.

Heat oil in a sauté pan over medium-high heat. Pour in 1/2 cup of batter and cook until golden brown on both sides. Repeat with remaining batter. Put prepared pancakes in a warm oven.

Peel and slice 6 peaches. Melt butter in a large saucepan over medium heat. Add peaches. Stir in sugar and flour and cook until the sugar is dissolved and the peaches soften. Puree the mixture.

Slice the remaining 2 peaches.

To serve, put a dollop of peach puree on each pancake, then place several peach slices on top.
Makes 4 servings.

*Recipe developed by Lisa White.*

## Homemade Oatmeal
Oregon Chai

1 1/2 cups of your favorite Oregon Chai* concentrate ❧Organic
2/3 cup organic rolled oats
1 tablespoon oat bran
1/4 cup oven-toasted thinly sliced almonds
1/4 cup dried cranberries or other dried fruit
Organic milk

Place chai, rolled oats and oat bran in a saucepan and bring to a boil. The chai concentrate can be diluted with water for individual taste preference.

Once the mixture is boiling, stir and turn off the burner. Cover and let it sit for at least 5 minutes in the saucepan.

Stir the oatmeal and spoon into bowls. Sprinkle with toasted almonds and dried fruit. Add a splash of milk. Makes 2-3 servings.

*\* Brands may vary by region; substitute a similar product.*

# Appetizers

## Peach Salsa
### I.M. Ripe

6 I.M. Ripe peaches, peeled and chopped

4 Roma tomatoes, chopped

2 serrano chiles, finely chopped

3 green onions, chopped

1 avocado, chopped

4 tablespoons extra-virgin olive oil

2 tablespoons sherry vinegar

2 tablespoons chopped fresh cilantro

Juice of 1 lemon

Juice of 1 lime

Salt

Tortilla chips, for serving

In a bowl, combine peaches, tomatoes, chiles, onions and avocado. Stir to blend.

In a small bowl, whisk together olive oil, vinegar, cilantro, and lemon and lime juice. Pour over the peach mixture and stir to blend. Add salt to taste.

Serve with tortilla chips. Makes 10-12 servings.

**Tip:** This also goes well with pork and shrimp.

## Fruit Salsa and Cinnamon Chips
### Sage Fruit

*FRUIT SALSA*

2 tablespoons granulated sugar

3 tablespoons brown sugar

3 tablespoons jam, any flavor

2 Sage Fruit* Fuji apples, peeled, cored and diced

1/2-3/4 pound Sage Fruit* Rainier or dark sweet cherries, pitted and diced

8-12 ounces frozen raspberries, thawed

12-16 ounces frozen strawberries (unsweetened), thawed and sliced

2 kiwis, peeled and diced

*CHIPS*

2 cups granulated sugar

1 tablespoon ground cinnamon

10  10-inch flour tortillas

Cooking spray

To prepare the fruit salsa, combine the sugars in a large bowl, then add the jam and mix. Add remaining salsa ingredients and stir to blend. Add more sugar if desired. Cover and chill for at least 15 minutes.

Preheat oven to 350°F.

To prepare the chips, place sugar and cinnamon in a gallon-size resealable plastic bag. Shake to mix. Coat both sides of a tortilla with cooking spray. Cut into 8 wedges. Place wedges in the bag and shake until coated. Arrange in a single layer on a baking sheet. Repeat with the remaining tortillas.

Bake for 15 minutes, turning the wedges over halfway through baking. The chips should be slightly crispy; they will crisp more as they cool. Let cool for about 15 minutes.

Serve the chips with the fruit salsa. Makes 4-6 servings.

*\* Brands may vary by region; substitute a similar product.*

# Gingered Cream Cheese Grapes
Unifrutti of America

6 ounces cream
   cheese, softened
2 tablespoons
   finely chopped
   crystallized ginger
30 green seedless grapes
1 cup pecans, toasted
   lightly, cooled
   completely and
   chopped fine

In a bowl, cream together cream cheese and ginger.

Put 1 teaspoon of the cream cheese mixture in the palm of your hand and roll it around a grape, using both palms to coat the grape completely. Place the coated grapes on a tray lined with waxed paper and chill for 15 minutes.

Roll the cheese-coated grapes in the pecans, coating completely. Chill until the coating is firm.
Makes 30 grapes.

# Melon-Teasers
Dulcinea

30-40  2-inch squares
   (about 1 inch thick)
   Dulcinea PureHeart
   mini watermelon
1 cup Tuscan-Style
   cantaloupe cut in
   1/4-inch dice
1 tablespoon white
   balsamic vinegar
4 strips of prosciutto
2 tablespoons thinly
   sliced fresh basil

Place watermelon squares on a serving platter. Scoop out a space in the center of each square (a melon baller works well for this).

In a bowl, toss together diced cantaloupe and vinegar. Spoon into the center of the watermelon squares.

Place prosciutto between double layers of paper towels and microwave on high for 3 minutes, or until crisp. Let cool slightly, then crumble and sprinkle over the watermelon.

Top with basil. Makes 8-10 servings.

**Tip:** Use small cookie cutters to make the watermelon shapes.

## Apple Cranberry Wonton Cups
Rainier Fruit Company

**Nonstick cooking spray**
**1 package small wonton wrappers (refrigerated)**
**1/4 cup butter or margarine, melted**
**Confectioners' sugar (optional)**

**FILLING**
**4 medium Rainier Fruit\* Cameo or Fuji apples**
**1 tablespoon lemon juice (optional)**
**3/4 cup sugar**
**1/2 teaspoon ground cinnamon**
**1/8 teaspoon grated nutmeg**
**1/2 cup dried cranberries**
**1 tablespoon water**
**2 tablespoons flour**

Preheat oven to 350°F. Lightly coat a mini muffin pan with cooking spray.

Brush one side of the wonton wrappers with melted butter and fit them into the muffin cups, butter side up. Bake for 10 minutes, or until lightly browned. Remove from the pan and let cool on a rack. Place the cooled wontons back in the pan.

Peel and core apples, cut into quarters and dice into 1/2-inch cubes. Place in a sturdy pan and mix in lemon juice, sugar, cinnamon and nutmeg. Bring slowly to a boil, stirring occasionally. Add cranberries and boil for about 5 minutes.

Make a thin paste by stirring water into the flour. Add this mixture slowly to the apples and cranberries; cook, stirring constantly, until the mixture has thickened.

Carefully pour the boiling mixture evenly into the wonton cups. Return to the oven for 15 minutes, or until the filling is bubbling.

Remove from the oven, let cool slightly and serve, sprinkled with confectioners' sugar if desired. Makes about 30 cups.

*\* Brands may vary by region; substitute a similar product.*

## Fresh Herb Yogurt Dip with Sliced Pears
California Pear Advisory Board

**3 cups plain regular yogurt**
**2 tablespoons chopped fresh tarragon**
**2 tablespoons chopped fresh chives**
**1 tablespoon chopped fresh dill**
**1 tablespoon sherry vinegar**
**Freshly ground pepper**
**Dash of allspice**
**6 fresh California\* pears, any variety or a mix, sliced**
**Honey (optional)**

Line a sieve with a coffee filter or double thickness of cheesecloth. Suspend the sieve over a deep bowl. Spoon the yogurt into the filter, cover with plastic wrap, place in the refrigerator and let stand to allow the whey to drip out. When the yogurt has the consistency of soft, velvety, spreadable cheese, about 6 hours, scrape into a bowl.

Add herbs, vinegar, pepper to taste and allspice to the yogurt cheese. Stir. Cover and refrigerate for 2 hours or up to 24 hours.

Serve with sliced pears and a dollop of honey. Makes 6-9 servings.

**Nutritional information:** Each serving (1 large pear, 5 tablespoons dip) has 182 calories, 7 g protein, 40 g carbohydrates, 1 g fat, trace saturated fat, 2 mg cholesterol, 5 g fiber, 58 mg sodium.

*\* Brands may vary by region; substitute a similar product.*

## Balsamic-Herb Marinated Strawberries with Peppered Mascarpone and Crisp Bacon
Naturipe Farms

$1/2$ pound bacon

8 ounces mascarpone cheese

2 teaspoons coarsely ground black pepper

15 Naturipe Farms* fresh strawberries

1 teaspoon balsamic vinegar

1 teaspoon chopped fresh basil

1 teaspoon chopped flat-leaf parsley

Cut bacon across the shorter width into strips about $1/4$ inch wide. Sauté over medium heat, stirring occasionally, until deep brown. Drain well. Transfer to absorbent paper to remove excess fat and let cool.

Place mascarpone and pepper in a bowl and gently mix with a spatula or beater to incorporate the pepper evenly. Transfer the mixture to a pastry bag with a plain tip (see tip below). Keep refrigerated.

Trim strawberries and cut in half lengthwise. Keep refrigerated.

To serve, gently toss strawberries with vinegar, basil and parsley. Arrange cut-side up on a tray. Pipe a small amount of cheese onto each berry. Garnish with bacon. Makes 30 appetizers.

**Tips:** A good pastry bag to use is an Ateco with a # 807 tip. If you don't have one, a small zip-top plastic bag does the trick. Just snip off a lower corner of the bag to pipe the cheese out. Also, freezing the bacon makes it easier to cut. Freeze it, cut it, then cook it.

*Brands may vary by region; substitute a similar product.*

## Blueberry Mini-Satays with Yogurt Dip and Spicy Pine Nut Topping
Naturipe Farms

1 cup yogurt, full-fat

1 teaspoon ground cumin

1 tablespoon sugar

2 teaspoons minced chives

$1/2$ cup toasted pine nuts, chopped

$1/2$ teaspoon ground roasted chiles (or $1/8$ teaspoon crushed red pepper)

1 teaspoon ground sesame seeds

$1/4$ teaspoon kosher salt

6 ounces (about 150) Naturipe Farms* fresh blueberries

30 small decorative skewers

In a shallow bowl, combine yogurt, cumin, sugar and chives. Whisk together until the sugar dissolves.

In another shallow bowl, combine pine nuts, ground chiles, sesame seeds and salt. Whisk until well blended.

Thread 5 blueberries onto each skewer.

Dip one side of each blueberry satay in the yogurt mixture. Then push that same side into the pine nut mixture to adhere. Makes 30 satays.

*Brands may vary by region; substitute a similar product.*

## Grilled Shrimp Cocktail Skewers
Mastronardi Produce/Sunset

6 metal skewers or 10-inch heavy wood skewers, soaked in water

1/2 medium sweet onion, cut into 1-inch chunks (or 18 pickled cocktail onions)

1 pint Sunset Splendido* grape tomatoes

12 medium raw shrimp, peeled and deveined

Oil for brushing

Salt and pepper

1/2 cup purchased cocktail sauce, plus more for serving if desired

2-3 cups lettuce or spinach leaves

Lemon wedges, for serving

Thread ingredients onto each skewer in the following order: onion, grape tomato, shrimp. Repeat. Finish with a piece of onion and a tomato.

Lightly brush skewers on each side with oil and season to taste with salt and pepper.

Preheat grill to medium-high.

Grill the skewers, turning and basting regularly with cocktail sauce, until the shrimp is cooked through, about 5-6 minutes.

Arrange the skewers on a platter of lettuce or spinach. Serve with lemon wedges and additional cocktail sauce if desired. Makes 6 skewers.

*Brands may vary by region; substitute a similar product.*

Goodness Grown Naturally™

## Crispy Wontons with Crab Salad, Melted Cheddar and Avocado Crème
Tillamook

Vegetable oil for frying

30 3-inch round wonton wrappers

20 ounces crab meat, well drained

3/4 cup minced celery

3 tablespoons minced chives, plus more for garnish

4 teaspoons grated lemon peel

3/4 cup mayonnaise

2 tablespoons lemon juice

1/4 teaspoon ground black pepper

8 ounces (2 cups) Tillamook* medium Cheddar, shredded

### AVOCADO CRÈME

1/2 cup avocado pulp

1/4 teaspoon salt

1 tablespoon lemon juice

1/4 cup heavy cream

Pour enough oil into a pan to cover the wontons; heat to 350°F. Working in batches, lay wonton wrappers in the oil and fry until light golden brown. Drain on paper towels; set aside.

In a medium bowl, combine crab, celery, chives and grated lemon peel. Stir in mayonnaise, lemon juice and pepper.

To prepare the Avocado Crème, place avocado pulp, salt, lemon juice and cream in a small bowl and stir until well blended. Refrigerate until ready to use.

Preheat oven to 400°F.

Top the wontons with crab salad. Sprinkle each wonton with 1 tablespoon shredded cheese. Place on a baking sheet in the oven and heat just until the cheese is melted.

Arrange 3 wontons on each plate with a spoonful of Avocado Crème. Garnish with chives. Makes 10 servings.

*Brands may vary by region; substitute a similar product.*

**Tillamook®**

# Salmon Carpaccio
## Kirkland Signature/Foppen

3 1/2 ounces Kirkland Signature Imported Norwegian Smoked Salmon
1/4 lemon
1/4 key lime, halved
1 tablespoon oil
Small handful of arugula
Cucumber, sliced into 4-6 thin ribbons
Capers, for garnish

Arrange salmon slices in a thin layer on a plate.

Squeeze the juice from the lemon and 1 piece of key lime into a small cup. Add oil and stir to blend.

Toss arugula and cucumber with some of the dressing and set in the center of the salmon.

Drizzle the remaining dressing over the salmon. Place capers in a circle around the salad. Cut the remaining piece of key lime into wedges and use as a garnish. Makes 1 serving.

**Tip:** Serve with toast and butter.

# Tilapia Ceviche
## Rain Forest Aquaculture

7 ounces Rain Forest* fresh tilapia (1 large fillet)
2 tablespoons minced leek (green part only)
2 tablespoons minced red onion
1 1/2 ounces boiled potato, cut in cubes
2 teaspoons chopped toasted hazelnuts
1 3/4 ounces lemon juice
A pinch of Chilean merken (smoked chile powder)
Salt and freshly ground pepper

Cut tilapia into small square pieces. Place in a bowl, then add leek, onion, potato and hazelnuts.

Pour lemon juice over the ingredients. Add merken and salt and pepper to taste. Gently mix to blend.

Serve immediately. Makes 2 servings.

*\* Brands may vary by region; substitute a similar product.*

30

# Seared Scallop Ceviche with Clementine Dressing
## Aconex

2 tablespoons extra-virgin olive oil, plus more for searing

12 bay scallops

1 cup clementine juice

1 tablespoon lemon juice

1/4-1/2 teaspoon grated clementine peel

1/4-1/2 teaspoon grated lemon peel

1 tablespoon minced Hungarian or banana pepper (or a few drops of hot pepper sauce)

Salt

Freshly ground black pepper

1 cup thinly sliced red onions

3 tablespoons chopped chives

8-12 clementine wedges, for garnish

Heat a nonstick sauté pan over high heat. Add enough olive oil to coat the pan. Add scallops and sear for just a few seconds on each side, until you get a nice golden coat. Do not overcook. Set aside and let cool. Cut the seared scallops into cubes about 1/4 by 1/4 inch.

In a bowl, combine clementine juice, lemon juice, 2 tablespoons olive oil, grated clementine and lemon peel, Hungarian pepper, and salt and pepper to taste. Mix well. Stir in the scallops, onions and chives. Chill in the refrigerator.

Serve in clear glass bowls over crushed ice and garnish with clementine wedges. Makes 4 servings.

## Spiced California Walnuts
### Diamond Foods

1 egg white

1 tablespoon water

2 cups Kirkland Signature California walnut halves and pieces

1/2 cup sugar

1 tablespoon ground cinnamon

1/2 teaspoon ground allspice

Preheat oven to 225°F. Line a large shallow baking pan with foil.

In a bowl, combine egg white and water; beat until foamy. Add walnuts and toss to coat. Pour the mixture into a strainer and let drain for 2-3 minutes.

Combine sugar, cinnamon and allspice in a plastic or paper bag; shake to mix. Add the walnuts; hold the bag shut and shake vigorously to coat the nuts. Spread the nuts in one layer in the baking pan.

Bake for 1 hour, stirring every 15 minutes.

Remove from the oven and let cool completely, stirring occasionally and breaking the nuts apart if they are stuck together. Don't worry if they stick to the foil—it's easy to peel them off. Store in a tightly capped jar. Makes 2 cups.

## Italian Meat Skewers with Mozzarella and Tomatoes
### Daniele

8 bamboo skewers

16 cherry tomatoes

16 basil leaves

1 16-ounce package Daniele* Gourmet Variety Pack thin-sliced Italian meats (Capocollo, Calabrese and Peppered Genoa)

1 16-ounce ball fresh mozzarella, cut into 32 1/2-inch cubes

Olive oil

Cracked black pepper

Soak skewers in water for 45 minutes.

Preheat broiler on low.

Wrap each tomato in a basil leaf.

On each skewer, thread slices of assorted meats, interspersed with 2 cherry tomatoes wrapped in basil leaves and 4 mozzarella cubes. Fit 8 meat slices onto each skewer.

Place on a nonstick baking sheet and set on the middle oven rack. Broil for about 1-2 minutes, being careful that the cheese does not melt.

Arrange on a serving platter. Drizzle with olive oil and sprinkle with cracked black pepper. Makes 8 servings.

*Brands may vary by region; substitute a similar product.*

# Hummus Chicken Salad
## Sabra Go Mediterranean

$^1/_2$ cup Sabra* Hummus

2 tablespoons finely diced celery

1 tablespoon finely chopped green onions

1 tablespoon finely chopped red bell pepper

$^1/_4$ teaspoon salt

Freshly ground black pepper

1 cup cubed ($^1/_2$ inch) grilled chicken breast (about 2 boneless breast halves)

1 tablespoon water

1 teaspoon finely chopped fresh parsley, for garnish

Bread or salad greens, for serving

In a large bowl, stir hummus, celery, green onions, bell pepper, salt and a sprinkling of pepper.

Add chicken and water and stir until mixed thoroughly.

Sprinkle with parsley. Serve with bread or atop your favorite salad greens. Makes 4 servings.

**Tip:** To grill chicken breasts, season with salt and pepper and cook on a grill or in a grill pan for about 4 minutes on each side.

*Recipe developed by Chef Colombe Jacobsen.*
*\* Brands may vary by region; substitute a similar product.*

# Nuts and Cream Stuffed Mushrooms
Cardile Brothers/Giorgio Fresh/
Monterey Mushrooms

1 pound Cardile Brothers*
  large white mushrooms

1 cup finely chopped pecans

3 tablespoons chopped
  fresh parsley

1/4 teaspoon chopped
  fresh thyme

Pinch of salt

Dash of pepper

1/4 cup softened
  cream cheese

1 garlic clove, minced
  to a paste

1/2 cup heavy cream

Preheat oven to 350°F.

Rinse mushrooms and pat dry. Remove stems from mushrooms and chop enough to make 1 cup. Arrange the caps in a shallow baking dish.

Mix the chopped stems, pecans, parsley, thyme, salt, pepper, cream cheese and garlic together. Spoon into the mushroom caps.

Pour cream over the mushrooms and bake for 20-25 minutes, basting with the cream once or twice. Serve warm. Makes 4-6 servings.

*Brands may vary by region; substitute a similar product.*

# Crimini Mushrooms in Tarragon Cream Sauce on Toasted Brioche

4 tablespoons
  unsalted butter

2 shallots, chopped

1 pound Monterey* crimini
  mushrooms, sliced

2/3 cup heavy cream

3 tablespoons chopped
  fresh tarragon

4 slices brioche, toasted

Melt butter in a sauté pan over medium heat. Add shallots and cook slowly until translucent; do not brown.

Add mushrooms and cook until tender.

Add cream and tarragon. Lower the heat and cook until thick and creamy.

Serve over toasted brioche. Makes 4 servings.

*Brands may vary by region; substitute a similar product.*

# Mushroom Quesadillas

3 tablespoons olive
  oil, divided

1 cup thinly sliced red
  bell pepper

1 cup thinly sliced red onion

2 cups sliced fresh
  Giorgio* white or baby
  bella mushrooms

1 cup thinly sliced jalapeño
  pepper (optional)

8 8-inch flour tortillas

2 cups shredded Cheddar
  and Jack cheese

Heat 2 tablespoons olive oil in a skillet over medium heat. Add peppers, onions and mushrooms (and optional jalapeños) and sauté until tender. Set aside on a plate.

Add remaining olive oil to the pan. Place a tortilla in the pan. Top with mushroom mixture and sprinkle with cheese. Place another tortilla on top. Cook until the bottom tortilla has browned, then flip and cook until the other side is browned and the cheese has melted.

Cut into quarters and serve. Makes 4-6 servings.

*Brands may vary by region; substitute a similar product.*

# Stuffed Portobello Mushrooms
Kirkland Signature

2 tablespoons olive oil

1 pound tomatoes, diced

3 tablespoons
  Kirkland Signature
  dried chopped onion

2 teaspoons
  Kirkland Signature
  granulated garlic

1 cup vegetable broth

1 pound 4 ounce focaccia
  bread, cut into
  1-inch cubes

5 ounces fresh
  baby spinach

8 ounces mozzarella
  cheese, shredded

2 large eggs, beaten

12 portobello mushrooms,
  stems removed

Preheat oven to 350°F.

Heat olive oil in a sauté pan over medium heat. Add tomatoes, onion, garlic and vegetable broth. Cook until heated through.

In a bowl, combine bread cubes, spinach, mozzarella, eggs and the tomato mixture. Mix until well blended.

Place mushrooms on a parchment-lined sheet pan. Form the stuffing mixture into round balls and place in the mushroom caps, spreading to cover.

Bake for about 20 minutes, or until internal temperature is 160°F. Serve immediately. Makes 12 servings.

# Party Cheese Log
## Raskas

16 ounces Raskas* cream cheese, softened

1  10-ounce package sharp Cheddar cheese, shredded

1 tablespoon chopped red bell pepper or pimiento

1 tablespoon finely chopped onion

2 teaspoons Worcestershire sauce

4 teaspoons lemon juice

Dash of ground red pepper

Dash of salt

Chopped pecans, for garnish

Chopped fresh parsley, for garnish

In a large mixing bowl, beat cream cheese and Cheddar cheese with an electric mixer at medium speed until well blended. Add bell pepper, onion, Worcestershire sauce, lemon juice, red pepper and salt; mix well. Chill for several hours or overnight.

Shape the cream cheese mixture into a log. Garnish with pecans and parsley.

Serve with crackers. Makes 6 servings.

**Tip:** To soften cream cheese, microwave in a bowl on medium (50%) for 2 minutes.

*\* Brands may vary by region; substitute a similar product.*

SCHREIBER™

## Mediterranean Flatbread
Panné Provincio

2 Panné Provincio ciabatta rolls

4 tablespoons prepared hummus

1/2 cup peeled, seeded and diced cucumber

1/3 cup plain yogurt

1 tablespoon chopped fresh mint

Salt and pepper

6 ounces roasted lamb, thinly sliced

1/2 cup thinly sliced red onion

1/3 cup crumbled feta cheese

2 tablespoons finely diced fresh tomato

Preheat oven to 400°F.

Slice each ciabatta in half and place on a cookie sheet. Spread each of the 4 halves with hummus. Bake for 4-6 minutes, or until the crust has crisped.

In a bowl, combine cucumber, yogurt, mint, and salt and pepper to taste. Set aside.

To assemble, top ciabatta halves with sliced lamb, red onion and feta. Top with cucumber yogurt sauce and diced tomato. Cut each sandwich into halves or quarters. Makes 2 servings.

**Tips:** Steak or chicken can be used instead of lamb. For a vegetarian version, use goat cheese instead of hummus and grilled or roasted vegetables.

## Classic Bruschetta
Panné Provincio

3 Panné Provincio ciabatta rolls

Kosher salt

Freshly ground black pepper

### TOMATO TOPPING

1 cup diced fresh tomatoes

2 tablespoons extra-virgin olive oil

1 tablespoon balsamic vinegar

1 tablespoon chopped fresh basil

### WHITE BEAN PUREE

1 cup canned white beans, drained

1 teaspoon fresh rosemary

2 tablespoons extra-virgin olive oil

### ARTICHOKE TOPPING

1 cup marinated artichokes, chopped

2 tablespoons thinly sliced green onions

Preheat oven to 400°F.

Using a bread knife, slice each ciabatta roll vertically into eight 1/8-inch slices and place on a cookie sheet. Toast for 6-8 minutes, or until golden brown.

To prepare the tomato topping, combine tomatoes, olive oil, vinegar and basil. Season to taste with salt and pepper.

To prepare the white bean puree, combine beans, rosemary and olive oil in a food processor and blend for 30 seconds, or until smooth. Season to taste with salt and pepper.

To prepare the artichoke topping, combine artichokes and green onions. Season to taste with salt and pepper.

Add toppings to the toasted slices and serve. Makes 4 servings.

## Feta and Goat Cheese Spread with Apricot Honey Marmalade
Kirkland Signature

**8 ounces cream cheese, softened**

**3 1/2 ounces feta cheese, crumbled**

**3 1/2-4 ounces goat cheese, crumbled**

**Bruschetta, for serving**

***APRICOT HONEY MARMALADE***

**1 tablespoon honey**

**3 tablespoons apricot preserves**

**1 tablespoon balsamic vinegar**

**2 tablespoons Kirkland Signature dried chopped onion**

**1 tablespoon chopped fresh thyme**

Place cream cheese in a bowl and beat until creamy. Add feta and goat cheese and beat on low speed until well blended. Set aside.

To prepare the marmalade, combine honey, apricot preserves, vinegar, onion and thyme in a saucepan. Cook over medium heat until thickened. Let cool to room temperature.

Add marmalade mixture to the cheese mixture and whip on low speed until well blended. Cover and chill for up to 1 hour, or until stiff.

Serve on bruschetta. Makes 24 (1 tablespoon) servings.

**Tip:** This can also be used on grilled chicken sandwiches.

## Ahi Bruschetta
Norpac Fisheries Export

**8 ounces fresh bigeye ahi tuna (with good red color)**

**2 tablespoons chopped green onions**

**3 tablespoons mayonnaise (homemade is best)**

**1 tablespoon seasoning: equal parts black and white pepper, red pepper and garlic powder**

**1 tablespoon toasted sesame oil**

**1 tablespoon sesame seeds, toasted**

**1 tablespoon Chinese mustard**

**Dill sprigs, for garnish**

**Baguette sliced into 1/2-inch slices, lightly toasted**

**Young pickled ginger, for garnish**

Mince tuna with a sharp knife into 1/4-by-1/4-inch cubes (or as uniform in size as possible).

Place the tuna in a bowl and add green onions, mayonnaise, seasoning, sesame oil, sesame seeds and mustard. Stir to blend.

Mold the tuna into a small cup and garnish with dill sprigs. Serve with toasted baguette slices and pickled ginger on the side. Makes 8-10 servings.

*Recipe courtesy of Wild Ginger restaurant, Seattle.*

# Bruschetta with Gorgonzola and Apples
## Holtzinger Fruit

$^{1}/_{3}$ cup (about 1 $^{1}/_{2}$ ounces)
   crumbled Gorgonzola cheese

2 tablespoons butter, softened

1 tablespoon brandy or cognac

$^{1}/_{8}$ teaspoon ground black pepper

Cooking spray

12 slices (12 ounces) diagonally cut
   French bread, about 1 inch thick

6 garlic cloves, halved

3 Holtzinger Fruit* Granny Smith
   apples, each cut into 8 wedges
   (about 18 ounces)

Combine cheese, butter, brandy and pepper in a small bowl, stirring until blended.

Heat the grill to medium and coat with cooking spray. Add the bread slices and cook for 2 minutes on each side, or until lightly browned.

Remove the bread from the grill and rub one side of each slice with the cut side of a garlic clove. Spread 2 teaspoonfuls of the cheese mixture over each bread slice.

Serve with apple wedges. Makes 12 servings.

*Brands may vary by region; substitute a similar product.*

## Veal Meatballs
Plume De Veau

1 pound Plume De Veau*
ground veal

2 eggs, lightly beaten

1 cup Italian seasoned
bread crumbs

8 garlic cloves,
finely chopped

1 cup grated Pecorino
Romano cheese

1/2 cup chopped
fresh parsley

Salt and pepper

1 1/2 cups vegetable oil,
for frying

In a bowl, combine ground veal, eggs, bread crumbs, garlic, grated cheese, parsley, and salt and pepper to taste. Mix until well blended and shape into balls.

In a frying pan, heat oil to 350°F. Add the meatballs and cook until evenly browned. Remove with a slotted spoon and place on paper towels to absorb excess oil.

Serve plain or with tomato sauce. Makes 8 servings.

**Tip:** This recipe makes about 50 meatballs, perfect for appetizers. Try a marinara sauce as a dip.

* Brands may vary by region; substitute a similar product.

## Zesty Fiesta Sausage Dip
Jimmy Dean

16 ounces Jimmy Dean*
Regular or All Natural
Regular Roll Pork
Sausage

1 large onion, chopped
(about 1 cup)

1 large red bell pepper,
chopped (about 1 cup)

1-2 jalapeño peppers,
seeded and chopped

2 8-ounce packages
cream cheese, cubed

1 large tomato, seeded
and chopped (about
1 cup), plus more
for garnish

1/2 cup sweet or hot yellow
banana peppers (from
a jar), drained, seeded
and chopped

1/4 cup chopped fresh
cilantro, plus more
for garnish

Tortilla chips or crackers,
for serving

In a large skillet, cook sausage, onion, bell pepper and jalapeño over medium-high heat, stirring frequently, until the meat is thoroughly cooked and no longer pink and the vegetables are tender. Drain.

Reduce the heat to medium and stir in cream cheese. Cook and stir until the cream cheese is smooth and completely melted.

Stir in tomato, banana peppers and cilantro; cook until heated through.

Serve warm in a chafing dish, with chips or crackers for dipping. Garnish with additional diced tomato and cilantro, if desired. Makes 20 servings.

**Variation:** Substitute 1/4 cup chopped pickled jalapeño peppers for the fresh jalapeño.

* Brands may vary by region; substitute a similar product.

# Reuben Dip
## Shenson/Mosey's

8 ounces cooked corned beef, coarsely chopped

1 cup sauerkraut, coarsely chopped, rinsed and drained

8 ounces cream cheese, softened

2 cups shredded Swiss cheese

1/2 cup Thousand Island dressing

Toasted cocktail rye bread slices and/or thick pretzel sticks, for serving

Preheat oven to 325°F.

Mix corned beef, sauerkraut, cream cheese, Swiss cheese and dressing together in an ovenproof dish.

Bake for 30-40 minutes, or until the internal temperature is 165°F.

Serve with cocktail rye bread and/or pretzels. Makes 8 servings.

# Organic Corn and Black Bean Salsa
Bybee Foods

2 cups Bybee Foods* Organic
    Supersweet White
    Cut Corn ❂Organic

1 15-ounce can black
    beans, drained

1 large ripe avocado,
    diced, plus extra slices
    for garnish

2 Roma tomatoes, diced

3/4 cup chopped
    green onions

1/2 cup chopped
    fresh cilantro

White, blue and red corn
    tortilla chips,
    for serving

DRESSING

1/4 cup Kirkland Signature
    extra-virgin olive oil

1/4 cup red wine vinegar

1 teaspoon ground cumin

2 garlic cloves, crushed

1 teaspoon lime juice

Salt and pepper to taste

In a bowl, combine corn, beans, diced avocado, tomatoes, green onions and cilantro. Cover and chill for 1 hour.

To prepare the dressing, combine all ingredients and whisk to blend. Stir into the vegetable mixture.

Garnish the salsa with avocado slices. Serve with tortilla chips. Makes 24 servings.

* Brands may vary by region; substitute a similar product.

# Easy Avocado Wreath
Chilean Hass Avocados

5 Chilean* Hass avocados

1/4 cup lime or lemon juice

Salt and pepper

Chopped red bell pepper,
    for garnish

Crackers, for serving

Rinse avocados. Cut each avocado in half. Spoon out the pits.

Spoon out the avocado flesh into a large resealable plastic bag. Add lime or lemon juice and salt and pepper to taste. Squeeze to press out the air. Seal the bag.

Mash the bag with your hands until the avocado is smooth but still has a few chunks.

With scissors, snip just the corner off one end of the bag. Pipe the avocado mixture into a wreath shape on a large serving plate. Garnish with chopped bell pepper.

Serve with crackers. Makes about 24 servings.

**Nutritional information:** Each serving has 53 calories, 1 g protein, 3.3 g carbohydrates, 4.7 g fat, 0.5 g saturated fat, 0 mg cholesterol, 1 g fiber, 48.5 mg sodium.

* Brands may vary by region; substitute a similar product.

# Ancient Sweets Roasted Pepper Spread
## Mastronardi Produce/Sunset

**6 Sunset\* Ancient Sweets red peppers**

**1/2 cup (1 1/2-1 3/4 ounces) sliced almonds**

**1/2 cup sun-dried tomatoes in oil, drained, and oil reserved**

**1/4-1/2 teaspoon crushed red pepper**

**1 teaspoon minced fresh garlic**

**Extra-virgin olive oil**

**1 tablespoon red wine vinegar**

**2 tablespoons fresh orange juice**

**1/4 teaspoon salt**

Preheat oven to 375°F.

Place peppers on a baking sheet and roast for 30-35 minutes, or until just starting to char on the outside. Immediately transfer peppers to a bowl and cover tightly with plastic wrap. Let sit, covered, until cool.

Meanwhile, spread almonds on a rimmed baking sheet and bake for about 4 minutes, or until golden and lightly toasted. Let cool.

Once the peppers are cool, the skin should slip off easily. Remove skin, seeds and stem, and discard. Coarsely chop the peppers.

In a food processor, combine the drained tomatoes, crushed red pepper, garlic and cooled almonds. Process until smooth, about 1 minute.

Meanwhile, measure the oil drained from the tomatoes, and add enough olive oil to make 1/4 cup total. Add to the processor along with the roasted peppers, vinegar, orange juice and salt, and continue processing until smooth.

The spread can be made up to 5 days in advance, covered and refrigerated until needed. Serve with bread, crackers or breadsticks or as a dip with veggies. Makes about 1 1/2 cups.

**Tips:** This recipe is easily doubled. It is also fantastic served on grilled chicken, veggies or lamb, as a sandwich spread or tossed with pasta.

*\* Brands may vary by region; substitute a similar product.*

SUNSET

*Goodness Grown Naturally*™

## Taco Casserole
McCormick

1 1/2 **pounds lean ground beef or turkey**

1/4 **cup McCormick Taco Seasoning Mix**

1 **15- to 16-ounce can pinto beans, drained and rinsed**

1 **15-ounce can tomato sauce**

1 **11-ounce can Mexican-style corn or whole kernel corn, drained**

1 **cup shredded Cheddar cheese**

1 **cup coarsely crushed tortilla chips**

**Assorted toppings: sour cream, sliced green onions, shredded lettuce and chopped tomatoes (optional)**

Preheat oven to 400°F.

Brown meat in a large skillet over medium-high heat. Drain off the fat.

Stir in seasoning mix, beans, tomato sauce and corn. Bring to a boil. Reduce heat to low; simmer for 5 minutes.

Spoon the mixture into a 2-quart baking dish. Sprinkle with cheese and tortilla chips.

Bake for 5-10 minutes, or until the cheese is melted.

Serve with assorted toppings, if desired. Makes 12 servings.

## Queso Blanco Dip
Don Miguel Mexican Foods

3/4 **cup half-and-half**

1/3 **cup finely chopped onion (the finer the better)**

2 **tablespoons ground cumin**

1 **teaspoon salt**

2 **serrano or jalapeño peppers, finely diced (adjust for your heat preference)**

12 **ounces Manchego cheese, finely grated**

6 **ounces cream cheese, cubed**

1/4 **cup finely chopped fresh cilantro (optional)**

In a small saucepan, combine half-and-half, onion, cumin, salt and peppers. Heat over low to medium-low heat until hot, but do not bring to a boil.

Add a small amount of Manchego and stir until it is melted. Gradually add the remaining cheese, stirring after each addition until thoroughly blended.

Add cream cheese and continue stirring until the mixture is smooth.

Remove from the heat, stir in cilantro and serve immediately. This dip is delicious with any of your favorite Don Miguel* products. Makes 4 servings.

*Brands may vary by region; substitute a similar product.*

# Rib Meat Nachos
## Curly's

1 12-ounce bag tortilla chips
1 tablespoon barbecue grilling spice
8 ounces chopped meat from Curly's baby back ribs
1/2 cup nacho cheese sauce
1/2 cup barbecue sauce
1 4-ounce can sliced jalapeños, drained

Toss tortilla chips with barbecue spice.

Spread the chips on a serving plate. Top with rib meat, cheese sauce, barbecue sauce and sliced jalapeños. Makes 8 servings.

# Pineapple-Ham Roll Ups
## Alpine Fresh

- **6 burrito-size tortillas, warmed**
- **12 tablespoons pineapple-flavored cream cheese**
- **2 cups or 1 pound diced Alpine Fresh\* fresh cut pineapple, well drained**
- **6 tablespoons dry-roasted sunflower kernels**
- **12 slices deli ham**
- **Toothpicks (optional)**

Lay tortillas on a flat work surface. Spread 2 tablespoons cream cheese over each tortilla. Divide diced pineapple evenly among the tortillas. Sprinkle each tortilla with 1 tablespoon sunflower kernels.

Place 2 slices of ham 1 1/2 inches from the top of each tortilla. Begin rolling from the bottom and secure with toothpicks, if desired. Slice in half.

Serve immediately. Makes 12 servings.

*Recipe developed by Kati Neville.*
*\* Brands may vary by region; substitute a similar product.*

# Turkey Sliders with Mango Poblano Relish
## Kirkland Signature

- **2 pounds ground turkey**
- **1 egg**
- **1 tablespoon Kirkland Signature dried chopped onion**
- **1 teaspoon Kirkland Signature California garlic salt**
- **1/8 teaspoon Kirkland Signature coarse ground pepper**
- **1 tablespoon grated Pecorino Romano cheese**
- **15 small dinner rolls, sliced in half**
- **15 pieces green leaf lettuce**

### MANGO POBLANO RELISH

- **2 ripe mangoes, cut in 1/8-inch dice**
- **1/2 cup diced red onion**
- **3 tablespoons diced grilled poblano chile**
- **Juice of 1 lime**
- **3 green onions, chopped**
- **3/4 teaspoon Kirkland Signature garlic salt**
- **1 tablespoon honey**

In a bowl, combine ground turkey, egg, chopped onion, garlic salt, pepper and Pecorino. Mix to blend well. Form into 15 round patties. Place in the freezer for 1 hour, or until frozen.

To prepare the relish, combine all ingredients in a bowl and mix until well blended. Place a third of the mixture in a blender and puree. Add to the remaining relish and blend well. Cover and chill.

Preheat the grill.

Place the burgers on the grill and cook over medium heat until the internal temperature is 165°F. Remove and place on the rolls.

Top each slider with a piece of lettuce and 1 tablespoon of relish. Close the rolls and serve immediately. Makes 15 servings.

# Tilapia Sliders
## Regal Springs

1/2 cup milk

2 eggs

1 cup flour

1/4 cup yellow cornmeal

1/2 cup grated Parmesan cheese

2 tablespoons chopped
    fresh parsley

Salt and pepper

4 Regal Springs tilapia fillets,
    cut into 16 equal pieces

3 tablespoons olive oil

1 package Parker House or
    Hawaiian rolls (16 rolls)

4 leaves romaine lettuce,
    cut into quarters

1/2 tomato, sliced

4 slices Cheddar cheese,
    cut into quarters

*TANGY TARTAR SAUCE*

1/2 cup mayonnaise

2 tablespoons pickle relish

1 tablespoon lemon juice

Salt and pepper to taste

In a medium bowl, whisk together milk and eggs.

In another medium bowl, mix together flour, cornmeal, Parmesan, parsley, and salt and pepper to taste.

Dunk fillets in the milk mixture and then dredge in the cornmeal mixture, coating both sides evenly.

In a large sauté pan, immediately heat olive oil over medium-high heat. When it is hot but not smoking, add the fillets to the pan. Cook on one side until the coating is light golden brown, about 4 minutes. Carefully turn the fillets and cook for 2-3 minutes more. Remove from the pan with a slotted spatula and drain on paper towels.

Meanwhile, whisk together the tartar sauce ingredients.

Slice the rolls and place a fillet on each bottom half, then top with lettuce, tomato, cheese and tartar sauce. Makes 8 servings.

**Tips:** A fun activity is to let your kids use mini spreaders to apply their own condiments. This recipe also works well with honey mustard, ketchup or barbecue sauce for condiments.

# Salads and Soups

## Pasta Fruit Salad
### Anthony Vineyards/Sun Date

1 1/2 cups dry rotini pasta

1/2 cup pitted and chopped Medjool dates

1 cup halved red seedless grapes

2-3 peaches, peeled and chopped (or nectarines)

1/2 cup sliced celery

1/4 cup chopped toasted walnuts

4 ounces soft cream cheese

1/4 cup low-fat vanilla yogurt

2-3 tablespoons honey

1/2 teaspoon grated lemon peel

2 tablespoons lemon juice

2 tablespoons whipping cream

Cook pasta according to package directions; drain and let cool.

In a large bowl, combine dates, grapes, peaches, celery, walnuts and pasta.

In a separate bowl, combine cream cheese, yogurt, honey, grated lemon peel and lemon juice. Beat with an electric mixer until smooth. Add whipping cream and beat until blended.

Pour the dressing over the fruit and pasta. Stir to blend. Cover and chill for 2-6 hours. Moisten with a little milk if necessary before serving. Makes 8 servings.

## Citrus Salad with Ginger Yogurt
### Diversified Citrus Marketing/ Noble Worldwide

1 red Florida grapefruit, peeled

2 large tangerines, peeled

1/2 cup dried cranberries

2 tablespoons honey

1/4 teaspoon ground cinnamon

1 16- or 17.6-ounce container Greek yogurt

2/3 cup minced crystallized ginger

Break grapefruit and tangerines into sections. Cut grapefruit sections into thirds. Cut tangerine sections in half. Transfer grapefruit, tangerines and all juices to a deep serving bowl.

Mix dried cranberries, honey and cinnamon into the fruit. Cover and refrigerate for at least 1 hour.

Mix yogurt and ginger in a bowl. (Fruit and yogurt can be prepared 1 day ahead. Store separately, covered, in the refrigerator.)

To serve, add ginger yogurt to the fruit mixture and stir to blend. Makes 6 servings.

*Recipe developed by Chef Brad Moore.*

## Festive Blackberry Waldorf Salad with Blackberry Vinaigrette Drizzle
Sun Belle

1 1/2 cups shelled walnuts
3/4 cup vanilla yogurt
2 tablespoons honey
Grated peel and juice of
    1 small lemon, divided
1/2 teaspoon salt, divided
1/4 teaspoon ground white
    pepper, divided
2 stalks celery
1 Granny Smith apple
2 Gala apples
1 cup golden raisins
18 ounces Sun Belle
    blackberries (4 cups),
    divided
1 tablespoon Dijon mustard
1 tablespoon wine vinegar
1 teaspoon dried tarragon
1/4 cup olive oil

Preheat oven to 350°F. Toast walnuts for 10 minutes.

In a large bowl, combine yogurt, honey and half *each* of the grated lemon peel, lemon juice, salt and pepper.

Chop celery into 1/4-inch pieces.

Core apples and chop into 1/2-inch cubes, leaving the skin on.

Fold apples, celery, raisins and 3 cups of blackberries into the yogurt dressing. Stir in the walnuts.

To make the vinaigrette, puree in a blender 1 cup blackberries, mustard, vinegar, tarragon and the remaining grated lemon peel, lemon juice, salt and pepper. Add olive oil slowly, blending until emulsified.

To serve, scoop the salad onto individual plates. Drizzle vinaigrette around and over each serving. Makes 8-10 servings.

## Fruit Salad
Top Ramen

1 head iceberg lettuce
10 strawberries
1 teaspoon
    balsamic vinegar
1 teaspoon sugar
2 cups cold water
1 teaspoon lemon juice
1 pear
1 apple
1  11-ounce can
    mandarin oranges
Prepared raspberry
    salad dressing
3-ounce package Top
    Ramen* Oriental Flavor

Break lettuce into bite-size pieces in a large bowl.

Trim and slice strawberries. Place in a small bowl and mix with vinegar and sugar.

Combine water and lemon juice in another bowl. Cut pear and apple into bite-size pieces and quickly place in the lemon water to prevent browning.

To assemble the salad, add pear and apple pieces, strawberries and mandarin oranges (with juice) to the lettuce. Mix in raspberry dressing to taste.

Crumble the ramen over the salad. Add half the seasoning packet. Mix everything together. Let sit for 5 minutes to allow the noodles to soften slightly. Makes 4 servings.

* *Brands may vary by region; substitute a similar product.*

# Grape and Quinoa Salad
## Divine Flavor

3 cups cooked quinoa, cooled

1 1/2 cups Divine Flavor* red and green seedless grapes, cut into quarters

1/2 cup dry-roasted hazelnuts, coarsely chopped

1/4 cup chopped green onion

1/4 cup canola oil

2 tablespoons fresh lemon juice

1 tablespoon sugar

1/4 teaspoon salt

Mix quinoa, grapes, hazelnuts and green onion in a medium bowl; set aside.

In a small bowl, whisk canola oil, lemon juice, sugar and salt. Pour dressing over the quinoa mixture and stir to combine.

Cover and refrigerate for 30 minutes before serving. Makes 6 servings.

*Recipe developed by Kati Neville.*
*\* Brands may vary by region; substitute a similar product.*

## Summer Oasis Salad
Richard Bagdasarian/Bard Valley
Medjool Date Growers

5 cups spring salad mix

1/2 cup sliced red
  seedless grapes

1/4 cup chopped
  Medjool dates

1/3 cup crumbled
  blue cheese

3/4 cup olive oil

1/4 cup balsamic vinegar

1 teaspoon salt

1 teaspoon pepper

*CANDIED PECANS*

1/4 cup pecans

2 tablespoons
  butter, melted

3 tablespoons
  brown sugar

To prepare the candied pecans, mix ingredients together and spread on a shallow pan covered with foil. Bake at 350°F until toasted. Let cool and then chop.

Toss salad mix, grapes, dates, pecans and cheese in a large salad bowl.

In a separate bowl, whisk together olive oil, vinegar, salt and pepper. Pour over the salad and toss. Makes 4 servings.

## Cara Cara and Asparagus Salad
Cecelia Packing/Kings River Packing

3 Cecelia Packing* or
  Kings River* Cara Cara
  oranges, divided

1 pound asparagus

1 avocado, peeled, pitted
  and diced

2 tablespoons finely
  minced red onion

3 tablespoons orange
  juice (from one of
  the oranges)

1 tablespoon extra-virgin
  olive oil

2 teaspoons honey mustard
  or Dijon mustard

1/8 teaspoon salt

Ground black pepper

1 head Bibb lettuce, torn
  into bite-size pieces

Gather zest from the peel of 1 orange. Peel and section 2 of the oranges. Cut the sections in half and place them in a large bowl. Squeeze and save the juice from the remaining orange.

Snap off and discard woody bases from asparagus, then cut the spears into 2-inch-long pieces. In a small saucepan, bring 1 cup of water to a boil. Place asparagus in boiling water for 1 minute, then drain and transfer immediately to a bowl of ice water. Drain.

Add avocado, red onion and the cooled, drained asparagus to the bowl of oranges.

In another bowl, whisk together the reserved orange juice, olive oil, mustard, salt and pepper to taste. Pour over the salad ingredients and gently toss.

Arrange lettuce on plates and top with the salad. Garnish with the reserved orange zest. Makes 4 servings.

*Recipe developed by Christine W. Jackson, food stylist.*
*\* Brands may vary by region; substitute a similar product.*

# Fresh Cara Cara Orange Mozzarella Towers
## Sunkist Growers

4 Sunkist Cara Cara oranges

12 baby lettuce leaves

12 1/4-inch slices fresh mozzarella

12 fresh basil leaves

Freshly ground black pepper

2 teaspoons chopped Sunkist fresh
orange zest

**ORANGE BALSAMIC
VINAIGRETTE**

1/4 cup freshly squeezed Sunkist
orange juice

1 tablespoon balsamic vinegar

3 tablespoons olive oil

Salt and pepper

Peel oranges and cut three 1/4-inch horizontal slices from the center of each orange. Lightly sear the slices in a hot pan or on a grill.

To prepare the vinaigrette, combine orange juice, vinegar, olive oil, and salt and pepper to taste in a small bowl and whisk together.

For each serving, arrange 3 lettuce leaves on a salad plate. Place 1 mozzarella slice on the lettuce, and top with 1 orange slice and 1 basil leaf. Repeat with 2 more layers of mozzarella, orange and basil leaf.

Drizzle each serving with 1 tablespoon vinaigrette. Sprinkle with black pepper to taste and 1/2 teaspoon orange zest. Makes 4 servings.

**Sunkist**

# Fruit Salad and Baby Greens with Poppy Seed Dressing
## Del Monte Fresh Produce

3 Del Monte bananas, sliced

1 1/2 teaspoons lemon juice

1 cup Del Monte Gold Extra Sweet fresh-cut pineapple chunks

1 cup Del Monte fresh-cut cantaloupe chunks, cut into bite-size pieces

2 kiwi fruit, peeled and sliced

1 cup blueberries

About 12 cups mixed baby greens

1/2 cup salted shelled pistachios

### POPPY SEED DRESSING

1 cup vegetable oil

3/4 cup sugar

1/3 cup white vinegar

2 tablespoons minced onion

1/2 teaspoon salt

1/2 teaspoon dry mustard

1 1/2 teaspoons poppy seeds

To prepare the dressing, combine oil, sugar, vinegar, onion, salt and mustard in a blender. Mix until blended. Stir in poppy seeds. Chill.

In a mixing bowl, sprinkle banana slices with lemon juice. Add the remaining fruit and stir.

Place mixed greens in a large serving bowl or on a platter. Pour the fruit mixture on top, distributing it evenly. Sprinkle with pistachios.

Serve with the dressing on the side. Makes 6 servings.

# Fuji Apple and Cucumber Salad with Sesame-Ginger Dressing
## Domex Superfresh Growers

1 tablespoon sesame seeds

1/3 cup vegetable oil

3 tablespoons rice wine vinegar

1 teaspoon toasted sesame oil

1 teaspoon finely grated
   fresh ginger

Salt

2 Superfresh Growers Fuji apples

1 large cucumber, peeled, seeded
   and thinly sliced

Put sesame seeds in a small dry skillet and lightly toast over medium heat, stirring often, for 3-5 minutes; set aside.

Combine vegetable oil, vinegar, sesame oil and ginger in a large bowl and whisk to blend. Season to taste with salt.

Quarter and core apples and cut into thin slices. Add them to the dressing with the cucumber slices. Toss gently to evenly mix. Cover with plastic and refrigerate for at least 30 minutes and up to 2 hours before serving, stirring once or twice.

To serve, arrange the salad on individual plates, drizzling a bit of the dressing over each. Sprinkle with toasted sesame seeds. Makes 4 servings.

# Low-Fat Apple Waldorf Salad
Pennsylvania Apple/New York Apple

- 1/3 cup low-fat mayonnaise
- 1/3 cup fat-free yogurt
- 2 medium Eastern* Fuji apples, cored and cut into bite-size chunks
- 1/2 fresh pineapple, peeled and cut into bite-size chunks, or one 20-ounce can pineapple chunks packed in juice, drained
- 2 celery stalks, sliced (7- to 8-inch stalks)
- 3/4 cup coarsely chopped walnuts, toasted
- 1/3 cup golden raisins

Mix mayonnaise and yogurt in a bowl until blended.

Add apples, pineapple, celery, walnuts and raisins to the bowl. Stir until well mixed. Makes 6 servings.

**Tip:** Other Eastern apple varieties such as Red Delicious, Empire, Jonagold or Ginger Gold are also great choices.

**Nutritional information:** Each serving has 204 calories, 3 g protein, 31 g carbohydrates, 9 g fat, 4 mg cholesterol, 4 g fiber, 117 mg sodium.

*\* Brands may vary by region; substitute a similar product.*

*Eastern* **Apples**
CRISPIER • JUICIER • TASTIER

# Asian Pear Chicken Salad
Trinity Fruit

- 3 boneless, skinless chicken breast halves
- Salt and pepper
- 1 cup walnuts
- 1 tablespoon butter
- 2 tablespoons brown sugar
- 1 head green leaf lettuce
- 2 cups chopped radicchio
- 1/2 cup chopped celery
- 1/2 cup chopped fresh cilantro
- 1 cup chopped Trinity Asian pear
- 1/2 cup shaved Parmesan cheese
- 3 Trinity Asian pears, cored and sliced, for garnish

*DRESSING*
- 1/2 cup olive oil
- 4 tablespoons citrus champagne vinegar (see note)
- 1/4 teaspoon salt
- 1/4 teaspoon ground pepper
- 1 tablespoon honey
- 1/2 teaspoon fresh lemon juice
- 2 tablespoons sugar

Preheat the grill.

Season chicken to taste with salt and pepper. Grill the chicken. Set aside and let cool.

Combine walnuts, butter and brown sugar in a sauté pan and cook over medium heat, stirring, until the walnuts are coated. Remove from the pan and let cool. Break walnuts apart and set aside.

In a large bowl, combine lettuce, radicchio, celery, cilantro, chopped Asian pear and Parmesan.

Whisk together all the dressing ingredients. Add to the salad and toss.

Arrange the salad on plates. Slice the chicken and place on top of the salad. Place Asian pear slices and some walnuts on the side of each serving.

Makes 6-8 servings.

**Note:** Citrus champagne vinegar is champagne vinegar made with a twist of lemon. For a substitute, use rice vinegar.

*Recipe developed by Lisa White.*

# Baby Mixed Greens with Apple Pear, Pecans and Feta
Kingsburg Orchards

### DRESSING
3 tablespoons extra-virgin olive oil

2 tablespoons red wine vinegar

2 tablespoons orange juice

3 tablespoons finely chopped pecans

2 tablespoons honey

Salt and freshly cracked black pepper

6 cups loosely packed baby mixed greens

1 Kingsburg Orchards apple pear, halved, cored and sliced into thin wedges

1/3 cup pomegranate seeds or dried cranberries

1/3 cup feta cheese

To prepare the dressing, combine olive oil, vinegar, orange juice, pecans, honey, and salt and pepper to taste in a salad bowl. Mix until well blended.

Add greens and toss to coat with the dressing.

Divide the salad among 4 plates. Top with apple pear slices. Sprinkle with pomegranate seeds or dried cranberries and feta. Makes 4 servings.

## Shrimp and Cherry Almond Bleu Salad
Dole

1 package Dole Cherry Almond Bleu Salad Kit

1 pound cooked and deveined shrimp

1/2 pound Dole asparagus, cooked, drained and cut into 2-inch pieces

1 1/2-2 cups sliced Dole strawberries

Combine salad greens, shrimp, asparagus and strawberries in a large bowl.

Toss with the dressing from the kit.

Arrange on 5 large plates. Top with cherries, bleu cheese and almonds from the kit. Makes 5 servings.

## Shrimp Salad with Clementines
Duda Farm Fresh Foods, Inc.

5 Dandy* sweet clementines

1 pound cooked medium (30-35 count) shrimp

1 on-the-vine tomato, seeded and chopped

1/3 cup thinly sliced Dandy* celery

1/3 cup finely chopped Dandy* red onion

1 teaspoon lemon juice, squeezed fresh from a Dandy* lemon

1 teaspoon salt

1/8 teaspoon ground black pepper

1 tablespoon extra-virgin olive oil

16 Bibb/Boston lettuce leaves

4 teaspoons chopped chives

Peel and section 4 of the clementines and place in a medium-size mixing bowl. Add shrimp, tomato, celery and onion to the bowl.

Cut the remaining clementine in half horizontally and squeeze the juice into a small bowl; there will be about 3 tablespoons. Add lemon juice, salt and pepper, and whisk until the salt dissolves. Whisk in olive oil.

Pour the dressing over the salad and toss with a fork until it looks moist.

Arrange lettuce leaves on 4 plates, placing the stem ends toward the center. Mound the salad in the center of each plate. Sprinkle 1 teaspoon of chives over each serving. Serve immediately. Makes 4 servings.

* Brands may vary by region; substitute a similar product.

# Living Lettuce with Citrus Grilled Shrimp
## Tanimura & Antle

### CITRUS DRESSING

Finely grated peel of 1
    Cara Cara* orange

1/3 cup fresh Cara Cara* orange juice

1 tablespoon fresh lime juice

1 tablespoon honey

1 teaspoon Dijon mustard

1/2 teaspoon salt

1/4 teaspoon freshly ground
    black pepper

2/3 cup extra-virgin olive oil

10 large (21-25 count) raw
    peeled and deveined shrimp

1 head Tanimura & Antle*
    Living Lettuce

1 Cara Cara* orange, peeled
    and sectioned

1 avocado, peeled and thinly sliced

4 ounces feta cheese, crumbled

1/3 cup dried cherries

1/4 cup thinly sliced Tanimura &
    Antle* Artisan Red onions

1/4 cup toasted slivered almonds

To prepare the dressing, combine grated orange peel, orange and lime juices, honey, mustard, salt and pepper in a bowl. Slowly whisk in olive oil until blended. This can be stored in the refrigerator for up to a week. Shake or blend before use.

Thaw shrimp and pat dry. Place in a small bowl, add 1/4 cup of dressing and toss to combine. Let stand for 30 minutes.

Gently remove each lettuce leaf from the root, rinse and drain.

In a large bowl, combine lettuce, orange, avocado, feta, dried cherries, red onions and almonds. Add dressing to taste and toss gently to coat.

Heat a nonstick frying pan over medium heat. Add shrimp and cook until pink, about 3 minutes. Remove from the pan with a slotted spoon and place on top of the salad. Makes 2 servings.

*Brands may vary by region; substitute a similar product.*

## Spinach Prawn Orange Salad
### River Ranch Fresh Foods

6 cups River Ranch Cello spinach

2 oranges, peeled and sectioned

12 precooked giant prawns or shrimp

1/4 cup dried cranberries

2 tablespoons olive oil

1 tablespoon lemon juice

1 tablespoon honey

1/4 teaspoon poppy seeds

1/2 teaspoon garlic powder

1/4 cup toasted slivered almonds (optional)

Salt and freshly ground pepper (optional)

Place spinach in a large bowl. Add oranges, prawns and cranberries. Toss lightly to mix.

For the dressing, in a screw-top jar combine olive oil, lemon juice, honey, poppy seeds and garlic powder. Cover and shake well. Pour the dressing over the salad. Toss lightly to coat.

Sprinkle the salad with toasted almonds. Season to taste with salt and pepper if needed.

Makes 6-8 servings.

## Shrimp and Spring Mix Salad with Jalapeño Dressing
### Taylor Fresh

1/2 cup fresh lime juice

1/2 cup extra-virgin olive oil

2 tablespoons finely chopped jalapeño

1 tablespoon chopped fresh cilantro

1/2 tablespoon honey

1 teaspoon minced garlic

Salt and freshly ground black pepper

4 cups Taylor Fresh Organic Spring Mix Organic

1/3 cup minced red onion

2 large heirloom tomatoes, cut into eight 1/2-inch-thick slices

2 avocados, peeled and diced

1 pound cooked shrimp

Lime wedges, for serving

To make the dressing, combine lime juice, olive oil, jalapeño, cilantro, honey and garlic in a bowl. Add salt and pepper to taste.

Gently toss spring mix and red onion with 4 tablespoons of the dressing.

Place 2 tomato slices in the center of each plate and top with spring mix. Arrange avocado and shrimp on top and drizzle with the remaining dressing.

Serve with lime wedges. Makes 4 servings.

# Go-with-the-Grain Salad

Kirkland Signature/Citterio/
Arthur Schuman/Zanetti

1 cup barley or brown rice
12 ounces Citterio Prosciutto di Parma
6 cherry tomatoes, quartered
3/4 cup diced red bell pepper
1/2 cup chopped green onions,
    including some of the
    green portion
1/3 cup chopped fresh basil

1 1/2 cups thinly shaved or coarsely
    grated Kirkland Signature
    Parmigiano Reggiano
    cheese, divided
2 tablespoons olive oil
4 teaspoons lemon juice
1/2 teaspoon salt
1/4 teaspoon ground black pepper
Basil sprigs, for garnish (optional)

Cook barley or brown rice according to package directions until tender. Transfer to a large bowl and let cool.

Meanwhile, cut enough prosciutto in 1-inch-wide strips to make 1/2 cup. Reserve the remaining slices.

In a large bowl, combine prosciutto strips, tomatoes, bell pepper, green onions, basil, 1/2 cup of the Parmigiano Reggiano, olive oil, lemon juice, salt and pepper. Add the cooled barley and toss to blend.

To serve, arrange the reserved prosciutto slices in a fan shape on 6 plates. Spoon some salad onto the center of each plate. Scatter the remaining 1 cup of Parmigiano Reggiano shavings over the salads. Garnish with basil sprigs. Makes 6 servings.

**KIRKLAND** Signature   **CITTERIO** The World's Most Celebrated Italian Specialty Meats

*arthur schuman inc.* **Zanetti**

## Summer Salad
Royal Flavor

$^1/_2$ cup diced Royal Flavor* mixed bell peppers (red, yellow and orange)

$^1/_2$ cup diced Royal Flavor* mini sweet peppers (red, yellow and orange) [or 1 cup of either mix]

$^1/_2$ cup diced Royal Flavor* long English cucumber

1 cup diced Royal Flavor* tomato (1 large beefsteak)

$^1/_3$ cup sliced green onion

$^1/_4$ cup sliced white onion

$^1/_3$ cup sliced olives

2 tablespoons extra-virgin olive oil

2 tablespoons white or balsamic vinegar

1 teaspoon dried basil or 1 tablespoon minced fresh basil

1 teaspoon dried oregano

$^1/_2$ cup mini ($^1/_2$ inch) fresh mozzarella balls

Salt and pepper

1 head romaine, butter or Bibb lettuce

In a salad bowl, mix diced peppers, cucumber, tomato, onions and olives.

In a small bowl, whisk together olive oil, vinegar, basil and oregano.

Add mozzarella balls to the veggies. Add the dressing and toss to blend. Season to taste with salt and pepper.

To serve, arrange lettuce leaves on plates. Top with the salad. Makes 4 servings.

**Tip:** Serve with toasted thinly sliced baguette that has been brushed with garlic olive oil.

*Recipe developed by Christine W. Jackson, food stylist.*
*\* Brands may vary by region; substitute a similar product.*

## Yucatan-Style Salad with Tomato, Avocado and Zesty Lime Dressing
Earth Source Trading

Juice of 4 Earth Source Trading* limes, plus lime slices for garnish

$^1/_4$ cup *each* red, yellow and orange bell peppers cut into medium dice

$^1/_4$ cup thinly sliced red onion

Kernels from 1 ear of fresh corn

$^1/_4$ cup sliced black olives

$^1/_2$ poblano chile, seeded, cut into small dice

2 large yellow tomatoes, cut into 1-inch cubes

1 pint grape tomatoes, halved

3 mini seedless cucumbers (or 1 large seedless cucumber), sliced

2 Hass avocados, cut into 1-inch cubes

1 garlic clove, minced

2 teaspoons kosher or sea salt

$^1/_4$ teaspoon freshly ground black pepper

$^1/_4$ cup extra-virgin olive oil

$^1/_4$ cup chopped fresh cilantro, plus a few additional sprigs for garnish

1 head butter or Boston lettuce, leaves separated

2 plum tomatoes, quartered

Place lime juice in a large mixing bowl. Add each of the ingredients up to and including the chopped cilantro, tossing gently after each addition. The lime juice will pull flavor out of each addition and result in a creamy yet vibrant vinaigrette.

Line a serving bowl with lettuce leaves and spoon in the salad. Garnish with tomato wedges, lime slices and cilantro sprigs. Makes 6-8 servings.

*\* Brands may vary by region; substitute a similar product.*

**Earth Source**
TRADING, INC.™

# Tomato and Bagel Salad
## Einstein Brothers Bagels/Noah's Bagels

3 Kirkland Signature plain bagels

2 medium tomatoes

1 bunch asparagus, blanched and cut into 2-inch pieces

12 ounces small fresh mozzarella balls, drained

1/2 red onion, thinly sliced

6 leaves fresh basil, cut in thin strips

**DRESSING**

2 medium tomatoes, halved

1 tablespoon chopped shallots

2 tablespoons chopped garlic

1/4 cup red wine vinegar

1/2 cup olive oil

2 teaspoons salt

1 teaspoon freshly ground black pepper

1/2 teaspoon crushed red pepper

Preheat oven to 375°F.

Cut bagels in half, then cut each half into 6 wedges. Spread in a pan and bake for 8-10 minutes, or until lightly toasted. Remove from the oven and let cool for 5-10 minutes.

To prepare the dressing, combine all ingredients in a blender and puree.

For the salad, cut tomatoes in half, then cut each half into 8 wedges. In a large bowl, combine tomato wedges, asparagus, mozzarella, onion, basil and bagel wedges. Add the dressing and stir to blend. Makes 8-10 servings.

## Italian Bread Salad
Alpine Fresh

**16 ounces Alpine Fresh\* French green beans, trimmed and cut into 1-inch pieces**

**3 cups Alpine Fresh\* grape tomatoes, sliced in half**

**2 cups seeded, chopped cucumber**

**1 cup diced red onion**

**1/2 cup chopped fresh basil**

**1/2 cup olive oil, divided**

**1/4 cup balsamic vinegar**

**1/2 teaspoon salt**

**1/2 teaspoon pepper**

**1/2 teaspoon sugar**

**1 loaf roasted garlic bread, cut into 1-inch cubes**

Set out 3 large mixing bowls. Divide green beans, tomatoes, cucumber, onion and basil evenly between two of the bowls.

In a small bowl, whisk together 1/4 cup olive oil, vinegar, salt, pepper and sugar. Pour over the vegetables and stir to combine. Set aside.

Toss bread cubes with 1/4 cup olive oil in the remaining bowl. Add bread to the vegetables and mix gently. Cover and refrigerate for 30 minutes before serving. Makes 14 servings.

*Recipe developed by Kati Neville.*
*\* Brands may vary by region; substitute a similar product.*

## Cheesy Garlic Croutons
Kirkland Signature

**4 ounces butter**

**1/8 teaspoon Kirkland Signature pure sea salt**

**1/8 teaspoon Kirkland Signature coarse ground pepper**

**1 teaspoon Kirkland Signature California granulated garlic**

**1/4 cup grated Pecorino Romano cheese**

**1/2 teaspoon dried oregano, crushed**

**1/2 teaspoon dried parsley, crushed**

**1/2 teaspoon dried basil, crushed**

**1 baguette, cut into 1-inch cubes**

Preheat oven to 350°F.

Melt butter in a saucepan over medium heat. Add salt, pepper, garlic, cheese, oregano, parsley and basil. Blend well.

Place bread cubes in a bowl. Drizzle the melted butter mixture over the bread cubes. Mix until well blended.

Spread the bread cubes evenly on a parchment-lined sheet pan. Bake for about 10 minutes, or until crisp and browned. Let cool. Store in a dry uncovered container.

Serve with salad or as a snack. Makes 12 servings.

## Grilled Hearts of Romaine
Andy Boy

**2 Andy Boy\* romaine hearts**
**Extra-virgin olive oil**
**Kosher salt**
**Freshly ground pepper**
**Freshly grated**
    **Parmesan cheese**

Slice romaine hearts in half lengthwise. Brush each cut side with olive oil. Sprinkle with salt and pepper to taste. Set aside.

Heat an outdoor grill to medium heat. If cooking indoors, heat a grill pan over medium heat.

Set romaine hearts, cut side down, on the grill and cook for 3 minutes. Flip to the other side and cook for another 2 minutes, or until slightly charred and beginning to wilt.

Sprinkle with grated Parmesan and serve. Makes 4 servings.

**Tips:** Serve as a light entrée, or as a side with grilled meat, fish, chicken or tofu. Or add your favorite salad dressing—try balsamic vinaigrette, Italian or even green goddess. For an extra-healthy twist, sprinkle with fresh lemon juice.

*\* Brands may vary by region; substitute a similar product.*

## Dilly Mini Cucumber and Red Onion Salad
Mastronardi Produce/Sunset

**1 small red onion,**
    **thinly sliced**
**1/2 cup cider vinegar**
**3 tablespoons sugar**
**1/2 teaspoon celery seed**
**1 tablespoon chopped**
    **fresh dill, or 3/4**
    **teaspoon dried**
    **dill weed**
**1/2 teaspoon salt**
**1/2 teaspoon fresh-cracked**
    **black pepper**
**12 Sunset\* mini-**
    **cucumbers, sliced**

Rinse onion in a strainer under cold water for 3 minutes to remove any harshness. Drain well.

Meanwhile, in a large bowl, whisk vinegar, sugar, celery seed, dill, salt and pepper until the sugar is dissolved. Toss in mini-cucumbers and onion.

Let marinate, refrigerated, for at least 15 minutes before serving. Makes 1 quart.

*\* Brands may vary by region; substitute a similar product.*

Goodness Grown Naturally™

# Kung Pao Tuna
## Chicken of the Sea

1 tablespoon soy sauce

2 tablespoons seasoned rice vinegar

2 teaspoons sake (Japanese rice wine) (optional)

1 teaspoon crushed red pepper

2 teaspoons chopped unsalted peanuts

2 teaspoons chopped green bell pepper

2 teaspoons chopped red bell pepper

1 tablespoon chopped green onion

1 7-ounce can Chicken of the Sea* chunk light tuna in water

Lettuce cups, for serving (optional)

In a bowl, whisk together soy sauce, vinegar, sake and crushed red pepper until well blended.

Stir in peanuts, bell peppers and onion.

Drain tuna, gently flake and add to the bowl. Mix until all ingredients are blended. Chill until ready to serve.

Serve in lettuce cups. Makes 3 servings.

**Tip:** This can also be heated and served with rice.

**Nutritional information:** Each serving has 100 calories, 16 g protein, 4 g carbohydrates, 2 g fat, 0 g saturated fat, 35 mg cholesterol, <1 g fiber, 740 mg sodium.

*Brands may vary by region; substitute a similar product.*

# Mandarin Orange Dijon Chicken Salad
## Crazy Cuizine

16 ounces Crazy Cuizine* Mandarin Orange Chicken

8 ounces Crazy Cuizine* Mandarin Orange Sauce

2 tablespoons Dijon mustard

6 ounces spring mix salad (or fresh spinach)

8 medium-sized fresh mushrooms, sliced

1/4 medium-sized red onion, thinly sliced

12 small cherry tomatoes, halved

1 avocado, peeled and sliced

1 cup mandarin oranges (approx. 1 11-ounce can)

1/2 red bell pepper, sliced

Crispy chow mein noodles

Heat chicken according to package directions. Let cool. Cut into pieces and set aside.

Thaw mandarin orange sauce under warm water. Combine with mustard and set aside.

In a large bowl, combine chicken, salad mix, mushrooms, onion, tomatoes, avocado, oranges and bell pepper. Add the dressing and toss to coat.

Top with chow mein noodles. Makes 4-6 servings.

*Brands may vary by region; substitute a similar product.*

## Summer Tomato Salad with Chicken Salad Rollers
Kirkland Signature

4 medium tomatoes, chopped into 1/2-inch pieces (or 2 pints small tomatoes)

1 medium seedless cucumber, chopped into 1/2-inch pieces

1/2 medium red onion, chopped into 1/2-inch pieces

1 tablespoon grated lemon peel

1/2 teaspoon table salt

1/4 teaspoon ground black pepper

Toss all ingredients together in a large bowl; let stand for at least 20 minutes.

Serve with Kirkland Signature Chicken Salad Rollers from your Costco deli. Makes 6 servings.

**Nutritional information:** Each serving of salad has 45 calories, 2 g protein, 9 g carbohydrates, 0 g fat, 0 mg cholesterol, 2 g fiber, 180 mg sodium.

## White Bean Turkey Chili
ConAgra Foods

Pam Original No-Stick Cooking Spray

20 ounces lean ground turkey

1 cup chopped onion (about 1 large)

1 cup chopped green bell pepper (about 1 medium)

1 14 1/2-ounce can Hunt's* diced tomatoes, undrained

2 15-ounce cans Great Northern beans, drained, rinsed

2 11 1/2-ounce cans tomato-vegetable juice

1 tablespoon Gebhardt* chili powder

1/2 teaspoon ground cumin

Spray a large saucepan with cooking spray. Add ground turkey, onion and bell pepper. Cook and stir over medium heat for about 8 minutes, or until the turkey is crumbled and no longer pink.

Stir in undrained tomatoes, beans, vegetable juice, chili powder and cumin. Bring to a boil, stirring occasionally. Reduce the heat to low; cover. Simmer for 15 minutes, stirring occasionally. Makes 8 servings.

**Nutritional information:** Each serving has 196 calories, 18 g protein, 18 g carbohydrates, 5 g fat, 1 g saturated fat, 43 mg cholesterol, 5 g fiber, 633 mg sodium.

*\* Brands may vary by region; substitute a similar product.*

## Lentil Chili
Tasty Bite

1 tablespoon cooking oil
1/4 cup chopped onion
1/2 cup chopped green
   bell pepper
2  10-ounce packs Tasty
   Bite* Madras Lentils
   (3 for vegetarian version)
1/2 pound ground turkey,
   cooked and crumbled
1 cup canned or fresh
   diced tomatoes
Dash of hot sauce, crushed
   red pepper or cayenne
   pepper (optional)

Heat oil in a saucepan over medium-high heat. Add onion and cook until soft and translucent.

Add bell pepper and continue cooking until soft.

Add lentils, turkey, tomatoes and hot sauce, mixing until well blended. Simmer for 5-10 minutes.

Serve with taco chips or over rice. Or add shredded cheese and eat as is. Makes 4 servings.

**Tip:** For a vegetarian version, omit the turkey and use 3 packs of lentils.

*\* Brands may vary by region; substitute a similar product.*

## Southwestern Turkey Chili
Del Monte Foods

3/4 pound ground turkey
1/2 cup chopped onion
1  14 1/2-ounce can
   Del Monte, S&W
   or Contadina
   diced tomatoes
1  8-ounce can Del Monte,
   S&W or Contadina
   tomato sauce
1 tablespoon chili powder
1  15 1/4-ounce can
   Del Monte or S&W
   whole kernel corn,
   drained (optional)
1  15-ounce can low-salt
   kidney beans, drained
Lime wedges, light sour
   cream and chopped
   fresh cilantro, for
   serving (optional)

In a large skillet over medium heat, cook turkey with onion for 5 minutes.

Add tomatoes, tomato sauce, chili powder, corn and beans. Cover and simmer for 10-15 minutes.

Serve with lime wedges and top with light sour cream and cilantro, if desired. Makes 4-6 servings.

**Nutritional information:** Each serving has 302 calories, 28 g protein, 25 g carbohydrates, 11 g fat, 0 g saturated fat, 90 mg cholesterol, 662 mg sodium.

# Roasted Red Pepper and Artichoke Bisque

## Kirkland Signature/Request Foods

When serving Kirkland Signature frozen lasagna, start the meal with this soup.

3 tablespoons olive oil
1/2 large onion, minced
2 stalks celery, minced (1/2 cup)
1 large carrot, minced (1/2 cup)
3 garlic cloves, minced
1 tablespoon salt
2 teaspoons ground black pepper
2 teaspoons dried thyme
1 teaspoon cayenne pepper
1 stick (4 ounces) butter
1 cup flour

3 14-ounce cans chicken broth
1 16-ounce jar roasted red peppers, pureed
2 cups water
2 tablespoons chicken-flavor instant bouillon
1 cup heavy cream
1 cup dry sherry
8 ounces marinated artichokes, minced
Shredded Parmesan or Asiago cheese

In a large saucepan, combine olive oil, onion, celery, carrots and garlic (you can mince garlic and vegetables in a food processor). Cook over low heat until soft. Season with salt, pepper, thyme and cayenne pepper.

Increase the heat to medium, add butter and melt. Stir in flour and cook, stirring, for 3-4 minutes.

Add chicken broth, roasted red pepper puree, water and chicken bouillon and stir until thickened.

Simmer, uncovered, for 20-30 minutes, adding water or broth as needed.

Stir in cream, sherry and artichokes and heat for 5-10 minutes.

Garnish with shredded Parmesan or Asiago. Makes 8-10 servings.

KIRKLAND Signature · REQUEST FOODS

# Sweet Sausage and Shrimp Chowder
## Premio

1 slice hickory-smoked bacon, minced

2 tablespoons butter

1 cup minced onion

4 medium garlic cloves, minced

1 pound Premio* sweet Italian sausage, removed from casings

2 tablespoons all-purpose flour

Salt and pepper

1 pound small raw shrimp, peeled and deveined

2 cups chicken broth

2 cups half-and-half

2 medium potatoes, boiled, peeled and diced

In a heavy-bottomed soup kettle over low heat, sauté bacon, butter, onion and garlic for 5 minutes. Do not brown.

Raise the heat to medium, add sausage meat and stir to break up. Cook for 5-7 minutes, or until almost cooked through.

Reduce the heat to low and stir in flour. Cook for 2 minutes; do not brown. Season to taste with salt and pepper.

Raise the heat to medium-high and add shrimp and chicken broth. Bring to a simmer, stirring. Add half-and-half.

Add potatoes. Return to a simmer and cook just until the shrimp are done. Do not boil or overcook. Makes 4 servings.

**Tips:** Hot sausage can be substituted for a spicier dish. Bay scallops can be used in place of shrimp.

*\* Brands may vary by region; substitute a similar product.*

# Side Dishes

## Broccoli Casserole
Eat Smart

1 10 3/4-ounce can
condensed cream of
mushroom soup

1/2 cup fat-free milk

1 teaspoon soy sauce

1/8 teaspoon ground
black pepper

4 cups Eat Smart*
bite-sized broccoli
florets, lightly steamed

1 1/3 cups French's French
Fried Onions, divided

3/4 cup shredded Cheddar
cheese, divided

Pinch of grated nutmeg

Preheat oven to 350°F.

Mix soup, milk, soy sauce, pepper, broccoli,
2/3 cup onions, 1/2 cup cheese and nutmeg in a
1 1/2-quart casserole.

Bake for 25 minutes, or until heated through.

Remove from the oven and sprinkle with the
remaining onions and cheese. Bake for 5 minutes,
or until the cheese has melted. Makes 8 servings.

**Tip:** This is a great substitute for the famous green
bean casserole.

*Brands may vary by region; substitute a similar product.*

## Balsamic Grilled Vegetables
Alpine Fresh

1 pound Alpine Fresh*
asparagus, trimmed
and cut into
1-inch pieces

2 cups Alpine Fresh*
snap peas

2 cups sliced carrots

2 cups broccoli florets

4 garlic cloves, sliced thin

1/2 cup extra-virgin
olive oil

1/3 cup balsamic vinegar

1 teaspoon dried basil

1 teaspoon dried oregano

1/2 teaspoon salt

1/2 teaspoon pepper

Cooked rice, for serving
(optional)

Place asparagus, snap peas, carrots, broccoli and
garlic in a large rectangular baking dish or bowl.

In a small bowl, whisk together olive oil, vinegar,
basil, oregano, salt and pepper. Pour over the
vegetables and stir to coat. Cover with plastic wrap
and marinate for 30 minutes, stirring occasionally.

Heat a gas or charcoal grill to medium, then place a
grill wok over the fire.

Carefully spoon the vegetables into the wok, to avoid
flare-ups. Cook, stirring, until the vegetables are
crisp-tender, about 15 minutes.

Serve over rice. Makes 6 servings.

*Recipe developed by Kati Neville.*
*Brands may vary by region; substitute a similar product.*

# Easy Baked Artichoke
## Ocean Mist Farms

1 whole large Ocean Mist artichoke, rinsed and trimmed

2 tablespoons olive oil

3 tablespoons balsamic vinegar (optional)

1/2 teaspoon sea salt (or preferred dry seasoning)

2 fresh garlic cloves, quartered

2 squares aluminum foil

Preheat oven to 450°F.

Spread artichoke petals open to season. Between the petals, drizzle olive oil and vinegar, sprinkle salt and stuff garlic pieces.

Tightly double wrap and seal the seasoned artichoke with foil.

Place the foil-wrapped artichoke in the oven and bake for 1 hour and 15 minutes.

Remove from the oven and let cool before unwrapping the artichoke. Makes 1-2 servings.

**Note:** You can easily bake more than one artichoke at a time for larger crowds. Increase the ingredients as needed.

**Tips:** Enjoy as is, or scoop out the fuzzy choke center and use as an edible bowl filled with chili or your favorite dip. Cooked artichokes can be cut in half and placed directly on the grill and charred for added flavor. Artichokes can be cooked ahead of time and stored in a ziplock bag for up to 3 days in the fridge.

# Green Beans and Shallots
## Bybee Foods

1 pound Bybee Foods* Organic Petite Whole Green Beans ☘Organic

1/3 cup water

2 tablespoons chopped shallots

2 tablespoons chopped garlic

1/4 cup olive oil

Place beans in a saucepan with water. Heat to a boil, then stir, reduce heat and cook, covered, for 3-5 minutes, or until heated through. Drain and place in a serving bowl.

In a small bowl, combine shallots, garlic and olive oil, stirring to blend.

Pour the dressing over the cooked beans. Toss and serve. Makes 4 servings.

**Variation:** After draining the cooked beans, immerse in ice water until cold. Drain well. Add 1/4 cup balsamic vinegar to the olive oil mixture. Pour over the chilled green beans, toss and chill for 1 hour. Serve cold.

*Brands may vary by region; substitute a similar product.*

# Orange Honey-Glazed Carrots
## Paramount Citrus

**1 pound carrots**
**4 Paramount Citrus\***
**oranges, divided**
**¼ cup honey**
**2 tablespoons**
**unsalted butter**
**Salt and pepper**

Peel carrots and slice crosswise into coins.

Grate the zest of 2 oranges. Peel and cut the 2 oranges into segments. Set aside.

Juice the remaining 2 oranges, to make ¾ cup of juice.

In a large sauté pan, combine the carrots and orange juice. Bring to a boil, then lower the heat and simmer until the carrots are fork-tender. Add honey, orange segments and the grated zest.

Remove from the heat and stir in the cold butter. Season to taste with salt and pepper. Serve immediately. Makes 6 servings.

*\* Brands may vary by region; substitute a similar product.*

**PARAMOUNT**
*Citrus*

# Organic Baby Carrots with Ginger-Soy Vinaigrette
## Grimmway Farms

**6 cups Grimmway Farms\***
**Bunny-Luv Organic**
**Baby Carrots ❦Organic**
**4 tablespoons rice vinegar**
**2 tablespoons soy sauce**
**2 tablespoons light**
**brown sugar**
**4 tablespoons finely**
**chopped green onions**
**4 tablespoons sesame oil**
**2 tablespoons peeled,**
**minced ginger**
**Salt to taste**

Steam carrots for about 6-8 minutes, or to desired tenderness. Remove and run under cold water to stop the cooking process.

Meanwhile, in a small bowl, whisk together vinegar, soy sauce and brown sugar. Add green onions and slowly whisk in sesame oil and ginger. Season to taste with salt.

Gently toss the baby carrots in the vinaigrette and serve at room temperature or chilled. Makes 8 servings.

*\* Brands may vary by region; substitute a similar product.*

## Montana Avenue's Fresh Tomato Sauce
### Eurofresh Farms

3 pounds Eurofresh* Roma tomatoes
1/4 cup olive oil
3 ounces Spanish onion, cut into small dice
1 tablespoon chopped garlic
1 tablespoon chopped fresh basil
Pinch of chopped fresh thyme
1 1/2 teaspoons kosher salt
3 grinds of fresh black pepper
1 teaspoon sugar

Prepare a pot of boiling salted water and a bowl of ice water.

With a paring knife, remove the stem from each tomato and score the opposite end. Drop tomatoes into the boiling water just long enough for the skin to crack; then remove and place immediately in ice water.

Peel the tomatoes and roughly chop.

Heat olive oil in a saucepot over medium heat. Add onions and cook until translucent. Add garlic and tomatoes. Reduce heat to a simmer and cook, uncovered, for 1 hour, stirring occasionally.

When the sauce has cooked down to the desired consistency, add herbs and season to taste with salt, pepper and sugar. Makes 4-6 servings.

*Brands may vary by region; substitute a similar product.*

EURO FRESH FARMS

## Roasted Roma Tomatoes
Houweling's Hot House

1/2 cup olive oil

4 garlic cloves, minced

1/4 cup chopped fresh basil

1/2 teaspoon crushed red pepper

1/2 teaspoon salt

1/4 teaspoon freshly ground black pepper

2 pounds Houweling's Hot House* Roma on the Vine tomatoes

Preheat oven to 400°F.

Line a baking sheet with foil, and coat lightly with some of the olive oil.

In a small bowl, combine the remaining olive oil, garlic, basil, crushed red pepper, salt and black pepper.

Cut tomatoes in half lengthwise and place them cut-side up on the baking sheet. Brush with the olive oil mixture.

Bake for 25-30 minutes, or until the tomatoes have softened and are sizzling, with the edges slightly charred. Serve while hot. Makes 6 servings.

*Brands may vary by region; substitute a similar product.*

## Spinach, Artichoke and Parm-Stuffed Roasted Sunset Campari Tomatoes
Mastronardi Produce/Sunset

Cooking spray

10-12 Sunset* Campari tomatoes (1-pound package)

1/4 cup purchased spinach, artichoke and Parmesan dip (see tip)

1 tablespoon Italian-style dry bread crumbs

Preheat oven to 475°F. Lightly coat a baking sheet with cooking spray.

Cut 1/4 inch off the top of each tomato. Lightly squeeze the tomatoes to remove some of the seeds. With a sharp knife, shave a tiny bit off the bottom of the tomatoes so they stand up. (Eat the removed tops and bottoms of the tomatoes!)

Top each tomato with 1 teaspoon of dip, then sprinkle with 1/4 teaspoon of bread crumbs.

Place tomatoes, spaced apart, on the baking sheet.

Bake for 3-5 minutes, or until the bread crumbs are lightly golden and the tomatoes are warmed through. Makes 4-6 servings.

**Tip:** Choose a thick spinach dip, the kind that is usually served warm and is thick with cheese. It is sold refrigerated. We used Stonemill Kitchens Spinach & Artichoke Parmesan Dip.

*Brands may vary by region; substitute a similar product.*

Goodness Grown Naturally™

Side Dishes

## Cherry and Nectarine Pilaf
### Stemilt Growers

1 14 1/2-ounce can chicken broth

1/2 cup water

1 cup brown rice (uncooked)

2 tablespoons butter, divided

1/3 cup chopped walnuts

4 green onions, chopped (including green tops)

1 teaspoon freshly minced garlic (about 1 clove)

10 fresh Stemilt* cherries

1 large ripe Stemilt* nectarine

Place chicken broth and water in a 1- or 2-quart saucepan with a lid that has a tight seal. (If the pan is too big, the rice won't steam properly.) Bring to a boil, add rice and reduce heat immediately to a simmer. Cover and leave the lid on until the liquid is absorbed, 45-60 minutes.

About 10 minutes before the rice is done, melt 1 tablespoon butter in a large skillet over medium-high heat. When the butter is foaming, add walnuts and sauté until toasted. Remove from the skillet.

With the heat still on medium-high, add the remaining tablespoon of butter to the skillet and let it melt. Add onions and garlic and sauté until both are softened and golden brown.

Pit and chop cherries. Peel and chop nectarine.

Toss the steamed rice with the walnuts, garlic and onion mixture, and cherries and nectarines. Serve warm. Makes 4 servings.

*Brands may vary by region; substitute a similar product.*

## Citrus Shrimp and Couscous Toss
### alli

2 large oranges

1 large red grapefruit

1 pound peeled and deveined large shrimp

1/2 cup uncooked whole-wheat couscous

2 cups chopped fennel

1/4 cup chopped red onion

1/2 cup pitted, chopped Kalamata olives

1/2 cup slivered almonds

Nonstick cooking spray

1/3 cup fat-free balsamic vinaigrette

1/2 large head Boston lettuce, separated into leaves

8 7-inch breadsticks, for serving

Grate enough orange peel to measure 2 1/2 teaspoons. Squeeze the juice from the oranges and grapefruit.

Place shrimp in a resealable plastic bag. Add 2 tablespoons orange and grapefruit juice mixture and 1 teaspoon grated peel.

Prepare couscous according to package directions, replacing 6 tablespoons of water with 6 tablespoons of orange and grapefruit juice mixture. Place couscous in a large bowl with fennel, onion, olives and almonds.

In a large nonstick skillet lightly coated with cooking spray, cook and stir shrimp over medium-high heat for 5 minutes, or until opaque. Add shrimp to the couscous mixture.

In a small bowl, stir remaining 1 1/2 teaspoons grated orange peel into the vinaigrette. Pour over the couscous mixture and toss to coat.

Arrange lettuce on 4 plates. Top with the couscous mixture. Serve with breadsticks. Makes 4 servings.

**Nutritional information:** Each serving (2 breadsticks per serving) has 518 calories, 30 g protein, 70 g carbohydrates, 15 g fat, 168 mg cholesterol, 11 g fiber, 823 mg sodium.

*Alli is the only FDA-approved, over-the-counter weight loss aid. It is proven to help boost your weight loss by 50% more than dieting alone.*

alli

# Asparagus Barley Risotto

Gourmet Trading/Jacobs Malcolm & Burtt/
NewStar Fresh Foods/Victoria Island Farms

10 cups chicken broth

4 tablespoons extra-virgin
olive oil, divided

2 large Vidalia onions,
finely chopped

8 garlic cloves, finely chopped

3 cups barley

2 1/2 cups dry white wine

2 1/4 pounds asparagus, cut on
diagonal into 2-inch pieces

Sea salt and freshly ground pepper

1 1/2 cups freshly grated
Parmesan cheese

Warm chicken broth in a saucepan over low heat.

In a large sauté pan, heat 2 tablespoons olive oil over medium-high heat. Add onions and cook until translucent, about 5 minutes. Add garlic and cook for another 1-2 minutes.

Add barley and cook, stirring constantly, for about 2-3 minutes. Add wine and cook until the liquid is absorbed.

Add the warmed broth 1/2 cup at a time, stirring occasionally after each addition, and waiting until it is absorbed before adding more.

Meanwhile, in another sauté pan, heat 2 tablespoons olive oil over medium heat. Sauté asparagus until bright green and slightly tender, about 3-4 minutes.

Once the broth is completely absorbed into the risotto, add the asparagus, season to taste with salt and pepper, and stir in Parmesan. Serve immediately. Makes 6-8 servings.

## Roasted Washington Red Potatoes and Vegetables
### Skagit Valley's Best Produce/ Wallace Farms/Valley Pride

8 Washington*
  red potatoes
2 tablespoons chopped
  fresh parsley
2 tablespoons chopped
  fresh thyme
2 tablespoons chopped
  fresh basil
1 garlic clove, minced
12 asparagus spears,
  trimmed
3 medium shallots,
  peeled and quartered
1 medium sweet onion,
  peeled and cut into
  1/2-inch squares
2 tablespoons olive oil
Kosher salt and ground
  black pepper

Preheat oven to 425°F.

Scrub potatoes under cold running water and cut into 2-inch pieces.

In a small bowl, combine parsley, thyme, basil and garlic. Set aside.

In a large bowl, toss potatoes and vegetables with olive oil. Arrange in a single layer on a baking sheet.

Roast for 15 minutes. Turn the vegetables. Return to the oven and roast until tender and golden, about 5 minutes longer.

Transfer the vegetables to a heated serving platter. Sprinkle with the herb mixture and season to taste with salt and pepper.

Serve immediately. Makes 6 servings.

**Nutritional information:** Each serving has 347 calories, 7 g protein, 71 g carbohydrates, 5 g fat, 1 g saturated fat, 0 mg cholesterol, 6 g fiber, 69 mg sodium.

*Brands may vary by region; substitute a similar product.*

## Potatoes au Gratin with Mushroom Crumb Topping
### Kirkland Signature

5 cups heavy cream
1 tablespoon Kirkland
  Signature California
  garlic salt
1/2 teaspoon Kirkland
  Signature coarse
  ground pepper
1 cup grated Pecorino
  Romano cheese
5 1/2 pounds baking
  potatoes, peeled
  and sliced thin

### TOPPING
4 cups panko
  bread crumbs
8 ounces butter, melted
2 ounces shiitake
  mushrooms, cut in
  1/4-inch slices
8 ounces domestic
  mushrooms, cut in
  1/4-inch slices
3/4 cup sliced (1/4 inch)
  green onions
1 teaspoon Kirkland
  Signature California
  garlic salt

Preheat oven to 350°F.

In a bowl, combine cream, garlic salt, pepper and cheese. Whisk until well blended. Add potatoes and mix until well blended.

Spread potato mixture evenly in a buttered 15-by-12-inch baking pan. Cover with parchment and foil. Bake for about 1 hour, or until the potatoes are tender.

In a bowl, combine all the topping ingredients and mix until well blended.

Remove covering from the potatoes and evenly distribute the topping over them. Return to the oven, uncovered, and bake for about 5 minutes, or until the topping is browned. Makes 28 servings.

**Tip:** This recipe can be halved.

# Pomme Soufflé au Fromage
Reser's Fine Foods

- **4 tablespoons (1/2 stick) butter, melted**
- **2 24-ounce packages Main St. Bistro\* Restaurant Style Mashed Potatoes**
- **3 large eggs, lightly beaten**
- **8 ounces Camembert (or other soft ripe cheese, e.g., Gorgonzola, Brie), cut into 12 pieces**

Preheat oven to 400°F. Position rack in center of oven.

Brush twelve 4-ounce ramekins with melted butter and set aside.

Place mashed potatoes in a large mixing bowl. With a rubber spatula, fold eggs into the potatoes to combine.

Fill the ramekins with the mashed potato mixture. Place a square of cheese in the center of each ramekin. Smooth the potato over the cheese with a rubber spatula. Brush the tops with the remaining melted butter.

Place the ramekins on a sheet pan. Bake for 30 minutes, or until golden brown. Makes 12 servings.

**Casserole variation:** Place the potato and egg mixture in a buttered 2 1/2-quart casserole. Insert pieces of cheese evenly into the potato mixture. Smooth the top with a spatula and brush with the remaining melted butter. Bake for 45 minutes, or until golden brown.

*\* Brands may vary by region; substitute a similar product.*

# Mediterranean Potatoes
Alsum Produce/Russet Potato Exchange

- **1/4 cup olive oil**
- **3/4 pound onions, cut into 1/4-inch slices**
- **2 1/4 pounds medium russet potatoes, cut into 1/4-inch slices**
- **1 1/2 pounds zucchini, cut into 1/2-inch rounds**
- **2 tablespoons minced garlic**
- **3/4 teaspoon crushed red pepper**
- **Salt and black pepper**
- **3 cups tomato puree**
- **1/2 cup chopped fresh basil**
- **1 tablespoon chopped fresh mint**

In a large braising pan, heat oil over medium-low heat; add onions. Spread potatoes over onions, cover and cook for 5 minutes.

Add zucchini, garlic and red pepper; season to taste with salt and pepper. Cook, uncovered, for about 5 minutes, stirring occasionally.

Add tomato puree, cover and cook for 8-10 minutes, or until the potatoes and zucchini are tender. Stir in basil and mint; adjust seasoning with salt and pepper. Makes 12 servings.

**Nutritional information:** Each serving has 156 calories, 4 g protein, 27 g carbohydrates, 5 g fat, 0 mg cholesterol, 4 g fiber, 118 mg sodium.

## Santa Fe Olive Toss
Lindsay Olives

1 1/2 cups drained and coarsely chopped Lindsay olives (combine 2 or 3 types of olives for flavor and color)

1 ear of corn, cooked, cooled and kernels cut off the cob, or 4 ounces canned sweet corn

1 small red bell pepper, seeded and diced

1 small yellow bell pepper, seeded and diced

5 green onions, thinly sliced

3/4 cup canned black beans, rinsed and drained

2 tablespoons freshly squeezed lime juice

4 tablespoons extra-virgin olive oil

1 teaspoon ground cumin

1 teaspoon chili powder

1/4 cup chopped fresh cilantro

Salt and freshly ground black pepper

Combine olives, corn, bell peppers, green onions and black beans in a bowl.

In a small bowl, whisk together lime juice and olive oil. Stir into the olive mixture.

Add cumin, chili powder and cilantro to the olive mixture; mix well. Taste and season with salt and pepper as needed. Makes 10 servings.

**Serving suggestion:** The olive toss goes great with beef or chicken. For a completely vegetarian version, serve it with salad or coleslaw.

**Tip:** This can be made up to 2 days in advance. Place in a covered container and refrigerate. Remove from the refrigerator 30 minutes before serving.

**Nutritional information:** Each 1/2-cup serving has 115 calories, 2 g protein, 8 g carbohydrates, 9 g fat, 3 g saturated fat, 0 mg cholesterol, 2 g fiber, 153 mg sodium.

## Honey Cornbread Muffins
Pacific Natural Foods

2/3 cup heavy cream

2/3 cup Pacific Natural Foods* Organic Free Range Chicken Broth

1 cup corn kernels

1/4 cup butter, melted

1/3 cup honey

6 ounces canned green chiles, chopped

1 egg

1 tablespoon vanilla extract

1 cup all-purpose flour

3/4 cup cornmeal

1/3 cup sugar

1 teaspoon baking powder

1 teaspoon baking soda

Dash of salt

Preheat oven to 350°F.

In a bowl, combine cream, chicken broth, corn kernels, butter, honey, chiles, egg and vanilla. Stir until well blended.

In a separate bowl, combine flour, cornmeal, sugar, baking powder, baking soda and salt.

Gently incorporate the wet ingredients into the dry until you have a smooth and moist batter. Be careful not to overmix. Spoon the batter into 12 greased or paper-lined muffin cups.

Bake for 25-30 minutes, or until a tester inserted in the center comes out clean. Makes 12 muffins.

*Brands may vary by region; substitute a similar product.*

# Chef's Choice

The world's best chefs have the special ability to infuse dishes with their unique personalities. We asked several top chefs to do their magic with the products supplied by these great companies:

94

98

100

108

## The Neelys

As co-owners of Neely's Bar-B-Que, Patrick and Gina Neely have turned their family restaurant into one of the most successful barbecue operations in the South and delighted viewers of their hit Food Network show, *Down Home with the Neelys*. Patrick and his three brothers opened their first restaurant in downtown Memphis with just a few tables and chairs, one barbecue pit and $20,000 borrowed from their grandmother. The Neelys now have two locations in Memphis and one in Nashville. Patrick and Gina are authors of the cookbook *Down Home with the Neelys* (Knopf, 2009).

Memphis-Style
Steaks with Beer and
Molasses Sauce

Swift & Company®

# Memphis-Style Steaks with Beer and Molasses Sauce

JBS Swift

Recipes developed by Patrick and Gina Neely

4 beef tenderloin steaks,
   1 1/2 inches thick

3 tablespoons
   vegetable oil

Kosher salt

Freshly ground
   black pepper

**BEER AND MOLASSES
   SAUCE**

2 teaspoons butter

2 strips thick-sliced bacon,
   cut into 1/2-inch pieces

1/2 medium onion,
   finely diced

1 garlic clove, minced

1 cup ketchup

1/4 cup molasses

1/4 cup apple cider

1/4 cup lager-style beer

1 tablespoon honey

1 tablespoon prepared
   yellow mustard

1 tablespoon fresh
   lemon juice

1 1/2 teaspoons
   Worcestershire sauce

1/2 teaspoon
   cayenne pepper

1/2 teaspoon paprika

Rub steaks with oil and season generously with salt and pepper.

To prepare the sauce, melt butter in a medium saucepan over medium heat. Add bacon, onion and garlic, and sauté for 3 minutes, or until softened. Add remaining ingredients, bring to a boil, then reduce the heat to low and simmer until the sauce is reduced and thickened, 15-20 minutes.

Preheat the grill or a grill pan to medium-high.

Grill the steaks for about 7-8 minutes per side for medium-rare, brushing with some of the sauce during the last 2 minutes of cooking time.

Let the steaks rest for 10 minutes, then slice on the diagonal and serve with the remaining sauce on the side. Makes 4 servings.

# Sweet and Tangy Pork Chops

JBS Swift

The secret behind many of the Neely's recipes is the special Barbecue Seasoning and Barbecue Sauce. You can use them in a variety of savory dishes.

**NEELY'S BARBECUE
   SEASONING**

1 1/2 cups paprika

3/4 cup sugar

3 3/4 tablespoons
   onion powder

4 boneless pork chops,
   1 inch thick

Kosher salt

1/2 cup Neely's
   Barbecue Seasoning

2 cups Neely's
   Barbecue Sauce
   (see page 87)

**For Neely's Barbecue Seasoning:** Stir together the ingredients in a small bowl.

Season pork chops with salt and Barbecue Seasoning and refrigerate for at least 1 hour. About 30 minutes before you are ready to cook the chops, take them out of the fridge and let them come to room temperature.

Preheat the grill to 250°F, preferably over hickory wood and charcoal.

Place the chops on the grill away from the flame, using indirect heat, and cook for about 30-35 minutes, turning once. Wrap the chops in a foil packet and return to the grill or place them in a 180°F oven, and cook until the meat is done, about 40 minutes more. Brush the chops with a generous amount of sauce during the last 10 minutes of cooking.

Serve the chops with additional sauce.
Makes 4 servings.

**Note:** Wrapping the chops in foil is a "low and slow" finish that allows the sauce to baste the chops and ensures moist meat.

# Memphis-Style Barbecued Pork Ribs
## JBS Swift

### NEELY'S BARBECUE SAUCE

4 cups ketchup

2 cups water

1/2 cup light brown sugar

1/2 cup granulated sugar

3 teaspoons freshly ground black pepper

3 teaspoons onion powder

3 teaspoons dry mustard powder

4 tablespoons fresh lemon juice

4 tablespoons Worcestershire sauce

1 cup apple cider vinegar

4 tablespoons light corn syrup

2 tablespoons Neely's Barbecue Seasoning (see page 86)

3 pork loin back ribs, about 2 1/2 pounds each

Kosher salt

2 cups Neely's Barbecue Seasoning, plus more, as desired

4 cups Neely's Barbecue Sauce

**For Neely's Barbecue Sauce:** Combine all ingredients in a large pot or a Dutch oven. Bring to a boil over high heat, stirring frequently to prevent sticking. Reduce the heat to very low and simmer, uncovered, for at least 2 hours, stirring occasionally.

Remove from the heat and let cool. This will make about 4 cups of sauce.

Rinse the rib slabs in cold water and pat dry with paper towels. Season both sides of the slabs liberally with salt and Neely's Barbecue Seasoning. Refrigerate for at least 1 hour or up to 24 hours.

Preheat the grill to 250°F, preferably using a combination of hickory wood and charcoal.

Place the rib slabs on the grill away from (not directly over) the flame, using indirect heat.

Cook the slabs curl-side up for about 2 hours. Flip the slabs over and cook for about 1 more hour, until you get the bend in the slab (see tip below).

Pull the ribs off the grill. For dry ribs, sprinkle with more Neely's Barbecue Seasoning. For wet ribs, pour Neely's Barbecue Sauce over the slabs. Slice between the bones and serve. Makes 4 servings.

**Tip:** When barbecuing ribs, try this tenderness test for doneness. When you're ready to pull the first slab off the grill, grab the ribs with tongs about halfway down. As you lift, the slab should be flexible, easily bending downward to a 45-degree angle. That's a good indication that the ribs are ready. The meat should pull away easily from the bones.

## Mark Bittman

Mark Bittman is the bestselling author of *Mark Bittman's Kitchen Express*, *Food Matters* and *How to Cook Everything*, among others. He writes the popular weekly *New York Times* column "The Minimalist," his work has appeared in countless newspapers and magazines, and he is a regular on the *Today* show. Bittman has hosted two public television series and is currently appearing in a third.

# Pasta with Broccoli Rabe, My Style
## Garofalo
### Recipes developed by Mark Bittman

I've turned the way I cook pasta upside down: Instead of making 1 pound of pasta with 1 or 2 cups of sauce, I double the sauce and cut the noodles in half. The benefit? More vegetables, maybe a little meat or seafood for flavor and fewer refined carbohydrates. This may go against everything you've learned about cooking pasta, but it tastes wonderful, and it works with just about any recipe, except those with heavy cheese or meat sauces.

Salt

1 pound broccoli rabe, trimmed and cut into pieces

1/4 cup olive oil, or more as needed

1/4-1/2 pound sweet or spicy Italian sausage (if using link sausage, squeeze it from the casing or cut it up a bit)

1 tablespoon chopped garlic, or more to taste

1/4 teaspoon red pepper flakes, or to taste

1 teaspoon fennel seeds (optional)

Freshly ground black pepper

1/2 cup white wine or water

1/2 pound Garofalo* organic penne ziti rigate pasta, ⦾Organic or any pasta from Garofalo's variety pack

1/2 cup freshly grated Parmesan cheese (optional)

Bring a large pot of water to a boil and salt it. Add broccoli rabe and boil until it's crisp-tender, 3-5 minutes, depending on the size of your pieces. Scoop the broccoli rabe out of the water with a slotted spoon or small strainer and set it aside.

Heat oil in a large skillet over medium heat. Crumble sausage into the pan and cook, stirring occasionally to break the meat into relatively small bits and brown it, about 5 minutes. Add garlic, red pepper flakes and fennel seeds if you're using them, and sprinkle with salt and pepper.

Continue cooking and stirring for another minute or so. Add broccoli rabe and wine and cook, mashing and stirring, until the broccoli rabe is quite soft, 2-3 minutes more. Turn the heat to low to keep the sauce warm.

Cook pasta in the boiling water for about 5 minutes before checking the first time. When the pasta is just tender but not quite done, drain it, reserving about a cup of the cooking water. Toss the pasta with the sauce, along with some of the pasta water to keep the mixture from drying out. Taste and adjust the seasoning and serve immediately, with Parmesan if you like. Makes 4 servings.

**Tip:** For a pure vegetarian version, skip the sausage and add about 2 cups of chickpeas to the garlic along with the red pepper flakes. Or if you'd like to add a bright flavor and a bit more moisture, replace the wine with a couple of fresh chopped tomatoes.

*\* Brands may vary by region; substitute a similar product.*

# Spaghetti with Butter and Parmesan
## Garofalo

Salt

4-6 tablespoons (1/2-3/4 stick) butter

1 pound Garofalo* organic whole wheat spaghetti, ⦾Organic or any other pasta

1 cup freshly grated Parmesan cheese, or more to taste

Freshly ground black pepper

Bring a large pot of water to a boil and salt it.

Bring butter to room temperature. (You can soften it in a microwave, but don't melt it.) Put it in a warm bowl.

Cook pasta until tender but not mushy; drain it, reserving some of the cooking water. Toss the pasta with the butter, adding a little of the cooking water if necessary to thin the sauce.

Toss with Parmesan, sprinkle with salt and pepper, and serve immediately, passing additional Parmesan at the table. Makes 4 servings.

**Tip:** For a twist, try Pasta with Butter, Sage and Parmesan. Heat butter with 20-30 fresh sage leaves over medium heat for about 3 minutes; the butter should brown and the sage sizzle. Toss the cooked pasta with the butter, sage and Parmesan, thinning the sauce with pasta-cooking liquid if necessary.

*\* Brands may vary by region; substitute a similar product.*

*Garofalo*

# Noodles with Mushrooms
## Garofalo

Salt

1/4-1/2 cup dried porcini mushrooms (optional)

1 cup hot water (optional)

1 pound fresh mushrooms (see note)

1/4 cup plus 1 tablespoon olive oil

Freshly ground black pepper

2 tablespoons minced shallot, or 1 tablespoon minced garlic

1 pound Garofalo* organic casarecce pasta, or any pasta from Garofalo's variety pack

1/2 cup chopped fresh parsley leaves, plus more for garnish

Bring a large pot of water to a boil and salt it. If you're using porcini, put them in a small bowl, cover with the hot water and set aside to soak for about 15 minutes.

Rinse the fresh mushrooms and trim off any hard, tough spots; cut into small chunks or slices. If you're using porcini, lift them out of the soaking water; save the water, undisturbed, so that the sediment settles on the bottom of the bowl.

Put 1/4 cup olive oil in a medium to large skillet over medium heat. When hot, add all of the mushrooms and sprinkle with salt and pepper. Raise the heat to medium-high and cook, stirring occasionally, until the mushrooms begin to brown, at least 10 minutes. Add shallot or garlic and stir until the mushrooms are tender, another minute or two. Turn off the heat.

Cook pasta until tender but not mushy. When it's almost done, add about 1/2 cup of the pasta cooking water to the mushrooms (or use the porcini soaking liquid, being careful to leave the sediment in the bowl), turn the heat to low and reheat gently. Drain the pasta, reserving a little more of the cooking water.

Toss the pasta and the mushrooms together with the remaining tablespoon of olive oil; add a little of the pasta cooking water (or porcini liquid) if the dish seems dry. Taste and adjust the seasoning. Stir in parsley and serve garnished with more parsley. Makes 4 servings.

**Note:** Shiitakes are nice here; remove the stems and save them for another use.

*\* Brands may vary by region; substitute a similar product.*

## Karine Bakhoum

Karine Bakhoum is a visionary of hospitality consulting, public relations
and networking who has had a passion for cooking since childhood. She is
the founder of KB Network News, a leading food consulting and PR firm.
A frequent judge on *Iron Chef America*, Bakhoum has entertained many
luminaries of the food world with her own cooking over her 20-year career.
In 2007, she became the only person to have her palate insured by Lloyd's of
London. A New York resident, she is also an avid Costco shopper!

Broccoli Rabe
and Olive Stuffed
Chicken Breasts

# Broccoli Rabe and Olive Stuffed Chicken Breasts

## Foster Farms

Recipes developed by Karine Bakhoum, the "Iron Palate"

4-6 Foster Farms* boneless, skinless chicken breast halves

3-4 tablespoons Kirkland Signature extra-virgin olive oil, divided

4 fresh garlic cloves, coarsely chopped

1 bunch broccoli rabe, rinsed and chopped to top of stems (discard stems)

Kosher salt

Freshly ground black pepper

1 tablespoon Italian seasoning (basil, thyme, rosemary, oregano)

1/2 cup pitted Kalamata olives, coarsely chopped

1/2 cup golden raisins

1/4 cup flour

1/4 cup organic chicken broth

1/2 cup white wine (Chardonnay or Pinot Grigio)

1 tablespoon unsalted butter

Rinse chicken and pat dry with paper towels. Discard paper towels. Place chicken breasts on a cutting board and slice into the middle to create a large pocket, but do not cut through.

In a sauté pan, heat 1-2 tablespoons olive oil over medium to low heat. Add garlic and cook for 1 minute, then add broccoli rabe, stirring constantly. Cover and cook, stirring occasionally, for 2-3 minutes, or until the broccoli is soft and dark green. Season to taste with salt and pepper and a little bit of the Italian seasoning.

Add olives and raisins and continue to simmer for 1 minute over medium heat. Transfer to a bowl and set aside.

Dredge chicken lightly in flour. Stuff each chicken breast with approximately 2 tablespoons of the broccoli rabe mixture and close the fold carefully. Season both sides of chicken with salt and pepper and Italian seasoning.

Add more olive oil to the sauté pan. Place breasts carefully in the pan and cook over medium-low to medium heat until golden, then carefully turn and cook the other side until golden.

Cover the pan and cook for about 4 minutes over low heat, or until the internal temperature of the chicken reaches 170°F. Remove carefully from the pan and place on a serving platter.

Add chicken broth to the pan, stirring and scraping the pan over medium heat. Add wine and continue to stir or whisk. Add butter and stir until blended.

Pour the sauce over the chicken and serve with sautéed potatoes or side of your choice. Makes 4-6 servings.

*Brands may vary by region; substitute a similar product.*

# Cumin and Clementine Chicken

## Foster Farms

1-2 tablespoons Kirkland Signature extra-virgin olive oil

1 large Vidalia onion, chopped

1 tablespoon Italian seasoning (basil, thyme, rosemary, oregano)

4 fresh garlic cloves, coarsely chopped

6-8 Foster Farms* boneless, skinless chicken thighs

1/4 cup flour

1 1/2 tablespoons ground cumin

Kosher salt

Freshly ground black pepper

1/4 cup Spanish sherry (medium sweetness)

6 fresh clementines, cut in half, skin on

1 cup organic chicken broth

2 bay leaves

Heat olive oil in a nonstick pot over medium-high heat. Add onion, sprinkle with Italian seasoning and cook until translucent. Add garlic and cook for 1 minute, stirring frequently.

Cut chicken thighs into 1-inch pieces with kitchen shears (it's easier). Lightly dredge chicken in flour and add to the pot. Add cumin, stirring to coat. Season to taste with salt and pepper. Cook and stir for several minutes, until the chicken is browned.

Reduce heat to medium-low. Add sherry and mix thoroughly so all the chicken absorbs the flavor. Squeeze clementines over the chicken and stir. Cook for a few minutes, until the liquid is absorbed a bit, then add chicken broth and bay leaves. Cover and simmer for 40 minutes, or until the chicken reaches 165°F and the sauce has a nice unctuous consistency. If it is too thick, add more broth and gently stir until it is the desired consistency.

Serve with rice, couscous, pasta or mashed potatoes or any side of your choice. Makes 4-6 servings.

*Brands may vary by region; substitute a similar product.*

# Grilled Chicken, Mango, Pecan and Asparagus Chopped Salad
## Foster Farms

2 pounds fresh asparagus, steamed and chilled, then cut into 1-inch pieces

6 pieces fresh mango, sliced in horizontal strips

1 red onion, thinly sliced

2 ripe but firm avocados, sliced and cut into 1/2-inch cubes

1 pint cherry tomatoes, cut in half

1/2 pound bacon (optional), cut into 1/2-inch pieces, cooked until crisp and drained on a paper towel

1/2 cup pitted Kalamata olives (optional)

Kosher salt

Freshly ground black pepper

1/2 package (about 1 1/2 pounds) Foster Farms* Frozen Grilled Chicken Breast Strips, thawed

4 tablespoons Kirkland Signature balsamic vinegar

1/3 cup Kirkland Signature extra-virgin olive oil

1 cup whole pecans, broken up by hand

Select a large salad bowl (I like to use a wooden bowl about 4 inches deep). Place asparagus pieces in the bowl. Add mango, red onion, avocado, cherry tomatoes, bacon and olives. Season to taste with salt and pepper and mix with your hands (or a wooden spoon, being careful not to smash the avocado).

Add grilled chicken strips.

Pour vinegar and olive oil evenly over the salad. Mix well, using your hands or a wooden spoon. Sprinkle pecans over the salad and serve. Makes 4-6 servings.

*Brands may vary by region; substitute a similar product.*

### Myra Goodman

Myra Goodman and her husband, Drew, founded Earthbound Farm in their Carmel Valley, California, backyard 25 years ago. Myra's cooking is inspired by the fresh, flavorful and healthy harvest of their organic farm, which led her to establish one of the country's first certified organic kitchens. She is the author of *Food to Live By: The Earthbound Farm Organic Cookbook* (Workman Publishing, 2006). Her second cookbook will be published in spring 2010.

## Mixed Baby Greens with Ruby Grapefruit, Avocado and Champagne-Shallot Vinaigrette
### Earthbound Farm
Recipes developed by Myra Goodman

6 cups (tightly packed, approx. 5 ounces) Earthbound Farm* Organic Mixed Baby Greens ᴥOrganic

1 grapefruit, peeled and segmented, juice reserved

1 avocado, seeded, cut into small pieces

¹/₂ cup walnut pieces, toasted

**VINAIGRETTE**

1 tablespoon minced shallot (approx. 1 small shallot)

3 tablespoons grapefruit juice

3 tablespoons champagne vinegar

¹/₄ cup toasted walnut oil

¹/₃ cup olive oil

¹/₂ teaspoon salt

¹/₄ teaspoon pepper

Place salad greens in a large bowl.

To prepare the vinaigrette, combine shallot, grapefruit juice and vinegar in a small bowl. Add the oils in a steady stream, whisking ingredients together until well blended. Season with salt and pepper.

Add the vinaigrette to the salad greens a little at a time and toss lightly.

Top with grapefruit sections, avocado and walnuts. Serve immediately. Makes 4 servings.

*Brands may vary by region; substitute a similar product.*

Earthbound Farm.
ORGANIC
*Food to live by.*

## Spinach Yogurt Dip
### Earthbound Farm

1 cup (tightly packed) Earthbound Farm* Organic Baby Spinach ᴥOrganic

1 tablespoon minced fresh parsley

1 teaspoon chopped garlic

¹/₂ teaspoon salt

Grated zest of ¹/₂ lemon

1 ¹/₂ teaspoons lemon juice

³/₄ cup plain yogurt

2 tablespoons extra-virgin olive oil

Cayenne pepper

Place spinach, parsley, garlic, salt, lemon zest and lemon juice in a food processor and purée, stopping the machine to scrape down the sides of the bowl once or twice.

Transfer the mixture to a bowl and whisk in yogurt and olive oil.

Season to taste with a dash or two of cayenne pepper. Cover and refrigerate for at least 4 hours.

Serve cold with fresh vegetables, such as Earthbound Farm* Organic Mini Peeled Carrots.

*Brands may vary by region; substitute a similar product.*

### Vefa Alexiadou

Vefa Alexiadou is the leading authority on Greek cookery. Since 1980 she has published dozens of bestselling cookbooks in Greece, many of which won awards and have been published in other languages. She has her own TV series, regularly writes articles for magazines and gives lectures and demonstrations on Greek recipes and gastronomic traditions. Her latest book, *Vefa's Kitchen*, was published in English by Phaidon Press in June 2009.

## Roast Rack of Lamb with Vegetables
### Australian Lamb
#### Recipes developed by Vefa Alexiadou

1 teaspoon dried thyme

Salt and pepper

2 frenched Australian racks of lamb (8 ribs each)

1/3 cup olive oil

1/2 cup dry white wine

1/2 pound Brussels sprouts

1/2 pound baby carrots

1/2 pound pearl onions (frozen)

1 pound fresh mushrooms, quartered

3 tablespoons butter

1 tablespoon sugar

Preheat oven to 450°F.

Mix thyme and salt and pepper to taste and rub the racks all over. Brush with some of the olive oil and place them, meat side up, in an ovenproof dish big enough to hold them. Pour over the remaining olive oil and the wine.

Roast for about 10 minutes to brown the meat. Lower the temperature to 350°F and continue roasting the racks, basting occasionally with the pan juices, for 15-20 minutes, or until the internal temperature is 135°F for medium-rare.

Meanwhile, blanch Brussels sprouts, carrots and onions in boiling water for about 5 minutes. Strain and place in a large sauté pan along with the mushrooms.

When the lamb is done, remove from the oven, transfer to a large serving dish, rib bones up, and loosely cover with foil. Let rest for 5-8 minutes.

Pour the pan juices over the vegetables. Cook on the stovetop over medium heat until tender, about 10 minutes. At the last minute, stir in butter and sugar to caramelize the vegetables. Surround the lamb racks with the vegetables, trim the rib bones with frills and serve immediately. Makes 6 servings.

THE
AUSTRALIAN LAMB
COMPANY INC.

## Lamb Loin Chops
### Australian Lamb

1/3 cup olive oil

8 Australian lamb loin chops

Salt and pepper

1 teaspoon dried thyme

1/3 cup cooking sherry

1/4 cup lemon juice

1 teaspoon prepared mustard

1 tablespoon finely chopped fresh dill, for garnish

Lemon wedges, for garnish

Preheat oven to 375°F.

Heat olive oil in a heavy-bottomed frying pan and sauté lamb chops over high heat for 3 minutes on each side.

Remove the pan from the heat and sprinkle each side of the chops with salt and pepper to taste and thyme. Transfer the chops to an ovenproof dish or pan.

Deglaze the sauté pan by pouring sherry into it and returning it to the burner. (Caution: To avoid a fire hazard, never pour alcohol into a pan near an open flame. And always stand back when returning a pan with alcohol to the heat.) With a spoon or spatula, work the sherry around the pan to loosen any browned bits—this will add flavor as well as cook off the alcohol in the sherry. Add lemon juice and mustard to the pan and stir to combine.

Spoon the mixture over the chops and roast in the oven for approximately 8-10 minutes.

Transfer the chops onto a hot serving dish and spoon any pan juices over the chops. Serve immediately, garnished with chopped dill and lemon wedges.

Accompany with fried potatoes and buttered vegetables. Makes 4 servings.

# Lamb Kebabs (Souvlakia)
## Australian Lamb

1 cup olive oil, plus more
   for grilling

2 tablespoons dried oregano, plus
   more for grilling

1/4 cup fresh lemon juice, plus
   grated peel of 1 lemon

1 1/2 teaspoons salt (kosher or
   sea salt is best), plus more
   for grilling

1 tablespoon ground black pepper,
   plus more for grilling

1 Australian boneless leg of lamb,
   cut into 1 1/2-inch cubes

10 large wooden skewers, soaked
   in water for 1 hour

2 onions, cut into 1-inch squares

2 green bell peppers, cut into
   1-inch squares

2 firm tomatoes, cut into 1-inch
   squares, or small cherry tomatoes

Pita bread, for serving

Lemon wedges, for serving

### TZATZIKI SAUCE

1 cucumber, peeled, seeded
   and grated

16 ounces Greek yogurt

1 tablespoon minced fresh garlic

1 tablespoon olive oil

2 teaspoons lemon juice

1 teaspoon kosher salt

1 tablespoon chopped fresh dill
   (optional)

1 tablespoon chopped fresh parsley
   (optional)

To prepare the tzatziki sauce, spread out a clean dish towel on a counter, place grated cucumber in the center, fold up the sides of the towel and squeeze cucumber over the sink to remove the liquid.

Transfer the cucumber to a medium mixing bowl and stir in yogurt, garlic, olive oil, lemon juice, salt and optional herbs. Cover and refrigerate for 2 hours before serving to allow flavors to develop.

In a large mixing bowl, combine olive oil, oregano, lemon juice and grated peel, salt and pepper. Add lamb cubes and toss to coat. Cover and marinate in the refrigerator for 6 hours or overnight, turning the cubes of meat from time to time to keep them well moistened. (Note: If marinating overnight, omit the salt until the next morning.)

Thread the skewers, beginning with a lamb cube and then alternating with vegetables. End each skewer with a lamb cube.

Brush the souvlakia with olive oil and lightly season with a little more oregano, salt and pepper.

Prepare and heat the grill to medium-hot.

Grill the skewers for about 8-10 minutes, or until the meat is done to your taste, turning every 2 minutes to cook evenly.

Serve immediately with warm pita bread, Tzatziki Sauce and lemon wedges. Makes 8-10 servings.

**Tip:** Prepared tzatziki sauce can be purchased at some Costco warehouses.

Home Cooking The Costco Way

## Nigella Lawson

Nigella Lawson is the author of *How to Eat*, *How to Be a Domestic Goddess*, *Nigella Bites*, *Forever Summer*, *Feast* and *Nigella Express*, which have more than 5 million combined copies in print worldwide. These books, along with several successful TV series, have made her a household name around the world. Her latest cookbook, *Nigella Christmas: Food, Family, Friends, Festivities*, will be published by Hyperion in November 2009. She lives in London with her family.

Italian Sausages
with Lentils

# Italian Sausages with Lentils
## Tarantino
### Recipes developed by Nigella Lawson

This is what Italians serve traditionally on New Year's Day. The coin-shaped lentils symbolize the prosperity that is hoped for over the coming year.

3-4 tablespoons olive oil (not extra virgin), divided
1 onion, finely chopped
Sprinkling of salt
2 3/4 cups (18 ounces) dried Puy lentils (see note)
1 fat garlic clove, squished and skin removed
8 Tarantino* mild Italian sausages
1/3 cup plus 1 tablespoon red wine
1/4 cup water
Chopped fresh flat-leaf parsley, for sprinkling

To cook the lentils, put 2-3 tablespoons of the oil into a good-sized saucepan (with a lid that fits) over medium heat. Add the chopped onion, sprinkle with salt and cook till soft, about 5 minutes. Add the lentils, stir well and cover generously with cold water. Bring to a boil, cover and let simmer gently for half an hour, until cooked and most, if not all, of the liquid is absorbed.

Coat a heavy-based frying pan with oil, add the garlic and cook for a few minutes over medium heat. Add and brown the sausages. When they are brown on both sides, about 5 minutes, add the wine and water and let it bubble. Cover the pan and cook for about 15 minutes. Using a fork, mash the garlic into the sauce and taste for seasoning (adding more water if it's too strong).

Remove the lentils to a shallow bowl or dish and cover them with the sausages and the gravy. Sprinkle with parsley. Makes 4 servings.

**Note:** Puy lentils were originally grown in the volcanic soils of Puy, in France. Now they're grown in Italy and North America. They're prized because they remain firm after cooking and have a rich flavor.

*Recipe from Nigella Bites (Hyperion, 2002).*
*\* Brands may vary by region; substitute a similar product.*

# Bacon-Wrapped Chipolatas
## Tarantino

25 Tarantino* breakfast sausage links
25 thin slices bacon, or 50 very thin slices of pancetta
3 tablespoons vegetable oil

Preheat oven to 400°F.

Twist each sausage in the center to form 2 cocktail-size sausages and snip with scissors on the twist to separate them.

Cut each slice of bacon in half vertically. Wrap each half-slice of bacon round each cocktail sausage. The bacon, when thin, seems to get sticky and adheres to the sausage.

Spoon the oil into a roasting pan and arrange the sausages, each with the end bit of bacon facing down (though they may roll), and roast for 30 minutes or so, until the bacon is crisp and the sausages are cooked.

Take the pan out of the oven and wrap it in aluminum foil. If you've let the sausages burn a little, however, it may be better to remove them to a large piece of aluminum foil and wrap them up, forming a loose but tightly sealed package; otherwise the sausages will continue to fry a little in the pan.

When you are almost ready to eat, reheat the sausages by placing the foil-wrapped pan, or parcel, in a hot oven for about 10 minutes. Or cook them from scratch about 45 minutes before you need them. Makes 10-16 servings as part of the Christmas feast, or 8-10 if not.

**Tip:** To make ahead of time, roll the sausages in bacon, as directed, cover and keep in the refrigerator for up to 2 days. Cook in the oven as directed.

*Recipe from Nigella Christmas (Hyperion, 2009).*
*\* Brands may vary by region; substitute a similar product.*

# Panettone and Italian Sausage Stuffing
## Tarantino

1 pound panettone, cut into
   1-inch cubes
1/4 cup olive oil, divided
2 onions, finely chopped
3 stalks celery, finely chopped

8 Tarantino* mild Italian sausages
4 eggs
2 cups chicken broth
Salt to taste
Handful of chopped parsley

Preheat oven to 400°F.

Lay out the panettone cubes on a large baking sheet, and toast them in the oven for 10 minutes, till they are crisp and golden at the edges. Allow to cool. (This step can be done in advance.)

Put 2 tablespoons of the oil into a sauté pan and, when warm, add onion and celery. Cook gently, stirring every now and again, for 10-15 minutes, or until softened.

Add the remaining oil to the pan, then squeeze the sausages out of their casings into the pan and squish and turn with a wooden spoon to break the pieces up as much as possible. Mix with the celery and onion. Cook the sausage meat for about 10 minutes, or until the pinkness has left it, stirring regularly.

Grease an ovenproof pan (9 by 12 inches), pretty enough to serve from, put in the toasted panettone cubes and add the sausage, celery and onion. I use my hands to blend everything together well.

In a bowl, whisk the eggs with the broth (adding salt if it isn't already salty, so taste the broth first) and pour this over the stuffing, leaving it to soak in for about 5 minutes before baking, uncovered, in the oven for 45 minutes. It will be dark golden and crisp on top, a bit soft—but utterly firm—underneath.

Sprinkle with chopped parsley and use a large spoon to serve. Makes 10-16 servings as part of the Christmas feast, or 8-10 if not.

*Recipe from Nigella Christmas (Hyperion, 2009).*
*\* Brands may vary by region; substitute a similar product.*

### Devin Alexander

Costco member Devin Alexander has maintained a 55-pound weight loss for more than 15 years and is committed to helping others find healthy comfort foods through her TV shows, bestselling cookbooks, foods and culinary products. She is the author of *The Most Decadent Diet Ever!*, *The Biggest Loser Cookbook* and *The Biggest Loser Family Cookbook*. For more from Devin, see her Web site, *www.devinalexander.com*.

## Great Grape Baby Green Salad
### Delano Farms
Recipes developed by Devin Alexander

12 cups mixed
   baby greens
2 cups Delano Farms red,
   green or black seedless
   grapes, cut in half
1/4 cup walnut pieces
3 ounces (about 3/4 cup)
   crumbled reduced-fat
   blue cheese
6 tablespoons light
   balsamic vinaigrette
   or light honey
   mustard dressing
   (I used Newman's Own
   light balsamic)
1 pound grilled boneless,
   skinless chicken breast
   strips or shredded
   rotisserie chicken

Place greens, grapes, walnuts and cheese in a large glass or plastic mixing bowl. Add dressing and toss well.

Divide the salad among 4 serving plates and top each with equal portions of chicken. Serve immediately. Makes 4 entrée-sized servings.

**Nutritional information:** Each serving has 329 calories, 34 g protein, 19 g carbohydrates, 13 g fat, 4 g saturated fat, 77 mg cholesterol, 3 g fiber, 738 mg sodium.

## Prosciutto-Wrapped Grapes
### Delano Farms

4 1/2 ounces very thinly
   sliced prosciutto, cut
   into 36 strips (about
   1 1/2 inches wide
   by 3 inches long,
   if possible)
36 Delano Farms black
   seedless grapes
36 decorative toothpicks

Wrap a strip of prosciutto around each grape.

Arrange on a large plate or platter and place a toothpick in the center of each grape. Serve immediately. Makes 6 servings.

**Nutritional information:** Each (6-grape) serving has 66 calories, 6 g protein, 6 g carbohydrates, 2 g fat, <1 g saturated fat, 17 mg cholesterol, trace fiber, 570 mg sodium.

# Grape Skewers with Cheesecake Dip
## Delano Farms

**96** Delano Farms red
    seedless grapes
**16** 6- to 8-inch skewers

### CHEESECAKE DIP
**8** ounces reduced-fat cream cheese,
    at room temperature
**1/4** cup sugar
**1** tablespoon fat-free vanilla yogurt
**1/2** teaspoon vanilla extract

Skewer 6 grapes lengthwise onto each of the skewers so they touch.

To prepare the Cheesecake Dip, place cream cheese and sugar in a medium mixing bowl. Beat with an electric mixer until well combined. Add yogurt and vanilla and beat on low until just blended.

Spoon the dip into a medium decorative bowl. Place the bowl in the center of a large serving plate or platter.

Arrange the skewers around the bowl pointing outward. Serve immediately.
Makes 16 servings.

**Nutritional information:** Each serving (1 skewer plus 1 1/2 tablespoons dip) has 66 calories, 2 g protein, 10 g carbohydrates, 3 g fat, 2 g saturated fat, 8 mg cholesterol, trace fiber, 43 mg sodium.

## Rocco DiSpirito

Rocco DiSpirito's passion for cooking began at the very young age of 11, and he has never looked back. At 16 he entered the Culinary Institute of America, and at 18 began working for legendary chefs worldwide. He has opened two popular New York restaurants, authored five cookbooks and starred in the hit series *The Restaurant* on NBC. In 2008, the cooking series *Rocco Gets Real!* was launched on A&E. He is a regular contributor on *The Biggest Loser* and judge on *Top Chef,* and recently was seen on ABC's *Dancing with the Stars.* His latest book is *Rocco Gets Real* (Wiley).

Grilled Chicken with
Avocado Relish

# Grilled Chicken with Avocado Relish
## Pilgrim's Pride/Gold Kist Farms
### Recipes developed by Rocco DiSpirito

**4 Gold Kist Farms\***
  **boneless, skinless
  chicken breast halves**

**3 tablespoons extra-virgin
  olive oil, divided**

**Salt and freshly
  ground pepper**

**3 large avocados, diced**

**1 large tomato, diced**

**1 medium red onion, diced**

**1 jalapeño, finely chopped**

**Juice of 1 lime**

**1/2 cup fresh cilantro,
  roughly chopped**

Preheat a grill/grill pan/broiler on high.

Take each chicken breast and cut in half lengthwise to make cutlets. You'll end up with 8 cutlets.

Coat chicken with 2 tablespoons of the olive oil and season generously with salt and pepper. Grill chicken until it is cooked throughout, about 3 1/2 minutes per side (total time depends on thickness).

While the chicken is grilling, make the relish: In a medium-size bowl, combine avocado, tomato, onion, jalapeño, lime juice and remaining olive oil. Season to taste with salt and pepper. Gently fold in cilantro.

Serve chicken alongside a mound of the relish. Makes 4 servings.

*Recipe from Rocco's Real Life Recipes (Wiley).*
*\* Brands may vary by region; substitute a similar product.*

# Broiled Chicken Thighs with Stew of Mushrooms, Corn and Cabbage
## Pilgrim's Pride/Gold Kist Farms

**5 tablespoons vegetable
  oil, divided**

**3 tablespoons garlic
  paste, or 9 garlic
  cloves, chopped**

**2 pounds Gold Kist
  Farms\* boneless, skin-
  less chicken thighs**

**Salt and freshly
  ground pepper**

**1 8-ounce package sliced
  cremini
  mushrooms**

**1 bunch scallions, sliced
  thin on a bias**

**1 16-ounce package
  coleslaw mix**

**1 1/2 cups frozen
  corn kernels**

**1 12.5-ounce jar
  House of Tsang
  General Tsao Sauce\*\***

**1/4 cup water**

Combine 2 tablespoons of vegetable oil with garlic paste. Rub the mixture over chicken thighs to coat. (If desired, put thighs in a resealable plastic bag in the refrigerator and marinate overnight.)

Preheat broiler on high.

Season chicken generously with salt and pepper. Place chicken on a roasting rack set on a foil-lined rimmed baking sheet. Broil for about 10 minutes. Turn and continue to broil until chicken is just cooked through, 5-6 minutes more.

Meanwhile, heat remaining 3 tablespoons oil over high heat in a large sauté pan. When oil is hot, add mushrooms and cook, stirring occasionally, until golden brown, about 6 minutes. Stir in scallions, coleslaw mix and corn, and season to taste with salt and pepper. Cover and cook until cabbage is tender, about 4 minutes.

Add General Tsao Sauce and water to the vegetable mixture. Season to taste with salt and pepper, if necessary. Serve vegetable mixture with chicken thighs. Makes 4 servings.

*Recipe from Rocco Gets Real (Wiley).*
*\* Brands may vary by region; substitute a similar product.*
*\*\* Your favorite bottled or jarred Asian sauce works here.*

# Broiled Chicken Legs with Onions, Apples and Chunky Lemon-Pepper Sauce

Pilgrim's Pride/Gold Kist Farms

2 1/2 pounds Gold Kist Farms* chicken drumsticks

Salt and freshly ground pepper

2 large Vidalia onions, peeled

2 Granny Smith apples, peeled, cored and cut in wedges

2 tablespoons extra-virgin olive oil

1 10-ounce jar Tabasco Spicy Pepper Jelly

3 lemons

Coarsely ground black pepper

Preheat broiler on low. Line a rimmed baking sheet with foil.

Season chicken generously with salt and pepper. Place chicken in center of pan.

Cut each onion into 12 thin wedges. Scatter onions and apples around chicken. Drizzle everything with olive oil and season with salt and pepper. Broil for 10 minutes. Turn chicken over and stir apples and onions to expose uncooked surfaces.

Turn broiler to high. Broil until chicken is charred and cooked through, about another 10 minutes.

Meanwhile, heat pepper jelly in a small saucepan over medium heat until melted. Peel lemons and remove the pith. Dice the lemons, reserving the juice. Remove jelly from the heat; add diced lemon and juice. Stir to combine and season to taste with salt and pepper.

To serve, spoon sauce on top of chicken, onions and apples and top with fresh coarsely ground pepper. Makes 4 servings.

*Recipe from Rocco Gets Real (Wiley).*

*\* Brands may vary by region; substitute a similar product.*

## Tony Mantuano

Chef Tony Mantuano operates the highly acclaimed Spiaggia, Cafe Spiaggia and Terzo Piano restaurants in Chicago. He is the James Beard 2005 Best Chef: Midwest winner. Chef Mantuano and his wife, Cathy, are authors of *The Spiaggia Cookbook: Eleganza Italiana in Cucina* and *Wine Bar Food*. Tony has been seen on national TV networks and shows, including *The Early Show* on CBS, PBS, CNN, Travel Channel, Fox and The Food Network.

# Chef Tony Mantuano's Flaming Ouzo Shrimp
SeaMazz
Recipe developed by Tony Mantuano

1/4 cup plus 1 tablespoon extra-virgin olive oil, divided

1 russet potato, very thinly sliced

1 jalapeño pepper, thinly sliced

2 garlic cloves, thinly sliced

1 1/4 pounds SeaMazz easy-peel U-15 shrimp, thawed

Sea salt and freshly ground black pepper

6 ounces ouzo

1/2 lemon

Crusty bread, for serving

Preheat oven to 500°F.

Heat a large skillet in the oven for 5 minutes.

Remove the pan from the oven and add 1/4 cup olive oil. Carefully layer potato slices in the pan, slightly overlapping them. Top with sliced jalapeño, garlic and finally the shrimp. Season to taste with salt and pepper. Drizzle with the remaining tablespoon of olive oil.

Return the pan to the oven and bake until the shrimp are opaque throughout, 5-7 minutes.

Remove the pan from the oven and add ouzo. Stand back and carefully hold a lit match to the juices to flame the dish. As the flame begins to die down, squeeze the lemon over the shrimp. Serve immediately with crusty bread to mop up the juices. Makes 6 appetizer servings or 4 entrée servings.

**Tip:** Make sure that the ouzo goes on while the dish is very hot, or it will not light. And remember to stand back when flaming the shrimp.

*Recipe by Tony Mantuano and Cathy Mantuano from Wine Bar Food.*

# Grilled Oregano Shrimp with Mediterranean Salad
SeaMazz

2 pounds SeaMazz large (U-8 or U-6) shrimp, thawed and peeled (tails left on)

Juice of 1 large lemon (about 1/3 cup juice)

2/3 cup Kirkland Signature extra-virgin olive oil

1 tablespoon minced garlic

1 teaspoon dried oregano

1 teaspoon dried thyme

1/2 teaspoon paprika

1/2 teaspoon sea salt

*SALAD*

4 cups coarsely chopped romaine lettuce

4 cups total of any combination of the following: grape tomatoes, cucumber or avocado chunks, pitted Kalamata olives, sliced celery or fennel, marinated artichoke hearts, thinly sliced red onion

1/2 cup crumbled feta or Gorgonzola cheese

3/4 cup bottled balsamic or vinaigrette salad dressing

Place shrimp in a gallon-size zip-top bag (or medium bowl).

In a small bowl, combine lemon juice, olive oil, garlic, oregano, thyme, paprika and salt; pour over the shrimp. Close the bag and turn to coat the shrimp. Marinate for 15-30 minutes.

Preheat the grill or broiler to medium-high.

Remove the shrimp from the marinade and grill or broil, turning once, until opaque throughout.

Combine romaine and the 4 cups of other salad ingredients; toss to blend. Arrange in the center of 4 plates.

Place the shrimp on top of the salads. Sprinkle with cheese and drizzle with dressing. Makes 4 servings.

*Recipe developed by Amy Muzyka-McGuire, dietitian/ Certified Culinary Professional.*

# Entrées

## Pork Chops with Fresh Cherry Reduction Sauce
Trinity Fruit

6 bone-in pork chops, approximately 1-1 1/2 inches thick

Kosher salt

Fresh cracked black pepper

1 pound fresh large Trinity Fruit Sales California cherries

1 cup ruby port or oloroso sherry

1/2 cup sugar

2 tablespoons balsamic vinegar

1 tablespoon orange blossom honey

6 fresh mint leaves, for garnish

Fresh cherry leaves or blossoms, for garnish (optional)

Preheat the grill.

Lightly season pork chops on both sides with salt and pepper. Place on the grill and sear on high direct heat for 4 minutes on each side, making a grill-mark pattern. Finish cooking the chops for an additional 6-10 minutes on indirect medium heat, or until the internal temperature is 160°F.

Stem and pit cherries with a cherry or olive pitter. Place the cherries in a large saucepan and add port, sugar, vinegar and honey. Cook over high heat, stirring slowly, until the sugar dissolves. Bring to a boil, reduce heat and simmer for approximately 12-15 minutes, or until the cherries are soft but still retain their shape.

To serve, spoon the cherry mixture on top of the chops. Garnish with mint and cherry leaves or blossoms if available. Makes 6 servings.

*Recipe developed by Maurice Cameron.*

## Caramel Apple Pork Chops
Borton & Sons

4 boneless pork loin chops, 3/4 inch thick

Vegetable oil

1/4 cup packed light brown sugar

1/4 teaspoon ground cinnamon

1/4 teaspoon grated nutmeg

Salt and pepper

2 tart Borton apples (Granny Smith, Pink Lady or Braeburn)

4 tablespoons butter

4 tablespoons chopped pecans

Heat a skillet over medium-high heat. Brush pork chops lightly with oil and cook for 5-6 minutes on each side, or until evenly browned. Remove from the pan and keep warm.

In a small mixing bowl, combine brown sugar, cinnamon, nutmeg, and salt and pepper to taste. Core apples and slice into 1/2-inch wedges.

Add butter to the skillet and stir in the apples and brown-sugar mixture. Cover and cook over medium-high heat for 3-4 minutes, just until the apples are tender. Remove the apples with a slotted spoon and arrange on top of the chops; keep warm.

Continue cooking the mixture in the skillet, uncovered, until the sauce thickens slightly. Spoon the sauce over the apples and chops. Sprinkle with pecans. Makes 4 servings.

# Marinated Pork Chops and Roasted Grapes
## Aconex

1 cup red wine
5 black peppercorns
1 clove
1 bay leaf
1 tablespoon dried oregano
2 garlic cloves, 1 minced and 1 whole
7 tablespoons olive oil, divided
Salt
4 pork chops
8 ounces Flame seedless grapes, separated into small bunches
12 new potatoes
Sea salt
Fresh black pepper

In a nonreactive container, combine wine, peppercorns, clove, bay leaf, oregano, minced garlic, 2 tablespoons olive oil and salt to taste. Mix well and add pork chops. Marinate in the refrigerator overnight.

Preheat oven to 200°F.

In a nonstick pan, heat 2 tablespoons olive oil over medium heat. Add garlic clove and grapes and cook until the grapes are seared. Transfer to the oven and roast until the grapes start to release their juices, about 8-10 minutes. Remove from the oven and set aside.

Cook potatoes in water until nearly tender, then slice and sear them in 1 tablespoon olive oil in a hot pan for a couple of minutes. Sprinkle with sea salt and black pepper. Set aside.

Heat a sauté pan over medium heat; add 2 tablespoons olive oil. Add the pork chops and cook for about 4 minutes on each side, or until they have a nice golden color and are pale pink in the center. Remove from the pan and let rest for about 1 minute.

Serve the pork chops with the grapes and grape juices on top and the potatoes alongside. Makes 4 servings.

## Sweet Onions and Apricot with Grilled Espresso Pork
Keystone

2 Keystone Certified Sweet Onions

1 teaspoon olive oil, plus more for brushing

Salt and pepper

4 tablespoons apricot preserves

1 teaspoon Dijon mustard

1 jalapeño pepper, seeded and minced

2 1-pound pork tenderloins

1 tablespoon espresso powder or fresh-ground beans

1 teaspoon ground thyme

Fresh or dried apricot slices, for garnish (optional)

Preheat the grill.

Peel and cut each onion into 3 thick slices. Brush with olive oil and season with salt and pepper. Grill over high heat for 4 minutes per side; remove from the heat and cut into quarters.

In a saucepan, combine preserves, 1 teaspoon olive oil, mustard and jalapeño. Cook for 2 minutes over medium-high heat. Add onions and cook for 1 minute.

Preheat oven to 450°F.

Cut pork into 1 1/2-inch-thick slices.

In a small bowl, combine espresso powder, thyme, and salt and pepper to taste. Apply the rub generously to cut sides of pork.

Grill the pork over high heat for 3 minutes on each side. Transfer to the oven for 3 minutes for medium, or until cooked to taste. Remove from the oven and let rest for 5 minutes.

Place the onion mixture on plates and top with pork. Garnish with sliced apricots. Makes 5-6 servings.

## Pork Tenderloin with Mushroom Sauce
Mr. Yoshida's

1 pork tenderloin

1 1/2 cups Mr. Yoshida's Original Gourmet Sauce

*MUSHROOM SAUCE*

2 tablespoons butter

1 teaspoon toasted sesame oil

1 garlic clove, minced

3/4 cup sliced fresh mushrooms

1/4 cup white wine

2 tablespoons Mr. Yoshida's Original Gourmet Sauce

Marinate pork in Gourmet Sauce in the refrigerator for 6 hours.

Preheat oven to 325°F.

Place pork on a baking sheet (discard the marinade). Set on the center oven rack and roast for 1-1 1/2 hours, or until the internal temperature is 160°F. Remove pork from the oven and let stand.

To prepare the mushroom sauce, melt butter and oil in a hot skillet over medium heat. Add garlic and mushrooms and sauté until tender. Pour in wine and cook for 1 minute.

Add Gourmet Sauce and cook for another 2-3 minutes.

To serve, place the pork on a platter and pour the sauce over and around it. Makes 6 servings.

# Cornbread-Stuffed Bacon-Wrapped Pork Tenderloin
## Farmland Foods

7 slices Kirkland Signature hickory-smoked bacon, divided

3 tablespoons butter or margarine

1/2 cup chopped onion

1/3 cup chopped red cooking apple (e.g., Rome, Jonathan)

1/4 cup chopped celery

1 garlic clove, finely chopped

1/2 teaspoon poultry seasoning

1/4 teaspoon salt

1/8 teaspoon ground pepper

3/4 cup cornbread stuffing mix

Apple cider (approximately 1/3 cup)

1 1 1/2- to 2-pound Farmland pork tenderloin

Preheat oven to 375°F.

Cook 3 slices bacon in a large skillet according to package directions; drain. Crumble.

Carefully pour all but 1 tablespoon bacon grease from the pan; add butter and melt. Add onion, apple, celery, garlic, poultry seasoning, salt and pepper; cook over medium heat until the onions are tender. Stir in crumbled bacon and cornbread stuffing. Stir in enough cider to moisten the stuffing.

Place 4 remaining slices of bacon about 2 inches apart across the center of a 15-by-10-by-1-inch baking pan.

Make a lengthwise cut down the center of the tenderloin but not all the way through. Lay flat on top of the bacon slices.

Spoon the stuffing over the tenderloin. Wrap the bacon slices around the tenderloin, overlapping on top, but leaving the tenderloin open.

Bake for 40-45 minutes, or until the internal temperature of the stuffing is 160°F. Let stand 10 minutes before slicing. Makes 4 servings.

# Crown Roast of Pork with Cranberry Stuffing
Mazola Oils

### SPICE RUB
1 tablespoon garlic salt
1 tablespoon poultry seasoning
1 tablespoon dried thyme leaves
2 teaspoons ground cinnamon
2 teaspoons medium-grind
black pepper
1 1/2 teaspoons paprika
1/4 teaspoon ground cloves

### STUFFING AND PORK
1/4 cup Mazola corn oil
1/4 cup butter or margarine
1 1/2 cups chopped celery
1 cup chopped onion
1/2 cup dried cranberries
1/2 cup chopped dried apricots
6 cups cubed firm white bread,
dried (about 6 slices)
1 cup reduced-sodium chicken broth
12- to 16-bone tied crown pork
roast (about 8 pounds)

Preheat oven to 350°F.

Combine the spice rub ingredients in a small bowl. Set aside.

Heat corn oil and butter in a large skillet over medium heat. Add celery, onions and 2 tablespoons of spice rub. Cook for 5-7 minutes, or until the vegetables are tender but not browned. Add cranberries and apricots; cook for 1-2 minutes, or until heated through. Transfer to a large bowl.

Add bread cubes to the cranberry-and-onion mixture and toss. Stir in chicken broth.

Rub remaining spice rub on the exterior and interior of the roast; transfer to a roasting pan. Fill cavity of roast with stuffing. Cover the stuffing and rib tips with foil. Place on lower oven rack and bake for 3 1/2-4 hours, or until the roast is well browned and internal temperature is at least 155°F. Remove from the oven and let rest for at least 10 minutes.

Slice the roast between the bones and serve with stuffing. Makes 8-10 servings.

**Mazola**

## Ol' Gramma's Stone Fruit Marinade
SunWest

- **3 SunWest\* nectarines, peaches or plums**
- **1/2 cup packed light brown sugar**
- **3 tablespoons olive oil**
- **1/4 cup seasoned rice vinegar**
- **1/2 teaspoon Worcestershire sauce**
- **2 tablespoons crushed red pepper (or to taste)**
- **1/2 teaspoon ground black pepper**
- **1 teaspoon garlic powder**
- **1 teaspoon onion powder**
- **1 3- to 4-pound boneless pork loin**

Remove pits from fruit, cut the fruit into chunks and place in a blender.

Add brown sugar, olive oil, vinegar, Worcestershire sauce, red pepper, black pepper, garlic powder and onion powder. Blend until pureed.

Pour the mixture over the pork and marinate in the refrigerator for 12-24 hours. Discard the marinade.

Barbecue pork over low heat until the internal temperature is 155°F. Makes 4-6 servings.

**Tip:** This can also be used to marinate one whole chicken.

*\* Brands may vary by region; substitute a similar product.*

## Pulled Pork and Coleslaw Sandwiches
Best Brands Corp.

- **1 package (1 dozen) Kirkland Signature fresh bakery sweet rolls**
- **Butter or margarine, softened**
- **36 ounces barbecued pulled pork, warmed**
- **12 ounces deli coleslaw, chilled**

Preheat the oven broiler.

Cut individual rolls in half horizontally. Spread cut sides of rolls with butter or margarine. Toast under the broiler.

Fill each roll with 3 ounces pulled pork and top pork with 1 ounce coleslaw.

Serve immediately. Makes 12 sandwiches.

Best Brands Corp.

# Ham with Apple-Cranberry Salsa
## Farmland Foods

1 Kirkland Signature/Carando
  spiral-sliced hickory-smoked
  ham
4 medium cooking apples
3 tablespoons lemon juice
1/2 cup butter

1 cup walnut pieces
1 cup dried cranberries
1/2 cup pure maple syrup
1 Kirkland Signature Spiral Ham
  Glaze Mix Packet

Preheat oven to 275°F.

Remove all packaging materials from ham, including the clear button on the bone. Place the ham flat, face-side down, in a shallow roasting pan. Cover tightly with foil.

Bake for approximately 2 hours, or until heated through. *Do not overcook*. Remove the ham from the oven and let stand, covered, for 20-30 minutes before serving.

To prepare the salsa, core and chop apples. Toss with lemon juice to keep from browning.

Melt butter in a large skillet over medium-high heat. Add walnuts and cook, stirring, until walnuts smell "toasted." Stir in apples, dried cranberries, maple syrup and ham glaze mix, stirring well to dissolve the glaze mix. Bring to a boil.

To serve, spoon salsa over ham slices. Makes 12-16 servings.

# Sweet and Hot Prune-Chipotle Ribs

Kirkland Signature/Sunsweet

1 large slab pork ribs
  (about 4 pounds)
1 cup Sunsweet* pitted dried plums
1 cup chicken or vegetable stock
1 cup chopped onion
3 tablespoons honey

2 tablespoons lime juice
1  8-ounce can tomato sauce
2-3 canned chipotle peppers in
  adobo sauce
2 teaspoons adobo sauce
Chopped fresh cilantro (optional)

Preheat oven to 400°F.

Place ribs in a large shallow baking pan. Add 1 inch of water to the pan and cover tightly with foil; bake for 1 hour.

Meanwhile, combine dried plums, stock, onion, honey, lime juice, tomato sauce, chipotles and adobo sauce in a medium saucepan. Bring to a boil, then reduce heat and simmer, uncovered, for 15 minutes. Let cool slightly, then puree in a blender or food processor. Return to the saucepan and cook until fairly thick.

Remove foil from the ribs and drain off the water. Bake, uncovered, for another 30 minutes, basting liberally with the sauce several times.

Serve the ribs with extra sauce, and sprinkle with cilantro, if desired.
Makes 4-6 servings.

*Brands may vary by region; substitute a similar product.*

# Barbecued Ribs with California Avocado-Mango Relish

California Avocado Commission

### RIBS
1 ½ tablespoons cumin seeds
1 tablespoon yellow mustard seeds
1 tablespoon coriander seeds
1 tablespoon anise seeds
18 green cardamom pods, husked
1 tablespoon smoked paprika
4 pounds pork spareribs
⅓ cup plain yogurt
1 tablespoon brown sugar
Salt to taste

### AVOCADO-MANGO RELISH
2 fresh, ripe California avocados, divided
1 cup plain yogurt
1 garlic clove
1 green onion, halved lengthwise and thinly sliced
1 jalapeño, seeded and minced
1 ½ tablespoons minced fresh cilantro
1 ½ tablespoons minced fresh basil
1 tablespoon minced fresh chives
2 cucumbers, peeled and diced
1 mango, peeled and diced
Salt to taste

To prepare the ribs, toast cumin, mustard, coriander, anise and cardamom in a skillet over medium heat, stirring frequently; cool. Grind in a spice grinder. Transfer to a bowl. Stir in paprika.

Arrange spareribs on a baking sheet. Massage with some of the spice rub, cover and refrigerate overnight. Remove 1 hour before cooking.

To prepare the relish, peel and chop 1 avocado and place in a food processor. Add yogurt and garlic; puree. Transfer to a bowl and stir in onion, jalapeño and herbs. Place in refrigerator; remove 1 hour before serving. Peel and dice second avocado; add to mixture with cucumber, mango and salt.

Preheat oven to 350°F. In a bowl, combine yogurt and brown sugar. Place foil on a baking sheet and arrange ribs on foil. Brush ribs with yogurt mixture, then wrap tightly in foil. Bake for 1 ¼ hours. Unwrap ribs; cool.

Preheat the grill. Grill ribs over medium heat until browned. Carve into individual ribs and sprinkle with spice rub and salt. Serve with relish. Makes 4 servings.

*Recipe provided by the California Avocado Commission.*

# Fettuccine Calabrese
## New York Style Sausage

1 pound New York Style*
    Italian sausage (hot
    or mild), removed
    from casings

1 tablespoon olive oil

1/4 cup butter

2 teaspoons crushed
    fresh garlic

2 tablespoons finely
    chopped shallots

3 cups sliced white mush-
    rooms (10-15 medium)

1/4 cup white wine

1 cup half-and-half

1 cup diced fresh tomatoes

1 1/4 cups prepared
    marinara sauce

1/4 cup chopped fresh basil

Salt and pepper

1 pound fettuccine,
    cooked until al dente
    and drained

Grated Parmesan cheese

Cook sausage in olive oil in a skillet over medium heat until crumbled and browned. Drain oil and remove sausage to a dish.

Add butter, garlic, shallots and mushrooms to the skillet. Cook over medium heat until tender and lightly browned.

Add wine and cook until reduced. Stir in half-and-half.

Add cooked sausage, diced tomatoes and marinara sauce to the pan and cook for about 5-7 minutes over medium heat, stirring occasionally. Add basil and salt and pepper to taste.

Pour over cooked fettuccine and toss. Garnish with grated Parmesan. Makes 4-6 servings.

*Brands may vary by region; substitute a similar product.*

# Sweet Sausage, Peppers, Onions and Potatoes with Mixed Greens
## Premio

1 pound Premio* sweet
    Italian sausage, cut
    into 1/2-inch chunks

1 large white onion,
    thinly sliced

1 large red bell pepper,
    seeded and sliced

1 pound small yellow
    potatoes, parboiled for
    5-7 minutes, skin on

4 fresh garlic cloves,
    crushed

Salt and pepper

1 tablespoon olive oil

5 cups arugula and
    watercress or mixed
    salad greens

### DRESSING

1/2 cup olive oil

3 tablespoons Dijon
    mustard

1 tablespoon light brown
    sugar

2 tablespoons red
    wine vinegar

2 tablespoons lemon juice

Preheat oven to 350°F.

Combine the first 5 ingredients in a large bowl. Toss with salt and pepper to taste and olive oil. Spread on a baking pan or sheet and roast for 15-20 minutes, or until the sausage is cooked and veggies are tender. Set aside and let cool to room temperature.

To prepare the dressing, combine all ingredients and whisk.

In a salad bowl, combine salad greens and the roasted sausage and vegetables. Add just enough dressing to coat and toss to blend. Season to taste with salt and pepper. Makes 4-6 servings.

*Brands may vary by region; substitute a similar product.*

# Broccoli Rabe and Sausage Frittata
Premio

2 tablespoons olive oil
1/2 cup finely diced onion
1/2 cup jarred or canned
   pimientos, diced
1 cup diced cooked potatoes
2 cups chopped cooked broccoli rabe
1 pound Premio* sweet Italian
   sausage, cooked and diced
   (follow package directions
   to precook)

1/4 cup chopped fresh basil, divided
1/4 cup chopped fresh chives, divided
Salt and pepper
8 large eggs, whisked
1 1/2 cups shredded cheese:
   fontina, Cheddar, mozzarella or
   a mixture, divided
1/4 cup grated Romano cheese
2 cups marinara sauce, heated,
   for serving

Preheat oven to 325°F.

On the stovetop, heat a large ovenproof casserole or skillet over medium heat.
Add olive oil and then onions and sauté until soft.

Add pimientos, potatoes, broccoli rabe and sausage; cook, stirring, until heated through.

Add half of the basil, half of the chives, and salt and pepper to taste; stir well.

Increase the heat to medium-high. Add eggs and 1 cup of shredded cheese; stir to combine.

Sprinkle the remaining shredded cheese and the Romano on top.

Bake for 8-10 minutes, or until set. Remove from the oven and let cool for 10 minutes, or until the sides come away from the pan.

Slide onto a cookie sheet or platter, slice into wedges and sprinkle with the remaining herbs.

Serve at room temperature with warm marinara sauce. Makes 4-6 servings.

*Brands may vary by region; substitute a similar product.*

## Home-Style Mexican Lasagna
Kirkland Signature

Cooking spray

8 ounces smoked or fresh hot chorizo sausage, diced

Vegetable oil

2 pounds organic lean ground beef

2 tablespoons chili powder

Salt

2 organic red onions, sliced

2 organic red bell peppers, seeded and sliced

1/2 cup chopped organic cilantro

3 cups Kirkland Signature organic salsa  Organic

16 6-inch soft corn tortilla shells (or soft flour tortillas)

1 cup organic sour cream

2 cups grated organic Cheddar cheese

Preheat oven to 375°F. Lightly coat a 12-by-9-by-2-inch baking pan with cooking spray.

Sauté chorizo in a little oil over medium heat. Add beef and chili powder and cook thoroughly. Drain and let cool. Add salt to taste.

Sauté onions and peppers in a little oil over medium heat until softened. Let cool, then mix in cilantro.

To assemble, spread 1/3 of the meat mixture in the prepared pan. Top with 1 cup of salsa. Add a layer of 4 tortillas. Spread with 1/3 of the onion/pepper mix, 1/3 cup sour cream and a thin layer of grated cheese. Repeat with 2 more layers. Top with the remaining 4 tortillas and grated cheese. Bake for 35-45 minutes, or until heated through. Makes 9 servings.

*Recipe created by Chef Brad Rombough.*

## Spambalaya Jambalaya
Hormel

1 12-ounce can Spam* Less Sodium, cubed

1 cup chopped onion

2/3 cup chopped green bell pepper

1/2 cup chopped celery

2 garlic cloves, chopped

1 14 1/2-ounce can tomatoes, cut up

1 10 1/2-ounce can reduced-sodium chicken broth

1/2 teaspoon dried leaf thyme

6 drops hot pepper sauce

1 bay leaf

1 cup long-grain rice

2 tablespoons chopped fresh parsley

In a large nonstick skillet or 3-quart nonstick saucepan, sauté Spam, onion, bell pepper, celery and garlic over medium to medium-high heat until the vegetables are tender.

Add tomatoes, chicken broth, thyme, hot pepper sauce and bay leaf. Bring to a boil; stir in rice. Cover. Reduce heat and simmer for 20 minutes, or until the rice is tender.

Discard the bay leaf. Sprinkle with parsley.

Makes 6 servings.

*\* Brands may vary by region; substitute a similar product.*

# Italian Sandwiches
## La Brea Bakery

**4 La Brea Bakery\* French Demi Baguettes**

**8 slices mortadella**

**12 slices capicola**

**8 slices salami**

**8 pepperoncini, sliced**

**1 cup shredded iceberg lettuce**

**4 slices provolone cheese**

### VINAIGRETTE

**3 tablespoons fresh lemon juice (about 1 1/2 lemons)**

**1/2 tablespoon finely chopped shallot**

**3 tablespoons extra-virgin olive oil**

**1/2 teaspoon kosher salt**

**Freshly cracked black pepper, to taste**

To prepare the vinaigrette, combine lemon juice and shallot in a small bowl and let sit for about 10 minutes. Whisk in olive oil, salt and pepper. Adjust the lemon juice and salt to taste.

Slice baguettes in half lengthwise. On the bottom half of each baguette, place a layer of mortadella, followed by a layer of capicola and a layer of salami. Scatter pepperoncini evenly over the meats.

In a small bowl, toss lettuce with 4 tablespoons of vinaigrette. Place the lettuce on top of the pepperoncini. Top with provolone and close the sandwich. Makes 4 servings.

*\* Brands may vary by region; substitute a similar product.*

## South Beach Brisket
### Horizon International

8- to 10-pound beef brisket
2 cups orange juice
2 cups applesauce
2 cups red wine
1 cup ketchup
2 packets Lipton onion
   soup mix
2 tablespoons cornstarch

Preheat oven to 350°F.

Place brisket in a Dutch oven. Stir together orange juice, applesauce, wine, ketchup and soup mix; add to the pot.

Set in the oven and cook 1 1/2 hours for every 5 pounds of meat, or until the brisket is tender.

Remove the brisket from the oven; let rest for 5 minutes before cutting.

To make a gravy, remove 2 cups of the cooking liquid to a small saucepan. Thicken with cornstarch mixed with 1/4 cup cold water. Heat and stir gravy until thickened, about 2 minutes. Makes 12-14 servings.

## Grilled Spice-Rubbed Loin Tip Steaks
### Morton's of Omaha

3 tablespoons paprika
1 tablespoon ground cumin
1 tablespoon dry mustard
2 teaspoons ground fennel
2 teaspoons ground
   black pepper
1 tablespoon kosher salt
2 1/2 pounds loin
   tip steaks
Flour tortillas, shredded
   cheese, sour cream and
   salsa, for serving

Combine the spices and salt and rub all over the meat. Store for 24 hours in the refrigerator.

Preheat grill to medium-high.

Let the meat sit at room temperature for 30 minutes while the grill is heating up.

Place the meat on the grill and cook for about 10 minutes per side for medium-rare (135°F). When the meat is done, remove it from the grill and let it rest for 10 minutes before slicing.

Slice the meat thin across the grain. Serve with flour tortillas, shredded cheese, sour cream and salsa. Makes 6-8 servings.

# Beer-Lime Grilled Steaks
## Market Source

Juice of 2 Market Source* limes

2 teaspoons honey

1  12-ounce bottle of your favorite beer, dark or light

2 garlic cloves, minced

2 tablespoons chopped fresh cilantro

1 teaspoon salt

1 teaspoon ground black pepper

4  8-ounce steak fillets, butterflied

In a bowl, combine lime juice, honey, beer, garlic, cilantro, salt and pepper. Mix until well blended.

Put steaks in a flat pan and pour the beer-lime mixture over the steaks. Marinate for 45 minutes on each side.

Preheat the grill to medium.

Remove the steaks from the marinade, letting excess marinade run off. Place the steaks on the grill and cook to desired temperature. Makes 4 servings.

* Brands may vary by region; substitute a similar product.

# Fiery Bacon-Wrapped Filet Mignon with Roasted Corn Ragout
Kirkland Signature/Tyson

2 ears of corn, husked

2 ounces chipotle peppers in adobo sauce

1/2 cup honey

4 8-ounce filets cut from Kirkland Signature beef tenderloin

12 slices Kirkland Signature hickory-smoked bacon, divided

Salt and pepper

2 tablespoons vegetable oil, divided

4 green onions, sliced into 1/2-inch pieces

1 jalapeño pepper, seeded and diced

2 cups shredded green cabbage

1 teaspoon ground cumin

Juice of 2 limes

Preheat oven to 350°F.

Roast corn in the oven for 30 minutes. Cut off kernels and reserve.

Preheat oven to 375°F.

In a blender, puree chipotles in adobo sauce and honey. Reserve half of the sauce.

Wrap each filet with 2 slices bacon, securing with toothpicks. Season with salt and pepper. Heat 1 tablespoon oil in a sauté pan over medium-high heat. Add filets and sear for 3 minutes on each side. Sear bacon for 1 minute. Brush with chipotle glaze, using about half the sauce. Place filets in an ovenproof pan, bake for 10 minutes and check internal temperature for doneness: 145°F for medium rare, 160°F for medium or 170°F for well done.

To make the ragout, cut 4 slices bacon into 1/2-inch pieces. Sauté over medium-high heat until it starts to crisp. Add 1 tablespoon oil, green onions and jalapeño; cook for 1-2 minutes. Add corn and cabbage and cook for 3-5 minutes, or until cabbage starts to wilt. Season with salt and pepper, cumin and lime juice.

Serve ragout with the filets and the reserved sauce. Makes 4 servings.

# Salisbury Steaks
Nature's Premium

1 1/2 pounds Nature's Premium* Organic Ground Beef ♥Organic

1 medium onion, finely chopped

1/3 cup fresh bread crumbs

1 egg, beaten

2 8-ounce jars beef gravy (Boston Market or Heinz), divided

1/4 cup finely chopped fresh parsley

Preheat oven to 350°F.

In a bowl, combine beef, onions, bread crumbs, egg, 1/2 jar of gravy and parsley. Mix well. Form into 4-6 oval patties and place in a baking dish. Pour the remaining gravy over the meat.

Cover the pan with foil and bake for 45 minutes. Remove the foil and bake for 15 minutes longer. Makes 4-6 servings.

* Brands may vary by region; substitute a similar product.

NATURE'S
PREMIUM
Make Every Meal More Natural

Entrées

# California Garlic Roast
Christopher Ranch

5 pounds boneless
  chuck roast

2 tablespoons olive oil

20 cloves Christopher
  Ranch California
  Garlic, peeled

1  12-ounce bottle beer

4 cups beef stock

1/2 cup cilantro leaves

2 sprigs fresh thyme

Leaves from 1 rosemary
  sprig, chopped

1 bay leaf

Pinch of cinnamon
  and nutmeg

1 teaspoon crushed
  red pepper

10 small cipolline*
  onions, peeled

8 carrots, peeled and cut
  into 1-inch chunks

Salt and pepper

Rice, for serving

In a Dutch oven, brown roast in olive oil over medium heat. Add garlic and sauté lightly (do not burn!). Use beer to deglaze the pan, scraping bits from the bottom.

Add stock and all the seasonings and bring to a boil. Reduce the heat, cover and simmer for 90 minutes, turning the meat every 20 minutes.

Add onions and carrots and simmer for 60 more minutes, turning the meat every 20 minutes. If the liquid reduces too much, add more stock. Season to taste with salt and pepper.

Serve over rice. Makes 6 servings.

*Cipolline are traditional Italian onions with a flat, oval shape, ranging from 1 to 3 inches in diameter.*

# Family Favorite Pot Roast
Heinz/Lea & Perrins

Nonstick cooking spray

3 pounds boneless beef tip
  or chuck roast

1 Wyler's beef
  bouillon cube

1 cup hot water

1/2 cup Lea & Perrins
  Worcestershire sauce

1 cup Heinz ketchup

2 tablespoons Heinz apple
  cider vinegar

2 tablespoons brown sugar

Coat a large saucepan with cooking spray.

Brown beef roast in the pan over medium-high heat for 4-5 minutes.

Add bouillon and hot water to the pan; bring to a boil. Reduce the heat to low, cover and simmer for 1 hour.

Stir in Worcestershire sauce, ketchup, vinegar and sugar. Continue to simmer, covered, for an additional 1 1/2-2 hours, turning occasionally, until the meat is tender. Makes 8 servings.

## Pot Roast Shepherd's Pie
### Morton's of Omaha

1 Morton's of Omaha All Natural Beef Pot Roast
$1/2$ cup frozen peas
$1/2$ cup frozen sliced carrots
$1/2$ cup frozen corn
1 cup prepared beef gravy
16 ounces prepared mashed potatoes

Preheat oven to 350°F.

Remove pot roast from the bag. Save the gravy from the bag and also wipe off any of the gravy on the meat and set aside. Dice the meat into small ($1/4$ inch) pieces.

In a bowl, mix together the diced meat, peas, carrots, corn, 1 cup gravy and the reserved gravy. Transfer to a baking dish. Spread mashed potatoes over the meat mixture.

Bake for about 45 minutes, or until the meat mixture starts to bubble. Makes 4-6 servings.

## Potato Lasagna
### Top Brass/Farm Fresh Direct

Cooking spray
2 medium russet, white or yellow-flesh potatoes, or 3-4 small red potatoes
1 15-ounce can pizza sauce
1 pound 85% lean ground beef
$1/2$ teaspoon salt
$1/2$ teaspoon black pepper
1 $1/2$ cups shredded mozzarella cheese
$1/4$ cup grated Parmesan cheese

Coat a 1-quart microwave-safe dish with cooking spray.

Cut potatoes into $1/4$-inch-thick slices.

Spread 2 tablespoons pizza sauce in the bottom of the prepared dish. Arrange half the potatoes in a single layer on top of the sauce. Crumble half the beef evenly over the potatoes. Season with half the salt and pepper. Sprinkle with half the mozzarella and half the remaining pizza sauce.

Repeat layers with the remaining potatoes, beef, salt, pepper, mozzarella and pizza sauce. Sprinkle Parmesan over the top.

Cover tightly with a lid or plastic wrap. Microwave on high for 20 minutes (cooking time may vary depending on your microwave), or until the potatoes and beef are done. Let sit for 2 minutes in the microwave. Use oven mitts or tongs to remove from the microwave. Remove plastic wrap carefully to prevent burns from steam. Makes 4 servings.

# Veal Meat Loaf
## Plume De Veau

Cooking spray
1 pound Plume De Veau*
   ground veal
2 eggs
1/4 cup ketchup

3/4 cup Italian seasoned
   bread crumbs
1 packet onion soup mix
5 slices Swiss cheese
5 slices bacon (optional)

Preheat oven to 325°F. Coat a baking pan with cooking spray.

In a bowl, combine ground veal, eggs, ketchup, bread crumbs and onion soup mix; blend well.

Flatten the mixture to about 3/4 of an inch. Place cheese slices in the middle. Fold the ends over first and then the left and right sides so that the cheese is completely covered.

Place the meat loaf in the center of the prepared pan. Lay bacon slices over the top.

Bake for 45 minutes, or until the internal temperature is 160°F. Makes 4 servings.

*Brands may vary by region; substitute a similar product.*

# Connie's Veal Cutlets
## Plume De Veau

2 eggs
1 cup grated Pecorino Romano
   cheese, divided
Italian seasoned bread crumbs
1 pound Plume De Veau*
   veal cutlets
Vegetable oil
2 hard-boiled eggs, chopped

¹/₂ cup pine nuts
¹/₂ cup chopped parsley
Salt and pepper
1 head of garlic, peeled and sliced
1 cup sliced green onions
1  28-ounce can plum
   tomatoes, crushed

Beat eggs in a shallow bowl; stir in ¼ cup grated cheese.

Place bread crumbs in another shallow bowl.

Dip veal cutlets in the egg mixture and then coat with bread crumbs.

Heat a frying pan over medium-high heat with enough oil to coat the pan.

Fry the veal cutlets for 2 minutes on each side. Remove from the pan and drain on paper towels.

In the center of each cutlet, place some chopped egg, pine nuts, chopped parsley, grated cheese, and salt and pepper to taste. Roll up the cutlets and secure with toothpicks.

Coat the frying pan with oil, add garlic and green onions, and sauté over medium-high heat for about 2 minutes. Add tomatoes and cook over low heat for 20 minutes.

Preheat oven to 325°F.

Place the rolled veal cutlets in a roasting pan, pour the tomato sauce over all and bake for 15 minutes, or until heated through.

Sprinkle with chopped parsley to serve. Makes 4 servings.

*Recipe developed by Connie Slater.*
*\* Brands may vary by region; substitute a similar product.*

## Stuffed Rib Veal Chops
Plume De Veau

1 cup balsamic vinegar
4 Plume De Veau*
 veal rib chops
8 slices prosciutto
4 slices mozzarella cheese
Cooking spray
3 mushrooms, sliced
1 head of garlic, peeled
 and sliced
1/2 teaspoon salt
1/2 teaspoon pepper

Preheat oven to 325°F.

Pour balsamic vinegar into a saucepan and simmer
until reduced by half.

Cut a pocket in the side of each veal chop. Stuff with
2 slices of prosciutto and 1 slice of mozzarella; secure
with a toothpick.

Coat a frying pan with cooking spray and sear the
chops over medium-high heat on both sides.

Brush the chops generously on both sides with half of
the reduced balsamic vinegar.

Coat a baking pan with cooking spray. Place the 4
stuffed veal chops, mushrooms and garlic in the pan.
Add salt and pepper. Pour the remaining reduced
balsamic vinegar over all.

Bake for 25 minutes, or until the internal temperature is 145°F, basting frequently. Makes 4 servings.

*Brands may vary by region; substitute a similar product.*

## Pesto Chicken with Sun-Dried Tomatoes
Kirkland Signature/Perdue

4 ounces oil-packed sun-
 dried tomato halves
1 container (about
 7 ounces) prepared
 basil pesto
4 Kirkland Signature/
 Perdue* Individually
 Wrapped Frozen
 Boneless, Skinless
 Chicken Breasts
1/3 cup chicken broth
8 ounces linguine, cooked
 according to package
 directions, and
 kept warm
Grated Parmesan cheese
 (optional)

Drain and chop sun-dried tomatoes. Combine tomatoes
with pesto in a small bowl.

Cook chicken in a large skillet according to package
directions. Remove to a platter, cover and keep warm.

Wipe the skillet with a paper towel. Reduce the heat
to low. Add the pesto mixture and chicken broth;
cook, stirring, just until softened and heated through.

Combine half of the pesto mixture with the hot
cooked linguine and toss to coat.

Serve the chicken with the linguine, spooning the
remaining pesto mixture over the chicken. Sprinkle
with grated Parmesan. Makes 4 servings.

*Brands may vary by region; substitute a similar product.*

# Rosemary-Scented Grilled Chicken

## Kirkland Signature/Filippo Berio

1 large chicken, at least 3 1/2 pounds, cut into quarters

1/3 cup Kirkland Signature Filippo Berio Organic Extra Virgin Olive Oil, plus more for brushing the grill ● Organic

3 tablespoons fresh lime juice

3 tablespoons minced green onion

1/2 tablespoon chopped fresh oregano

1 tablespoon chopped fresh rosemary leaves

1/2 teaspoon kosher salt

1/2 teaspoon freshly ground black pepper

4 rosemary sprigs

1 lime, cut into 4 wedges

Place chicken in a gallon-size resealable bag.

Combine 1/3 cup olive oil, lime juice, green onion, oregano, chopped rosemary, salt and pepper. Pour over the chicken. Shake the bag to coat chicken, and press out the air as you seal it. Refrigerate for 3-5 hours.

Soak rosemary sprigs in water for at least 30 minutes.

Lightly oil the grill grate with olive oil. Preheat the grill. When the grill is ready, place rosemary sprigs on the grate.

Place chicken bone-side down on the grill (near rosemary sprigs) about 4 inches above the coals, and cook for 12 minutes, basting frequently with the marinade. Turn and grill for 12 minutes more. Do not baste during the last 5-6 minutes of grilling. The chicken is done when juices no longer run pink.

Serve with lime wedges. Makes 4 servings.

## Smoky Tomato Chicken Breasts with Mediterranean Couscous
Kirkland Signature/Tyson

1 1/2 tablespoons smoked paprika

1 teaspoon salt

3/4 teaspoon ground pepper

4 Kirkland Signature/Tyson boneless, skinless chicken breasts

1 teaspoon vegetable oil

1/2 medium onion, cut in small dice

6 garlic cloves, minced

1 14 1/2-ounce can diced tomatoes

1/2 cup chicken broth

### COUSCOUS

2 cups chicken broth

5 tablespoons dried currants

5 tablespoons golden raisins

1/4 teaspoon ground cinnamon

1/8 teaspoon turmeric

1/2 teaspoon salt

1 cup couscous

1/4 cup pistachios

1/2 tablespoon chopped fresh mint

Blend paprika, salt and pepper; season the chicken.

Heat oil in a large sauté pan over medium-high heat. Add chicken and sear for 3 minutes on one side. Turn chicken over, add onions to the pan and cook for 3 minutes. Add garlic and cook for 30 seconds.

Reduce heat to medium-low; add tomatoes and chicken broth. Simmer until the sauce thickens and the chicken is cooked (165°F).

To prepare the couscous, combine chicken broth, currants, raisins, cinnamon, turmeric and salt in a saucepan and bring to a boil. Stir in couscous and pistachios. Remove from heat, cover and let sit for 5 minutes, or until the broth is absorbed. Add mint and fluff with a fork.

Serve the couscous with the chicken. Makes 4 servings.

## Cherry Olive Moroccan-Style Chicken
Grant J. Hunt Company

1 tablespoon olive oil

1 large onion, halved and thinly sliced

Salt and pepper to taste

2 garlic cloves, thinly sliced

1 tablespoon grated fresh ginger

2 teaspoons paprika

1 1/2 teaspoons ground cumin

1 teaspoon ground cinnamon

1 14-ounce can low-fat chicken broth

2 (about 1 1/2 pounds) chicken breast halves, cut in half

2 (about 12 ounces) chicken drumsticks

2 (about 12 ounces) chicken thighs

1 lemon, cut into 8 wedges

1 1/2 cups pitted Northwest* cherries, divided

3/4 cup pitted green olives

2 tablespoons lemon juice

Heat oil in a large skillet over medium-high heat. Add onions and sprinkle with salt and pepper. Sauté for 6-8 minutes, or until golden brown. Add garlic, ginger, paprika, cumin and cinnamon; cook, stirring, for 1 minute. Add chicken broth and bring to a boil.

Season chicken with salt and pepper. Add chicken and lemon wedges to the pan; return to a boil. Cover, reduce heat and simmer for 20-30 minutes, or until chicken is cooked. Remove chicken from the pan; keep warm.

Add 1/2 cup cherries, olives and lemon juice to the pan. Increase heat to high and cook, uncovered, for 5-10 minutes, or until slightly thickened. Add 1 cup cherries and simmer for 1 minute. Pour sauce over the chicken. Makes 4-6 servings.

**Tip:** When cherries aren't available, substitute Blue Goose* Italian prune plums. Pit and cut into wedges to measure 1 1/2 cups.

*Brands may vary by region; substitute a similar product.*

# Chicken Breasts with Citrus-Basil Pan Sauce
## Sunkist Growers

2 Sunkist grapefruits*

1/4 cup plus 1 teaspoon flour, divided

1/2 teaspoon salt

1/2 teaspoon ground white pepper

4 boneless, skinless chicken breast halves (about 1 pound)

3 tablespoons vegetable oil

1 shallot, diced

1/2 cup freshly squeezed Sunkist orange** juice

6 fresh basil leaves, torn into bits

Fresh basil leaves, for garnish

Juice 1 grapefruit. Peel the other grapefruit and cut the segments away from the membrane. Set aside.

Mix 1/4 cup flour with salt and pepper. Coat chicken in the flour mixture, shaking off excess.

Heat oil in a large skillet over medium heat. Add shallot and cook for 1 minute, until soft. Add chicken and cook for about 3-4 minutes on each side, browning evenly.

In a small bowl, combine grapefruit juice and orange juice, then whisk in 1 teaspoon flour until there are no lumps. Pour into the pan, stir well and reduce the heat to low. Cover and simmer for 5-10 minutes, or until the chicken is cooked through and the sauce is slightly thickened.

Gently stir in basil and grapefruit segments.

Serve the chicken with the sauce and garnish with basil leaves. Makes 4 servings.

*Use Sunkist grapefruit, Pummelo, Oro Blanco or Melo Gold.*
**Use Sunkist Navel, Valencia or Cara Cara oranges.*

**Sunkist**

## Jerk Chicken with Spicy Mango Topper
### Freska Produce

2 ripe Freska mangoes, peeled, pitted and cut into 1/4-inch dice

1/4 cup lime juice

2 tablespoons brown sugar

1/2 teaspoon crushed red pepper

1/4 teaspoon garlic powder

1/4 teaspoon ground cinnamon

1/4 teaspoon ground allspice

4 boneless, skinless chicken breast halves, flattened slightly (about 1 1/2 pounds)

2 tablespoons Jamaican jerk seasoning blend

1 lime, cut in half

In a medium bowl, stir together mangoes, lime juice, brown sugar, red pepper, garlic powder, cinnamon and allspice. Set aside.

Preheat the grill.

Rinse chicken and pat dry. Sprinkle on both sides with jerk seasoning and let stand for 10 minutes.

Cook chicken on a well-oiled grill over medium heat for about 5-7 minutes on each side, or until cooked through.

Remove from the grill and squeeze lime halves over the chicken. Serve with mango topper.

Makes 4 servings.

## Mango Barbecued Chicken
### Profood

25-30 strips Philippine Brand* dried mango

3 tablespoons apple cider vinegar

2 tablespoons dark brown sugar

1 garlic clove, minced

1/4 cup ketchup

6 boneless, skinless chicken breast halves

Preheat the grill.

Soak dried mango in hot water for about 5 minutes, or until tender.

Combine mango, vinegar, brown sugar, garlic and ketchup in a food processor and blend until smooth.

Brush chicken with some of the sauce and grill over medium-high heat, basting with the sauce, until it is fully cooked. Makes 6 servings.

**Tip:** To cook in the oven, cover the chicken with sauce and bake at 350°F for 30 minutes. Or cook in a slow cooker on low for 6-8 hours.

*Brands may vary by region; substitute a similar product.*

## Chipotle Honey Tangerine Glazed Chicken
### Seald Sweet

1 cup fresh tangerine juice (about 3 Seald Sweet* tangerines)

1/3 cup chopped fresh parsley

1/3 cup chopped fresh cilantro

3 tablespoons chopped fresh thyme

3 tablespoons minced peeled fresh ginger

3 tablespoons unseasoned rice vinegar

2 tablespoons olive oil

2 tablespoons finely grated tangerine peel

1 tablespoon coarse kosher salt

6 boneless, skinless chicken breast halves

Salt

*GLAZE*

2 cups fresh tangerine juice (about 6 Seald Sweet* tangerines)

5 tablespoons honey

1/4 cup soy sauce

2 tablespoons finely grated tangerine peel

2 teaspoons minced canned chipotle peppers in adobo sauce

Whisk the first 9 ingredients together. Place chicken in a dish and add the marinade, turning to coat. Cover and chill for 4 hours, turning occasionally.

To prepare the glaze, boil juice, honey and soy sauce in a medium saucepan until reduced to 2/3 cup, about 20 minutes. Mix in grated tangerine peel and chipotles.

Preheat the grill.

Remove chicken from the dish and discard the marinade. Sprinkle the chicken with salt to taste and grill over medium-low heat until nearly cooked through, turning for even cooking, about 20 minutes. Brush the chicken with glaze and grill for 2 minutes on each side. Makes 6 servings.

*\* Brands may vary by region; substitute a similar product.*

**Seald Sweet**
INTERNATIONAL

## Thai Chicken Fettuccine
### Campbell's

1 tablespoon vegetable oil

1 pound boneless, skinless chicken breast, cut into strips

1 cup Pace* picante sauce

1/4 cup chunky peanut butter

2 tablespoons honey

2 tablespoons orange juice

1 teaspoon soy sauce

1/2 teaspoon ground ginger

3 cups hot cooked fettuccine (16 ounces)

Chopped fresh cilantro (optional)

Heat oil in a skillet over medium-high heat. Add chicken and cook for 5 minutes, until it's lightly browned, stirring often.

Stir in picante sauce, peanut butter, honey, orange juice, soy sauce and ginger. Cook and stir until the chicken is cooked through.

Add fettuccine. Toss the mixture until evenly coated.

Top with cilantro if desired. Makes 4 servings.

*\* Brands may vary by region; substitute a similar product.*

Entrées

# Walnut Pesto Penne with Grilled Chicken
## California Walnuts

3 cups packed fresh basil leaves

3 large garlic cloves

2/3 cup Kirkland Signature walnuts, lightly toasted, divided

1/3 cup extra-virgin olive oil

1/3 cup freshly grated Parmesan cheese, plus more for topping

Salt and pepper

Cooking spray

4 boneless, skinless chicken breast halves

1 pound penne pasta

1/2 cup chopped sun-dried tomatoes (optional)

To make the walnut pesto, place basil leaves and garlic in a food processor or blender and mix well. Add 1/3 cup walnuts and continue to blend until the nuts are finely ground. With the machine running, drizzle in olive oil. When you have a smooth paste, transfer to a bowl and stir in Parmesan. Season to taste with salt and pepper.

Chop the remaining 1/3 cup walnuts; set aside.

Preheat grill to medium. Coat the grill rack with cooking spray.

Sprinkle chicken with salt and pepper to taste. Grill for 10 minutes, or until done, turning once. Cut into bite-size pieces and keep warm.

Cook pasta according to package directions. Drain.

In a large bowl, combine pasta, pesto, chicken and sun-dried tomatoes. Stir until evenly coated.

Top each serving with Parmesan and chopped walnuts. Makes 6 servings.

# Chicken and Mushroom Manicotti
## Kirkland Signature

- 4 tablespoons olive oil, divided
- 4 ounces shiitake mushrooms, cut in 1/4-inch dice (2 cups)
- 4 ounces domestic mushrooms, cut in 1/4-inch dice (2 cups)
- 2 tablespoons Kirkland Signature dried, chopped onion
- 1 tablespoon Kirkland Signature California granulated garlic
- 1 tablespoon chopped fresh thyme
- 1 tablespoon chopped fresh oregano
- 2 teaspoons Kirkland Signature pure sea salt
- 2 cups heavy cream
- 6 cups Alfredo sauce, divided
- 2 tablespoons grated Pecorino Romano cheese
- 2 pounds ground chicken
- 24 manicotti or cannelloni shells, cooked per package directions

Heat 2 tablespoons olive oil in a sauté pan over medium-high heat. Add mushrooms and chopped onion; sauté until mushrooms are soft. Add garlic, thyme, oregano, salt and cream. Simmer until the cream is reduced by half. Add 3 cups Alfredo sauce and grated cheese; whisk until well blended. Set aside.

Heat 2 tablespoons olive oil in a sauté pan over medium-high heat. Add ground chicken and cook, stirring to break up into small crumbles. Add 3 cups Alfredo sauce.

Preheat oven to 350°F.

Place chicken mixture in a piping bag. Pipe the mixture into the cooked pasta, being careful not to split the shells. Place evenly in a buttered baking dish.

Top evenly with the mushroom sauce. Cover with parchment and foil. Bake for about 20 minutes, or until the internal temperature is 165°F.

Makes 12 servings.

# Chicken Cacciatore
## Classico

- 2 1/2 tablespoons flour
- 1 1/2 teaspoons Italian-style seasoning
- 4 boneless, skinless chicken breast halves (about 1 1/3 pounds)
- 2 tablespoons olive oil
- 2 cups sliced fresh mushrooms
- 1/2 cup chopped onion
- 1 32-ounce jar Classico Tomato & Basil Pasta Sauce
- 1 1/3 cups shredded mozzarella or provolone cheese
- 8 ounces fettuccine, cooked according to package directions

In a shallow dish, combine flour and Italian-style seasoning. Coat chicken with the mixture.

Heat olive oil in a large skillet over medium-high heat. Add chicken and cook until browned. Remove chicken from the skillet.

Add mushrooms and onion to the skillet; cook, stirring, until tender.

Add pasta sauce and chicken to the skillet; cover and simmer for 15 minutes, or until the chicken is fully cooked.

Top each chicken breast with cheese. Serve with hot pasta. Makes 4 servings.

# Sweet Pepper Fajitas
## BC Hot House

2 tablespoons vegetable oil, divided

1 boneless, skinless chicken breast, cut into thin strips

1 garlic clove, crushed

1 teaspoon finely chopped fresh ginger

2 teaspoons sesame seeds, white or black

1 tablespoon soy sauce

1/4 white onion, cut into long strips

1 *each* BC Hot House* sweet red, yellow and orange pepper, cut into long strips

### ACCOMPANIMENTS

Soft tortilla shells

Red tomato salsa

Sour cream

Guacamole

Mixed shredded Monterey Jack and Cheddar cheese

Heat 1 tablespoon oil in a wok over high heat. Add chicken and cook, stirring often, for 30 seconds. Add garlic, ginger and sesame seeds; cook for 1 minute. Add soy sauce and cook for 1 minute. Transfer the mixture to a bowl.

Wipe out the wok and return to high heat. Add 1 tablespoon oil. When oil is hot, add onions and cook for 1 minute, stirring often. Add peppers and cook, stirring often, until they begin to soften, about 3 minutes. Return chicken to the pan and cook for 30 seconds. Pour the mixture into a serving bowl.

Serve immediately with accompaniments.

Makes 2 servings.

*\* Brands may vary by region; substitute a similar product.*

# Whole Grain Santa Fe Chicken Quesadillas
## Mars Foods

1 8 1/2-ounce pouch Uncle Ben's* Ready Whole Grain Medley Santa Fe

4 whole wheat tortillas, burrito size

1 cup shredded Monterey Jack

6 ounces packaged precooked chicken breast strips

Cilantro, for garnish

Prepared guacamole, for serving

Heat rice in the microwave according to package directions.

Making 1 quesadilla at a time, heat a tortilla in a large skillet over medium-high heat. Sprinkle with a quarter of the cheese, 4 chicken strips and a quarter of the rice.

Fold the tortilla in half and continue to heat on both sides until the cheese has melted.

Garnish with cilantro and serve with guacamole.

Makes 4 servings.

*\* Brands may vary by region; substitute a similar product.*

**Uncle Ben's.**

# Turkey, Spinach and Apple Wraps

Boskovich Farms/Fresh Innovations
of California

1 tablespoon mayonnaise
(for a healthier option, use
reduced-fat mayonnaise)

2 teaspoons mustard

2 whole wheat tortillas or
lavash* wraps

2 cups Fresh 'n' Quick spinach leaves

4 slices turkey breast
(approx. 4 ounces)

8 slices Prize Slice** organic sliced
apples,  Organic
sliced very thin

Combine mayonnaise and mustard. Spread on the wraps.

Top with a layer of spinach leaves and turkey. Lay apple slices lengthwise
across the turkey.

Fold over one end of each wrap, then the two sides. Roll as tightly as possible
toward the opposite side. Cover each wrap tightly in plastic wrap and refrigerate
for up to 4 hours before serving.

To serve, cut each wrap in half. Makes 2 servings.

*Lavash is a thin, soft flatbread popular in Middle Eastern countries.
** Brands may vary by region; substitute a similar product.

## Sweet Curry Chicken Salad
### Four Star Fruit

1/2 cup plain low-fat yogurt

1/4 cup sour cream

2 tablespoons honey

1/2 teaspoon mild
    curry powder

1/4 teaspoon salt

2 cups cubed cooked chicken

1 cup Four Star Fruit
    crimson seedless grapes,
    cut into quarters

1/4 cup diced celery

1 small apple, peeled,
    cored and shredded

Pita bread or wraps,
    for serving

Whisk yogurt, sour cream, honey, curry powder and salt in a small bowl until smooth; set aside.

Mix chicken, grapes, celery and shredded apple in a medium bowl.

Pour the sauce over the chicken mixture and stir to combine.

Use as a filling for pita bread or wraps, or as a luncheon salad. Makes 6 servings.

*Recipe developed by Kati Neville.*

## Pesto-Rubbed Turkey Breast
### Willow Brook

1 Willow Brook Kettle
    Fried Turkey Breast

6 ounces prepared basil
    pesto, divided

Preheat oven to 350°F.

Remove turkey from the wrapper. Place in a baking dish. Using a knife, score the top of the breast in a diamond pattern 1/8 inch deep.

Spread half of the pesto over the top of the breast.

Loosely cover the turkey with foil.

Bake for 35 minutes. Remove the foil and spread on the rest of the pesto. Return to the oven for 10-15 minutes, or until the turkey is hot. Remove from the oven and let rest for 10 minutes before slicing. Makes 10-12 servings.

**Tip:** Serve with roasted potatoes and tomato salad.

# Asian Mushroom Lettuce Wraps
Foxy Vegetables

2 tablespoons
    vegetable oil
1 pound ground chicken or
    diced boneless, skinless
    chicken thigh meat
3 cups finely chopped
    white mushrooms
1/2 teaspoon
    ground ginger
1 1/2 tablespoons
    crushed garlic
1/3 cup soy sauce
1/3 cup hoisin sauce
1/3 cup rice vinegar
1 Foxy romaine heart or
    1 head Foxy iceberg
    lettuce, leaves
    separated

GARNISHES

Grated carrots
Diced cucumbers
Chopped peanuts
Chopped fresh mint
Peanut sauce
Hot chili oil

Heat vegetable oil in a large skillet over medium-high heat. Add chicken and stir, breaking ground chicken into small pieces. Stir in mushrooms, ginger and garlic. Continue to stir and cook for about 4-5 minutes, or until the mushroom liquid has evaporated.

Stir in soy sauce, hoisin sauce and vinegar. Reduce the heat and simmer for about 4-5 minutes to blend flavors. Transfer to a serving bowl.

Arrange lettuce leaves on a platter. Spoon the filling into the lettuce leaves and garnish as desired. Makes 6 servings.

# Chicken Satay with Spicy Peanut Sauce
Skippy

1 cup Wish-Bone* Italian
    Dressing, divided
1 tablespoon firmly
    packed brown sugar
1 tablespoon finely
    chopped cilantro
1 tablespoon finely
    chopped fresh ginger
4 boneless, skinless
    chicken breast halves
    (about 1 1/4 pounds),
    pounded thin and cut
    into thin strips
1/2 cup Skippy* Creamy
    Peanut Butter
1/4 teaspoon curry powder
1/4 teaspoon ground
    red pepper

CUCUMBER RELISH

1 large cucumber, peeled,
    seeded and diced
1/3 cup finely chopped
    red onion
1/4 cup Wish-Bone*
    Italian Dressing
1 tablespoon finely
    chopped cilantro

To make a marinade, combine 1/2 cup Italian dressing, brown sugar, cilantro and ginger.

Place chicken in a large, shallow nonaluminum baking dish. Pour 1/4 cup marinade over the chicken; turn to coat. Cover and marinate in the refrigerator, turning occasionally, for 30 minutes to 3 hours. Refrigerate the remaining marinade.

Blend peanut butter, 1/2 cup Italian dressing, curry powder and red pepper; refrigerate until ready to serve.

To prepare the relish, combine all ingredients; refrigerate until ready to serve.

Preheat the grill or broiler.

Remove chicken from the marinade, discarding marinade. Thread chicken onto skewers. Grill or broil chicken, turning once and brushing frequently with refrigerated marinade, until chicken is thoroughly cooked.

Serve with peanut sauce and Cucumber Relish. Makes 4 servings.

**Nutritional information:** Each serving (not including relish) has 360 calories, 35 g protein, 9 g carbohydrates, 20 g fat, 0 g saturated fat, 85 mg cholesterol, 0 g fiber, 540 mg sodium.

*Brands may vary by region; substitute a similar product.*

# Grilled Salmon with Blueberry-Cabernet Coulis
## Meduri Farms

6 salmon fillet portions

Salt and pepper

1 3/4 cups Kirkland Signature dried blueberries

2 cups Cabernet Sauvignon or other dry red wine

2 tablespoons minced shallots

2 tablespoons minced fresh ginger

1 1/2 tablespoons sugar

1 tablespoon butter

Julienne-sliced fresh ginger and parsley sprigs, for garnish

Preheat the grill.

Season salmon with salt and pepper to taste. Grill skin side down over direct medium heat (350-450°F) for about 10 minutes, then turn and grill for about 2 minutes longer, or until cooked to taste.

To prepare the coulis, place blueberries in a food processor or blender and chop into small pieces. Add wine and blend until pureed.

Pour the puree into a sauté pan and add shallots, ginger and sugar. Bring to a boil over medium-high heat and cook, stirring constantly, until reduced to about 1 cup (approx. 7 minutes). Remove from the heat and stir in the butter until melted.

Remove the salmon from the grill, spoon the coulis over the top, and garnish with ginger and parsley. Serve immediately. Makes 6 servings.

# Henriette's Salmon with Tomato Sauce
## Kirkland Signature/Marine Harvest

4 Kirkland Signature frozen salmon portions, thawed
4 tablespoons bread crumbs
4 tablespoons chopped fresh chives
4 tablespoons butter, melted
Salt and pepper

*TOMATO SAUCE*
2 tablespoons olive oil
2 tablespoons finely chopped shallots
1 red or green chili pepper, minced
2 garlic cloves, minced
1 1/2 cups peeled and chopped fresh tomatoes
1 teaspoon honey
1 teaspoon vinegar
Salt
2 teaspoons chopped fresh basil leaves

Preheat oven to 425°F.

Place thawed salmon in a greased baking pan.

In a small bowl, mix bread crumbs, chives, melted butter, and salt and pepper to taste. Spread evenly over the salmon.

Bake the salmon for about 10 minutes, or until cooked to taste.

To prepare the tomato sauce, heat olive oil in a medium skillet over medium heat. Add shallots, chili pepper and garlic and sauté until the shallot is just soft.

Add tomatoes, honey, vinegar and salt to taste. Cook, uncovered, for 10 minutes, or until most of the liquid has evaporated. Stir in basil.

To serve, garnish salmon with the tomato sauce. Makes 4 servings.

# Salmon in Citrus Emulsion
## AquaChile

1/4 cup orange juice

1/4 cup grapefruit juice

1 1/2 tablespoons
lemon juice

2 tablespoons butter

3 tablespoons
Dijon mustard

2 fresh AquaChile*
salmon portions,
6 ounces each

Salt

3 tablespoons heavy cream

Pour orange juice, grapefruit juice and lemon juice into a saucepan large enough to hold the salmon in one layer. Add butter and mustard, and then simmer until reduced by half.

Sprinkle each salmon portion with a pinch of salt. Place salmon in the saucepan and cook over low to medium heat for 5 minutes, turning halfway through. Remove and set aside.

Add cream to the pan and simmer over medium heat until the sauce has the desired consistency. Return salmon to the pan and heat for 1 minute. Makes 2 servings.

*Brands may vary by region; substitute a similar product.*

AquaChile

# Citrus Salmon with Orange Relish
## McCormick

1/4 cup orange juice

2 tablespoons olive oil

1 1/2 teaspoons
McCormick* Gourmet
Collection thyme
leaves, divided

4 salmon fillets
(about 1 pound)

1 tablespoon brown sugar

1 teaspoon McCormick*
Gourmet Collection
paprika

1/2 teaspoon salt

### ORANGE RELISH

1/2 teaspoon grated
orange peel

2 seedless oranges,
peeled, sectioned and
cut into 1/2-inch pieces

2 tablespoons chopped
red bell pepper

1 tablespoon honey

1 tablespoon chopped
red onion

1 tablespoon chopped
fresh parsley

1/2 teaspoon McCormick*
Gourmet Collection
ground ginger

Mix orange juice, olive oil and 1 teaspoon of the thyme in a large glass dish. Add salmon; turn to coat well. Refrigerate for 30 minutes. Remove from the marinade. Discard any remaining marinade.

To prepare the orange relish, combine all ingredients and stir to blend.

Preheat oven to 400°F.

Mix brown sugar, paprika, remaining 1/2 teaspoon thyme and salt. Rub salmon evenly with the paprika mixture. Place on a foil-lined baking pan.

Bake for 10-15 minutes, or until cooked to taste.

Serve with relish. Makes 4 servings.

**Nutritional information:** Each serving has 283 calories, 25 g protein, 21 g carbohydrates, 11 g fat, 2 g saturated fat, 62 mg cholesterol, 3 g fiber, 354 mg sodium.

*Brands may vary by region; substitute a similar product.*

McCormick

## "In a Heartbeat" Sautéed Orange Ginger Salmon
Camanchaca

2 tablespoons olive oil

1/2 teaspoon freshly ground black pepper

1 tablespoon peeled and chopped fresh ginger

4 6-ounce boneless, skinless Camanchaca* Atlantic salmon portions

3 tablespoons ponzu sauce (see note)

1 orange, peeled and sliced, with each slice cut in half (or substitute 1/2 cup fresh orange juice with pulp)

Heat olive oil in a nonstick pan over medium-high heat. Add pepper and ginger and sauté for about 2 minutes.

Add salmon and sear for about 1 minute on each side.

Add ponzu sauce, lower the heat to medium and cook for 2 minutes.

Add orange slices and cook over medium-high heat for 2 minutes, or until the salmon is cooked to taste.

Transfer the salmon to plates and garnish with orange slices. Makes 4 servings.

**Note:** Ponzu sauce, common in Japanese cuisine, is known for its distinctive sweet, sour and slightly salty flavor.

*Brands may vary by region; substitute a similar product.*

## Grilled Fish and Peppers
JC Seafood/Sal Mar

4 6-ounce portions Norwegian Atlantic salmon

6 tablespoons white wine

3 tablespoons olive oil

6 tablespoons Mr. Yoshida's Original Gourmet Sauce

Salt and freshly ground black pepper

3-4 sweet mini peppers, sliced into strips

Preheat the grill.

Place each fillet on an individual 8-by-10-inch piece of aluminum foil skin-side down.

Mix wine, olive oil and Mr. Yoshida's sauce in a bowl. Brush over the top of each fillet.

Season with salt and pepper to taste.

Lay pepper slices over the fish. Fold the sides of the foil to enclose the fish, sealing the packets.

Place on the grill over medium heat for 6 minutes, or until cooked to taste. Remove from the foil and serve with a salad or pasta. Makes 4 servings.

# Captain John's Salmon with Maple Mustard Sauce

## Icicle Seafoods

4  6-ounce Atlantic or sockeye
   salmon portions, skin removed
Salt
Pepper
1 tablespoon vegetable oil
3 tablespoons water

2 tablespoons pure maple syrup
2 tablespoons Dijon mustard
2 garlic cloves, finely chopped
2 teaspoons mustard seed
1/4 cup chopped scallion greens

Pat salmon dry and season to taste with salt and pepper.

In a large nonstick skillet, heat oil over medium-high heat until hot but not smoking. Place salmon in the pan and sauté, turning once, until just cooked through, 3-4 minutes per side. If necessary, cook in 2 batches. Transfer to a platter, cover and keep warm.

Remove the skillet from the heat and let cool for about 1 minute. Add water, maple syrup, mustard, garlic, mustard seed and scallions to the pan and whisk together. Add salt and pepper to taste.

Pour the sauce over the salmon and serve. Makes 4 servings.

ICICLE
SEAFOODS, INC.

## Wild Alaskan Sockeye Salmon and Alaskan King Crab with Wilted Spinach Oscar-Style
Trident Seafoods

**4 tablespoons butter, divided**

**4 sockeye or coho salmon fillet portions**

**Salt and black pepper**

**1 tablespoon fresh lemon juice**

**2 tablespoons whipping cream**

**1 cup king crab meat**

**2 tablespoons extra-virgin olive oil**

**4 garlic cloves, sliced**

**1 pound clean spinach, stems removed**

**Coarse salt**

In a skillet, heat 2 tablespoons butter over medium heat. Season salmon with salt and pepper to taste. Place the fish in the skillet skin side down and cook for 4-5 minutes, or until the skin is crispy. Turn off the heat, turn fillets over and let sit in the pan for 2-3 minutes to finish cooking. Remove to a serving plate.

Add lemon juice, 2 tablespoons butter and cream to the pan. Cook over medium heat, stirring, for 1 minute. Stir in crab and turn off the heat.

Meanwhile, add olive oil and garlic to a large skillet. Cook over medium heat until the garlic is cooked through. Remove garlic.

Add spinach to the pan, turning to wilt. Season to taste with coarse salt and pepper.

Immediately place the spinach on the salmon fillets. Top with the crab and drizzle with the rest of the sauce. Makes 4 servings.

## Potato-Wrapped Stuffed Salmon
Orval Kent Foods

**2 large russet potatoes, peeled**

**Parchment paper**

**Salt and pepper**

**1 package Kirkland Signature stuffed salmon entrée (4 portions)**

**3 tablespoons olive oil**

**Arugula tossed with lemon vinaigrette, for serving**

Using a mandoline slicer, cut potatoes lengthwise into paper-thin slices. Place 4 slices lengthwise on a piece of parchment paper in a row, overlapping the long sides slightly. Make another row parallel to the first one, overlapping the short ends of the slices in the first row and forming approximately a 6-by-7-inch rectangle. Season to taste with salt and pepper.

Cut one of the salmon portions in half lengthwise, making sure the stuffing is evenly distributed. Place one of the halves on the center of the potatoes. Fold the potatoes up over the fish, forming a packet and pressing to make the potato slices adhere. Season again with salt and pepper. Repeat for as many portions as needed.

Heat olive oil in a skillet over medium heat. Gently lift the salmon packets from the parchment paper, place them seam-side down in the pan and cook until the potatoes are tender and golden brown, about 3 minutes. Carefully flip over and cook for an additional 2-3 minutes. Remove from the pan and cut in half diagonally before serving.

Serve on a bed of dressed arugula. Makes 4-6 servings.

## Zesty Atlantic Salmon Pasta
True North Salmon

2 cups light sour cream

2 teaspoons grated
lemon peel

2 teaspoons dried
dill weed

4 cups penne pasta

1 tablespoon olive oil

1 pound True North
Salmon* fillet, skinned,
cut into 1-inch cubes

1 leek, rinsed and sliced

1 red bell pepper, seeded
and chopped

2 cups sugar snap peas

Salt and pepper

In a bowl, combine sour cream, lemon peel and dill weed. Mix well and set aside.

Cook pasta according to package directions until al dente, then drain.

Heat olive oil in a large skillet over medium-high heat. Add salmon, and cook and stir until the salmon's color lightens, about 4 minutes. Remove from the skillet.

Add leeks to the skillet and cook, stirring, for 1 minute. Add bell pepper and peas and cook for 3 minutes longer, stirring constantly.

Reduce the heat to medium-low and add the cooked and drained pasta, salmon and sour cream mixture. Add salt and pepper to taste. Stir gently to coat and heat through. Makes 4 servings.

*Brands may vary by region; substitute a similar product.*

## Seasoned Grill Salmon with Spaghetti
Morey's

4 6-ounce portions
Morey's* Seasoned Grill
Marinated Salmon

8 ounces whole
wheat spaghetti

1 cup seasonal vegetables
(such as sun-dried
tomatoes, snow peas
or broccoli) cut in
bite-size pieces

3 tablespoons extra-virgin
olive oil

1 1/2 teaspoons
minced garlic

2 tablespoons chopped
green onions

1/2 cup shredded
Parmesan cheese

Salt and pepper

Cook salmon according to package directions. Break into flakes.

Bring a large pot of water to a boil. Add spaghetti and cook for 5 minutes. Add vegetables to the pot and continue cooking for 4-5 minutes, or until the pasta is tender and the vegetables are hot. Drain.

Return the pasta and vegetables to the pot. Stir in olive oil, garlic, green onions and flaked salmon. Add Parmesan cheese and toss to coat. Season to taste with salt and pepper. Makes 6 servings.

**Variations:** Slice the salmon and fan out on top of the pasta. Use linguine or angel hair pasta. Try shredded Romano, Asiago or a combination of shredded cheeses.

*Brands may vary by region; substitute a similar product.*

## Crusted Salmon with Onion Apple Compote
Kirkland Signature/Puratos

**2 Kirkland Signature croissants**

**1/2 cup hazelnuts, coarsely chopped**

**2 tablespoons olive oil**

**1 tablespoon sugar**

**Grated peel of 1 lemon**

**1/2 teaspoon salt**

**1/2 teaspoon ground pepper**

*SALMON*

**1 tablespoon olive oil**

**4 Atlantic salmon fillet portions, bones and skin removed**

**Salt and pepper**

**Chopped flat-leaf parsley, for garnish**

*ONION APPLE COMPOTE*

**2 Granny Smith apples, cut in small dice**

**1 medium red onion, cut in small dice**

**5 celery stalks, cut in small dice**

**1/2 cup white vinegar**

**1/2 cup sugar**

Preheat oven to 325°F.

Cut croissants into 1/4- to 3/8-inch pieces. Spread in an even layer on a sheet pan and bake until crisp, about 10 minutes. Let cool. Combine with hazelnuts, olive oil, sugar, lemon peel, salt and pepper in a bowl and blend with fingertips until well coated.

Preheat oven to 350°F.

To prepare the salmon, heat a nonstick sauté pan over medium-high heat, then add olive oil. Sprinkle salmon with salt and pepper to taste, place in the pan and sear for 1 minute on each side. Transfer to a baking dish and add a thick layer of croissant crust. Place in the oven and bake for approximately 5-6 minutes.

To prepare the compote, place all ingredients in a saucepan and bring to a quick simmer. Then turn off the heat, cover and let sit for 2 minutes to blend the flavors and soften the ingredients.

To serve, place the salmon on plates, then liberally spoon the compote around the dish and garnish with parsley. Makes 4 servings.

## Apple-Pear Fish Tacos
Oneonta Starr Ranch Growers

**1 orange**

**2 pounds halibut or other white fish**

**Sea salt and pepper**

**12-16 corn tortillas**

*APPLE-PEAR SALSA*

**1/2 bunch cilantro, chopped**

**1 cup chopped green cabbage**

**5 Roma tomatoes, chopped**

**1 serrano pepper (2 if you like it hot), chopped**

**1 Starr Ranch Growers* Granny Smith apple, cored and chopped**

**1 Diamond Starr Growers* Red D'Anjou pear, cored and chopped**

**1/4-1/2 cup chopped red onion**

**1 garlic clove, chopped**

**Juice of 2 limes**

**Sea salt and pepper**

*CHIPOTLE SAUCE*

**1 garlic clove**

**1 chipotle pepper in adobo sauce**

**1 teaspoon adobo sauce**

**2 6-ounce containers plain yogurt**

Squeeze orange over the fish; add salt and pepper to taste. Marinate in the refrigerator for about 1 hour.

To prepare the salsa, in a medium bowl combine cilantro, cabbage, tomatoes, serrano pepper, apple, pear, onion and garlic. Sprinkle with lime juice and season to taste with salt and pepper. Toss well, cover and chill.

To prepare the chipotle sauce, mix all ingredients in a blender. Cover and chill.

Preheat the grill. Preheat oven to 350°F.

Grill the fish until cooked to taste (or bake in the marinade).

Wrap tortillas in foil and heat in the oven.

To serve, fill warm tortillas with flaked fish and salsa. Serve with sauce. Makes 4 servings.

*\* Brands may vary by region; substitute a similar product.*

# Spicy Grilled Catfish
## Consolidated Catfish Producers

2 tablespoons olive oil

1/4 cup lime juice

1 cup dry white wine

2 tablespoons dry mustard

2 tablespoons chili powder

2 teaspoons ground pepper

1/2 cup chopped fresh cilantro or parsley

1/2 teaspoon salt (optional)

1 pound fresh U.S. Farm-Raised Catfish fillets

Prepare grill or preheat broiler.

Mix olive oil, lime juice, wine, mustard, chili powder, pepper, cilantro and salt in a medium bowl. Transfer half of the marinade mixture to another bowl and reserve for basting the catfish.

Add catfish to the first bowl and marinate for at least 15 minutes. If marinating longer than 15 minutes, cover and refrigerate.

Drain fillets and discard marinade. Place fillets on a lightly oiled grill rack or broiler pan rack. Grill or broil 4 inches from the heat source, basting with the reserved marinade, for about 4 minutes on each side, or until the fish flakes easily when tested with a fork. Makes 4 servings.

# Salsa Catfish
## Heartland Catfish

6 Heartland Catfish* U.S. farm-raised catfish fillets, 6-8 ounces each

1/2 teaspoon freshly ground white pepper

3/4 teaspoon garlic salt

2 cups Fresh Garden Relish or prepared salsa

### FRESH GARDEN RELISH

4 medium ripe tomatoes, chopped

1 green bell pepper, seeded and chopped

1 yellow bell pepper, seeded and chopped

1/4 cup snipped fresh chives

1/2 cup minced red onions

1 jalapeño, seeded and minced

1 1/2 teaspoons sea salt

1/2 teaspoon freshly ground black pepper

Sprinkle catfish with pepper and garlic salt.

Prepare a hot fire.

To prepare the relish, combine all ingredients and mix to blend. Cover and chill until ready to serve.

Place catfish on an oiled perforated grill rack over the fire. Grill until the fish is opaque and just beginning to flake when tested with a fork, about 10 minutes per inch of thickness, turning once halfway through cooking.

Serve the fish topped with relish or salsa.

Makes 6 servings.

**Nutritional information:** Each serving has 258 calories, 26 g protein, 10 g carbohydrates, 2 g fiber, 13 g fat, 75 mg cholesterol, 683 mg sodium.

*Source: Fish & Shellfish, Grilled & Smoked, by Karen Adler and Judith M. Fertig.*

*\* Brands may vary by region; substitute a similar product.*

# Halibut with Chunky Tomato and Pepper Compote
## Windset Farms

1/2 small red onion, thinly sliced

Juice of 2 limes

1/2 jalapeño pepper, seeded and finely chopped

12 Windset Farms* Concerto grape tomatoes, halved

4 Windset Farms* Dolce Super Sweet baby bell peppers, seeded and chopped

1/2 Windset Farms* Fresco cucumber, seeded and diced

2 tablespoons chopped fresh cilantro

1 teaspoon kosher salt, divided

1/4 cup canola oil

4 6-ounce fresh halibut fillets

In a small bowl, marinate red onion in lime juice for at least an hour. Add jalapeño, tomatoes, bell peppers, cucumber, cilantro and 1/2 teaspoon salt. Set aside.

Preheat oven to 450°F.

Heat a large nonstick ovenproof skillet over medium-high heat. Add canola oil. Season halibut fillets with 1/2 teaspoon salt and place in the hot skillet. Cook until the flesh is nicely browned, about 2 minutes. Turn the fish over and place in the oven for 3 minutes, or until cooked through.

Remove the fish from the pan and serve with the salsa. Makes 4 servings.

**Tip:** This compote also works nicely with salmon, sablefish or chicken.

*Recipe developed by executive chef Dana Reinhardt.*
*\* Brands may vary by region; substitute a similar product.*

## Roasted Halibut on a Bed of Vegetables
American Fish/S.M. Products

8-12 small new potatoes

1/2 cup plus 2 tablespoons extra-virgin olive oil, divided

Salt and pepper

6-10 ripe plum tomatoes, or 1  14 1/2-ounce can diced tomatoes

3-4 leeks, washed, trimmed and sliced lengthwise

1 large fennel bulb, diced

1 tablespoon chopped fresh parsley

1 tablespoon chopped fresh basil

1 tablespoon grated lemon peel

2 garlic cloves, peeled

4 fresh halibut portions (approx. 6-8 ounces each)

Preheat oven to 450°F.

Steam potatoes until just tender, about 10 minutes. Let cool, then cut in quarters and place in a large bowl. Add 2 tablespoons olive oil, toss to coat and sprinkle with salt and pepper to taste. Set aside.

Cut tomatoes in half lengthwise.

Arrange leeks, fennel, potatoes and tomatoes in a roasting pan. Roast for 10 minutes.

Blend 1/2 cup olive oil, parsley, basil, lemon peel and garlic in a food processor.

Brush halibut with the olive oil mixture. Set fish on top of the vegetables and bake until the fish is opaque, about 10-12 minutes. Makes 4 servings.

## Our Favorite Halibut Tacos
Alaska Glacier·Seafoods

2 pounds Alaska Glacier Seafoods* wild-caught halibut fillets, cut into 8 equal pieces

8 flour or corn tortillas

1 cup very thinly sliced green cabbage

1/2 cup diagonally sliced green onions

1/2 cup fresh cilantro leaves, chopped

1 lime, cut into wedges

### MARINADE

1 1/4 cups white wine

1/4 cup fresh lemon juice

1/2 cup olive oil

3 tablespoons crushed garlic

Juice and grated peel of 1 lime

1 green onion, thinly sliced

1/4 teaspoon salt

### SALSA

4-5 ripe tomatoes, diced

1 avocado, diced

1/4 cup fresh lime juice

1/4 cup fresh cilantro leaves, chopped

1-2 jalapeños, minced

1/2 cup finely chopped red onion

Salt and pepper to taste

Mix marinade ingredients. Add halibut and marinate in the refrigerator for 1-3 hours, turning several times.

Combine all salsa ingredients in a bowl and chill.

Preheat the grill.

Remove fish from marinade and grill over medium heat for several minutes per side, or until it is no longer translucent in the center and starts to flake. Crumble fish into a bowl and keep warm.

Fill tortillas with halibut, cabbage, onions, cilantro and salsa. Add a squeeze of lime. Makes 8 servings.

*Brands may vary by region; substitute a similar product.*

# Fruit Salsa over Walnut-Crusted Fish
## Primavera

1 cup Prima Noce* shelled walnut pieces

4 tablespoons firmly packed light brown sugar

1 tablespoon grated orange peel

1 teaspoon coarsely ground black pepper

1 teaspoon sea salt

4  8-ounce fillets of any fresh white fish

1 ripe mango, peeled and chopped into 1/4-inch pieces

1 Crystal Market* Granny Smith apple, peeled and chopped into 1/4-inch pieces

1 cup fresh Primavera* cherries, pitted and halved

2 tablespoons chopped fresh cilantro

1 tablespoon balsamic vinegar

1/4 teaspoon crushed red pepper

Preheat oven to 350°F.

Place walnuts, brown sugar, orange peel, pepper and salt in a food processor. Pulse until coarsely chopped.

Place fish in a shallow baking dish. Press the walnut mixture onto the top of the fish. Bake for 20-25 minutes, or until the fish flakes easily. Do not turn the fish.

Meanwhile, combine mango, apple, cherries, cilantro, vinegar and red pepper in a bowl and toss to blend.

Remove the fish from the pan and place on a serving platter. Spoon the fruit salsa over the warm fish. Serve immediately. Makes 4 servings.

*Brands may vary by region; substitute a similar product.*

## Dijonnaise-Crusted Cod
Trident Seafoods

4 Trident Seafoods* frozen cod fillet portions

2 tablespoons extra-virgin olive oil, divided

Salt and freshly ground black pepper

2 garlic cloves, crushed

A few sprigs of fresh thyme

3 tablespoons Dijon mustard

1 cup fresh bread crumbs

2 tablespoons minced chives

Thaw cod portions according to package directions, then remove from the bag and pat dry on paper towels.

Heat 1 tablespoon olive oil in a sauté pan over medium-high heat. Season the fillets with salt and pepper to taste and slip them into the pan, along with the garlic and thyme. Sear the fillets for 3 minutes, then turn them over and cook for 3 minutes more. Reduce the heat to medium and cook for another 3-4 minutes, or until the fish is opaque but still moist and flakes apart lightly when pressed with a fork.

Preheat the broiler.

Place the seared cod in an oven pan. Spread mustard evenly over the portions. Mix together bread crumbs, chives and 1 tablespoon olive oil and pat evenly over the fish. Broil just until the crumbs are golden brown. Makes 4 servings.

**Tip:** Serve with garlic wilted spinach and basmati brown rice.

*Brands may vary by region; substitute a similar product.*

## Wild Pacific Cod with Hunan Sauce and Green Beans
Copper River Seafoods

2 tablespoons vegetable oil

2-3 garlic cloves, minced

1 cup chopped onions

2 pounds Copper River Seafoods wild Pacific cod portions, thawed

2 pounds green beans (frozen or fresh)

6 tablespoons oyster sauce

2 tablespoons dark sweet soy sauce

1/2 cup water

1 teaspoon cornstarch

Heat a sauté pan over medium heat. Add oil, garlic and onions and cook, stirring occasionally, until slightly browned.

Raise the heat to high, add cod and cook for 2 minutes on each side. Remove from the pan.

Add green beans, oyster sauce and soy sauce to the onion and garlic mixture.

In a small bowl, mix water and cornstarch. Stir into the green bean mixture.

Place the cod back in the pan and baste with the sauce. Simmer for 5 minutes over medium heat. Makes 5-6 servings.

# Dover Sole with Coconut Curry Sauce, Shiitakes and Green Beans
## Pacific Seafood Group

1 teaspoon plus 1 tablespoon vegetable oil, divided
1/4 cup finely chopped onion
1 tablespoon minced fresh ginger
2 tablespoons curry powder
1/2 teaspoon crushed red pepper
1 cup chicken stock
1 14-ounce can coconut milk
2 tablespoons flour
2 tablespoons cornstarch
1 tablespoon sesame seeds

Salt and pepper
1 pound Dover sole or flounder fillets
1 cup sliced shiitake mushrooms
1 pound fresh green beans, trimmed
4 cups cooked jasmine rice
1/4 cup chopped green onions, for garnish
1 tablespoon chopped fresh basil, for garnish
Black sesame seeds, for garnish

In a saucepan, heat 1 teaspoon oil over medium heat. Add onion and ginger and sauté until translucent. Add curry powder and red pepper and cook for another 2 minutes. Add stock and cook until reduced by half. Add coconut milk and cook until thickened. Keep warm.

Heat 1 tablespoon oil in a nonstick skillet over medium-high heat.

In a shallow bowl, mix flour, cornstarch, sesame seeds, and salt and pepper to taste. Dredge sole in the flour mixture and place in the heated skillet. Brown the fillets on each side, flipping only once. Drain on paper towels.

Add mushrooms and green beans to the skillet and sauté until tender.

Divide the rice and the mushroom/bean sauté among 4 plates, place the fish on the rice and pour the sauce over the fish. Garnish with green onions, basil and sesame seeds. Makes 4 servings.

*PacificSeafood*™

# New England Pine Nut Crusted Haddock with Clams Puttanesca Style
## North Coast Seafoods

$^1/_2$ cup toasted pine nuts

$^1/_2$ cup fresh bread crumbs

$^1/_2$ cup grated Parmesan cheese

2 tablespoons chopped fresh parsley

1 tablespoon minced garlic

Salt and pepper

$^1/_2$ cup flour

2 eggs, beaten

4  8-ounce North Coast Seafoods*
   skinless haddock fillets

3 tablespoons olive oil

In a food processor, combine pine nuts, bread crumbs, Parmesan, parsley, garlic, and salt and pepper to taste. Pulse until the nuts are roughly chopped.

Set up 3 bowls, with flour in the first, eggs in the second and pine nut mixture in the third.

Dredge each haddock fillet in the flour, shake off excess and then dip in the egg. Place in the pine nut mixture and turn to coat.

Heat a sauté pan over medium-high heat. Add olive oil. Carefully place haddock in the hot pan and cook until golden brown, then turn and brown on the other side, about 3-4 minutes per side.

Serve with Clams Puttanesca Style (recipe page 167). Makes 4 servings.

*Brands may vary by region; substitute a similar product.*

# Toasted Crumb Tilapia Tacos
## Slade Gorton

1 cup sour cream
1/2 tablespoon canned chipotle in adobo sauce, pureed
1 teaspoon lemon juice
4 fillets Slade Gorton* Toasted Crumb Tilapia
Cooking spray
8 flour tortillas (8-10 inch)
1/2 cup salsa
1/2 cup sliced green onions

### SLAW

2 cups shredded Savoy cabbage
2 teaspoons lemon juice
2 teaspoons lime juice
1 tablespoon orange juice
2 teaspoons minced garlic
1 teaspoon salt
1/4 teaspoon freshly ground black pepper
2 teaspoons sugar
Dash of Cholula hot sauce or Tabasco sauce

To prepare the slaw, mix cabbage, citrus juices, garlic, salt, pepper, sugar and hot sauce. Refrigerate for at least 2 hours and up to 1 day before serving.

Combine sour cream, chipotle, lemon juice and a pinch of salt. Set aside.

Preheat oven to 375°F.

Lightly coat tilapia fillets with cooking spray. Bake tilapia until flaky and opaque. Flake each portion into bite-size chunks.

Place tortillas between damp paper towels and heat in the microwave for 30-60 seconds, or until lightly warmed and softened.

Place some flaked tilapia on each tortilla. Top with 1/4 cup of slaw, 1 tablespoon of salsa, 1 tablespoon of green onions and about a teaspoon of chipotle sour cream. Makes 4 servings.

*Brands may vary by region; substitute a similar product.*

# Spicy Lime Tilapia
## Aquamericas

4 Mountain Stream* tilapia fillets
2 tablespoons olive oil
Juice of 1 lime, plus lime slices for garnish
4 tablespoons spicy dry rub seasoning (Emeril's Essence or other Cajun blend)
Prepared pineapple mango salsa (optional)

Oil and heat a grill pan over medium-high heat.

Brush tilapia fillets with olive oil and lime juice. Season liberally with dry rub.

Grill the fillets for 3-4 minutes on each side, or until tender and flaky.

Garnish with salsa and lime slices. Makes 4 servings.

*Brands may vary by region; substitute a similar product.*

aquamericas

# Tilapia with Pistachio Pesto
## Tropical Aquaculture Products, Inc.

4 fresh Tropical Brand* tilapia fillets

Kosher salt

3 tablespoons shelled pistachios

2 cups packed chopped fresh
    basil leaves

1 garlic clove, peeled

1/2 cup plus 1-2 tablespoons
    extra-virgin olive oil, divided

1/4 cup freshly grated
    Parmigiano-Reggiano

Remove fresh tilapia fillets from the refrigerator and let sit for 8-10 minutes, bringing them to room temperature. Season both sides with a pinch of salt.

Combine pistachios, basil, garlic and 2 pinches of salt in a stone mortar. Grind with the pestle until fine. Drizzle in 1/2 cup olive oil. Continuously grind while adding Parmigiano-Reggiano 1 tablespoon at a time. (This can also be done in a food processor or blender.)

Heat a large nonstick skillet over medium-high heat. Place 1-2 tablespoons of olive oil in the hot pan, enough to coat it. Carefully place tilapia in the pan. Shake the pan slightly to make sure the fillets do not stick. Let cook undisturbed for 2-3 minutes. Flip fillets and cook for another 3 minutes, or until golden brown. Make sure they are cooked through by testing the thickest section with a fork.

Place tilapia on plates and top with pesto. Makes 4 servings.

**Tip:** Pesto will keep for 7-10 days in the refrigerator. Store in a jar topped with a thin layer of extra-virgin olive oil.

*\* Brands may vary by region; substitute a similar product.*

# Southwest Chile Lime Albacore Pasta
## Kirkland Signature

8 ounces dry gemelli pasta

1/4 cup chopped fresh cilantro, plus more for garnish

1 garlic clove, minced

3 tablespoons extra-virgin olive oil, divided

1/2 cup chicken broth

2 tablespoons tequila (optional)

1/4 cup lime juice

1 tablespoon taco seasoning or chili seasoning

1 1/2 cups half-and-half

1 tablespoon grated Parmesan cheese, plus more for garnish

1 cup canned corn, drained

1/2 medium red bell pepper, julienne sliced

1/2 medium red onion, sliced

1 large Anaheim green chile, seeded and chopped

2 7-ounce cans Kirkland Signature solid white albacore tuna, drained and flaked

Salt and pepper

Crushed red pepper, for garnish

Prepare pasta according to package directions.

In a saucepan, sauté cilantro and garlic in 1 tablespoon olive oil over medium heat for 2-3 minutes. Add broth, tequila and lime juice; bring to a boil and cook until reduced, 8-10 minutes. Stir in taco seasoning, half-and-half, Parmesan and corn. Bring to a boil, then simmer for 2-3 minutes, or until slightly thickened.

In a large saucepan, sauté bell pepper, onion and chile in 2 tablespoons olive oil over medium heat until softened, 3-4 minutes. Add tuna and sauce. Cook, stirring gently, until heated through. Add pasta and toss gently. Add salt and pepper to taste.

Garnish with cilantro, Parmesan and crushed red pepper. Makes 4 servings.

**Nutritional information:** Each serving has 640 calories, 41 g protein, 62 g carbohydrates, 24 g fat, 9 g saturated fat, 85 mg cholesterol, 4 g fiber, 690 mg sodium.

# Seared Ahi Tuna with Mixed Greens
## Western United Fish Company

2 Western United* ahi tuna steaks

Canola oil

Fresh mixed salad greens

*MARINADE*

2/3 cup soy sauce

2/3 cup water

1 cup mirin (see note)

Freshly ground pepper to taste

2 large knobs fresh ginger, thinly sliced

2 teaspoons sugar

4 teaspoons wasabi paste

Juice of 1 lemon

1 tablespoon chopped fresh cilantro leaves

In a bowl, mix all the marinade ingredients. Reserve half the marinade and set aside.

Place ahi steaks in the remaining marinade and refrigerate for up to 45 minutes.

Preheat the grill to high and brush with canola oil.

Grill ahi for 2 minutes per side, or until seared.

Slice the ahi into 1/4-inch strips and arrange over the mixed greens.

Drizzle the reserved marinade over the ahi and mixed greens, or use it as a dipping sauce. Serve immediately. Makes 4 servings.

**Note:** Mirin is a popular Japanese sweet cooking wine, often referred to as rice wine.

*\* Brands may vary by region; substitute a similar product.*

*Your Direct Source*

# Seared Ahi Tuna Salad with Pomegranate Vinaigrette
## Ready Pac Foods, Inc.

1 16-ounce bag Ready Pac* Grand Parisian Complete Salad

1/4 cup pomegranate juice

1/2 cup canola oil

5 wonton wrappers, cut into 1/8-inch strips (optional)

4 6-ounce fresh tuna steaks

2 tablespoons olive oil

3/4 teaspoon salt

1/2 teaspoon ground white pepper

1/4 cup black sesame seeds

1/4 cup white sesame seeds

Remove the dressing packet from the salad bag. In a small bowl, combine dressing and pomegranate juice; mix well and set aside.

Reserve frosted almonds, dried cranberries and feta cheese from the salad bag. Chill the salad greens.

Heat canola oil in a sauté pan to 325°F. Fry wonton strips for 3-4 seconds, or until golden brown. Remove and drain on paper towels; set aside.

Preheat the grill or a sauté pan over high heat.

Brush tuna steaks with olive oil. Sprinkle with salt and pepper. Coat the steaks with black and white sesame seeds. Sear for 2-3 minutes (for medium-rare) on each side. Remove from the heat and let rest for several minutes before slicing.

Toss half the pomegranate vinaigrette with the chilled salad greens. Mound equal portions of tossed salad greens on plates. Sprinkle with almonds, cranberries, feta and wonton strips.

Cut the tuna into diagonal slices and arrange on top of the salads. Drizzle with the remaining vinaigrette. Makes 4-6 servings.

*Brands may vary by region; substitute a similar product.*

## Trout with Pecan Rice Stuffing
Clear Springs

3/4 cup black and mahogany rice or gourmet wild rice blend

1/2 cup diced crimini mushrooms

1/3 cup finely chopped toasted pecans

1 tablespoon half-and-half

Sea salt

4 Clear Springs* dressed trout

2 medium vine-ripened tomatoes, sliced

1/2 cup shredded Asiago cheese

Prepare rice according to package directions. Stir in mushrooms, pecans, half-and-half and salt to taste.

Preheat oven to 375°F.

Stuff trout with the rice mixture and place in an oiled baking pan.

Top with lightly salted sliced tomatoes and shredded cheese.

Bake for 20-25 minutes, or until the internal temperature is 140°F. Makes 4 servings.

**Tip:** Serve with asparagus.

*\* Brands may vary by region; substitute a similar product.*

## Zesty Italian-Marinated Baked Rainbow Trout
Idaho Trout Company

4 Idaho Trout* whole dressed rainbow trout

Zesty Italian salad dressing

Salt and pepper

Lemon pepper

Italian seasoning salt (optional)

Garlic salt (optional)

1 medium yellow or white onion, sliced (optional)

2 tablespoons butter or margarine, melted

Marinate trout in Italian dressing in the refrigerator overnight.

Preheat oven to 350°F.

Place trout in a well-greased shallow baking dish; discard the marinade. Season trout cavities with salt, pepper, lemon pepper, Italian seasoning salt and garlic salt to taste. Fill the cavities partially with onions.

Drizzle melted butter over the fish.

Cover the dish with aluminum foil and bake for 20 minutes. Remove the foil and bake until the fish flakes easily with a fork. Allow 5-6 minutes for each half inch of thickness. Makes 4 servings.

*\* Brands may vary by region; substitute a similar product.*

# Grilled Sea Scallops with Mango and Tomato Salad

## American Pride Seafoods

Olive oil

8 American Pride all-natural, dry, Grade A sea scallops

1 tablespoon kosher salt

1 tablespoon ground black pepper

### SALAD

4 mangoes, cut into small dice

2 yellow tomatoes, cut into wedges

2 roasted red tomatoes, drained and chopped

1 red onion, cut into thin strips

### DRESSING

$1/2$ cup red wine vinegar

Juice of 1 lime

2 garlic cloves, minced

2 tablespoons chopped fresh cilantro

2 teaspoons sugar

1 cup Spanish extra-virgin olive oil

Preheat grill to medium-high. Clean the grill with a brush and oil it to prevent sticking.

To prepare the salad, combine mangoes, tomatoes and onion in a bowl.

To prepare the dressing, combine vinegar, lime juice, garlic, cilantro and sugar in a bowl. Whisk until the sugar is dissolved. Slowly drizzle olive oil into the vinegar, whisking continuously.

Toss half of the dressing with the salad and refrigerate. Set aside the remaining dressing.

Toss scallops in olive oil to coat and sprinkle with salt and pepper. Grill for 3-4 minutes per side, or until cooked to taste.

To serve, add half of the remaining dressing to the salad and toss to mix. Arrange the grilled scallops on top and drizzle with dressing. Makes 4 servings.

# Sautéed Sea Scallops with Kalamata Olive and Asiago Salsa

## Atlantic Capes Fisheries

1 large red onion
1 red or yellow bell pepper
1 cup plus 1 tablespoon olive oil, plus more for coating vegetables
Salt
1 cup Kalamata olives, pitted and cut in half
6 ounces (3/4 cup) grated Asiago cheese (or Manchego or Parmesan)

1/2 cup sherry vinegar
1 teaspoon Dijon mustard
1 teaspoon honey
1 tablespoon chopped fresh thyme
Freshly ground pepper
1 1/2 pounds Atlantic Capes sea scallops, thawed

Preheat oven to 375°F.

Remove the skin from the onion. Place onion and bell pepper on a cookie sheet; coat with olive oil and sprinkle with salt to taste. Roast in the oven for 30-40 minutes, or until browned and tender. Transfer the pepper to a bag and seal until it cools; peel off the skin, remove the seeds and slice. Slice the roasted onion.

Place the sliced onions and peppers in a bowl and mix with olives and cheese.

In another bowl, whisk together 1 cup olive oil, vinegar, mustard, honey, thyme, and salt and pepper to taste. Pour dressing to taste over the onion mixture, stirring to blend. Set aside.

Season scallops with salt and pepper to taste. Heat a sauté pan over high heat. Add 1 tablespoon olive oil and scallops, and cook until they begin to brown on one side. Flip the scallops over and cook until browned but still translucent in the center (don't overcook).

Place the scallops on a serving plate and cover with the salsa. Makes 4-5 servings.

**Tip:** Serve with crusty bread and grilled asparagus or other green vegetable.

## Roasted Littleneck Clams Puttanesca Style
North Coast Seafoods

Olive oil

1 onion, diced

2 garlic cloves, chopped

1  28-ounce can whole peeled tomatoes, roughly chopped with liquid

4 tablespoons tomato paste

12 Kalamata olives, pitted and chopped

2 anchovy fillets, minced

1 teaspoon dried basil

24 North Coast Seafoods* littleneck clams, washed

1 lemon

Kosher salt and pepper

2 tablespoons chopped fresh Italian parsley

Crusty bread, for serving

Preheat oven to 375°F.

Heat a 12-inch cast iron skillet over medium heat. Add about 2 tablespoons of olive oil and sauté the onion and garlic until soft. Add tomatoes, tomato paste, olives, anchovies and basil. Simmer for 10 minutes.

Arrange clams in the skillet and place in the oven for about 10 minutes, or until the clams open.

Remove from the oven, drizzle with olive oil, squeeze the lemon over the clams, and season to taste with salt and pepper. Garnish with parsley.

Bring to the table in the pan and serve with crusty bread. Makes 2-3 servings.

*Brands may vary by region; substitute a similar product.*

## Clams Marinara
Cedar Key Aquaculture Farms

1 large onion, chopped fine

4 tablespoons olive oil

2 large tomatoes, peeled and chopped

1/2 cup dry white wine

48 Cedar Key Sweets* farm-raised clams, scrubbed

1/2 cup chopped fresh parsley

Salt and pepper to taste

Cooked pasta, for serving

In a large pan, sauté onion in olive oil over medium heat until golden.

Add tomatoes and cook, stirring, until slightly thickened.

Stir in wine, and then clams. Cover and cook until the clams have opened, about 5-10 minutes.

Add parsley, salt and pepper.

Serve over pasta. Makes 4 servings.

*Brands may vary by region; substitute a similar product.*

# Wok-Fried Clams
## Quality Ocean International

5 pounds New Zealand cockles (littleneck clams)

3 tablespoons olive oil

1 green or red bell pepper, thinly sliced

About 2 cups thinly sliced broccoli or French green beans

2 teaspoons soy sauce

1/2 cup dry white wine or verjuice*

1 small red chile, seeded and finely sliced

1 teaspoon grated fresh ginger

2 garlic cloves, crushed

Freshly ground black pepper

1 teaspoon cornstarch, dissolved in a little cold water

Rice or pasta, for serving

Scrub clams thoroughly.

Heat oil in a wok over high heat. Stir-fry clams until the shells spring open. Remove from the wok, saving 4 tablespoons of juices from the wok.

Add vegetables to the wok and stir-fry until crisp-tender. Add soy sauce, wine, chile, ginger, garlic and pepper. Return the reserved juices to the pan. Bring to a boil and thicken with the cornstarch mixture. Add the clams and stir to blend.

Serve on a bed of rice or pasta. Clams are naturally salty, so there is no need to add salt. Makes 4 servings.

*Verjuice is a sour juice made from unripe fruit such as grapes or crab apples.*

# Steamed Prince Edward Island Mussels in Garlic and Wine
## North Coast Seafoods

Vegetable or olive oil

2 tablespoons minced garlic

2 pounds North Coast Seafoods* PEI mussels

1 cup Chardonnay

Juice of 1 lemon

1 tablespoon chopped fresh parsley

1 tablespoon sliced green onion

Salt and pepper

1/4 pound butter

Crusty bread, for serving

In a large sauté pan, heat enough oil over medium heat to cover the bottom of the pan. Add garlic and cook for about 3 minutes. Do not let it burn.

Increase the heat to high. Add mussels and wine and cover the pan. Cook for 3-4 minutes, or until the mussels have opened.

Add lemon juice, parsley, green onion, and salt and pepper to taste. Cut butter into pieces, add to the pan and toss until blended. Transfer to a serving bowl.

Serve with crusty bread. Makes 2 servings.

**Tip:** This dish will serve 4 as an appetizer.

*Brands may vary by region; substitute a similar product.*

# Dungeness Crab Cake Salad with Berry Sweet Onion Salsa
## Pacific Seafood Group

1 pound Dungeness crab meat

2 teaspoons chopped green onions

1 tablespoon mayonnaise

1 egg, beaten

1/4 teaspoon crushed red pepper

1 tablespoon chopped fresh parsley

1 cup panko bread crumbs

Salt and pepper

1 tablespoon vegetable oil

1 pound spring greens

4 Walla Walla spring onions, grilled and chilled

1 pound asparagus, grilled and chilled

### BERRY SWEET ONION SALSA

2 tablespoons chopped Walla Walla sweet onion

1 cup mixed fresh blackberries, raspberries, blueberries and sliced strawberries

1 tablespoon balsamic vinegar

1 teaspoon sugar

1 tablespoon chopped fresh mint

Salt and pepper to taste

In a bowl, combine crab, green onions, mayonnaise, egg, red pepper, parsley, panko, and salt and pepper to taste, mixing until blended. Shape into 4 cakes.

Heat oil in a sauté pan over medium heat. Add the crab cakes and sauté until browned on both sides.

To prepare the salsa, combine all ingredients in a bowl and stir gently to blend; set aside.

Arrange spring greens, grilled onions and asparagus on 4 plates. Place a crab cake on the greens and garnish with the berry salsa. Makes 4 servings.

*PacificSeafood*™

# Sautéed King Crab with Wine and Garlic
## Harbor Seafood

3 1/2 **pounds frozen king crab legs, thawed**

5 **tablespoons unsalted butter**

2 **garlic cloves, chopped**

1/2 **cup dry white wine**

1/8 **teaspoon cayenne pepper**

1 **tablespoon chopped fresh parsley**

**Salt**

**Lemon or lime wedges**

Remove crab meat from the shells. Rinse in cold water to remove glaze and brine.

Melt butter in a skillet over medium heat. Add garlic and sauté for about 1 minute, or until golden brown. Add wine, cayenne and parsley. Raise the heat to high and cook until reduced by half, about 1 minute.

Reduce the heat to medium and add the crab meat. Cook for 2-3 minutes, stirring occasionally, until heated through. Add salt to taste.

Serve with lemon or lime wedges. Makes 4 servings.

# Shrimp and Tropical Fruit Summer Rolls
## Chestnut Hill Farms/Legend Produce

1 **small mango, peeled, pitted and cut into julienne strips**

1 **small pineapple, peeled, cored and cut into julienne strips**

1 **cup julienned cantaloupe**

1/4 **cup golden raisins**

1/4 **cup shaved coconut**

2 **tablespoons orange blossom honey**

3 **sprigs fresh mint, torn**

2 **tablespoons tangerine juice**

1 **pinch sea salt**

12 **12-inch rice paper rounds, softened in warm water**

24 **jumbo cooked shrimp**

In a bowl, combine mango, pineapple, cantaloupe, raisins, coconut, honey, mint, tangerine juice and sea salt. Mix lightly, cover and refrigerate for 30 minutes.

For each roll, lay out a piece of softened rice paper. Place 2 shrimp and some of the fruit mixture at the bottom center. Roll the bottom toward the middle, fold in both sides and continue to roll. Makes 6 servings.

*Recipe courtesy of Chef Allen Susser.*

# Shrimp and Cashew Curry
## Ann's House of Nuts/Harvest Manor Farms

2 tablespoons butter

3 tablespoons curry powder

1/4 cup finely chopped onion

1/4 cup finely chopped celery

1/4 cup finely chopped red or
green bell pepper

1/4 teaspoon grated nutmeg

1 cup white wine

1 cup papaya nectar

1 pound raw shrimp, peeled
and deveined

1 pound Kirkland Signature
Whole Fancy Cashews

Melt butter in a 2-quart sauté pan over medium heat. Add curry powder and sauté for 1 minute. Add onion, celery, bell pepper and nutmeg and cook until tender.

Add wine, papaya nectar and shrimp. Simmer over low heat for 20 minutes, or until the mixture thickens. Note: Cornstarch can be added for additional thickening.

Gently stir in cashews.

Serve immediately. Makes 4 servings.

HARVEST MANOR FARMS

# Spinach Ravioli Lasagna with Pesto Panko Bread Crumbs

## Monterey Pasta Company/Cibo Naturals

Nonstick cooking spray

1 23-ounce package Cibo Naturals Alfredo Sauce, divided

1 38-ounce package Monterey Pasta Co. Spinach & Cheese Ravioli, cooked according to package directions

1/4 cup Kirkland Signature by Cibo Naturals Basil Pesto

1 cup roasted red peppers (jarred or canned), sliced into 1/2-inch strips

### PESTO PANKO BREAD CRUMBS

1 cup panko bread crumbs

1/2 cup Kirkland Signature by Cibo Naturals Basil Pesto

1 cup shredded mozzarella cheese

1/4 cup grated Parmesan cheese

Preheat oven to 350°F. Coat a 13-by-9-inch baking pan with cooking spray.

To prepare the bread crumbs, mix all ingredients in a small bowl until thoroughly combined. Set aside.

Smooth 1 1/2 cups of Alfredo sauce over the bottom of the prepared pan. Layer 18 of the ravioli in slightly overlapping rows—3 across and 6 lengthwise. Smooth 1/2 cup Alfredo sauce over the ravioli. Dot with pesto.

Layer the remaining ravioli in slightly overlapping rows—3 across and 6 lengthwise. Tuck any extra ravioli into this layer. Smooth 1/2 cup Alfredo sauce over the ravioli.

Place red pepper strips evenly across the top. Sprinkle with Pesto Panko Bread Crumbs.

Cover with foil and bake until the sauce is bubbling, about 35 minutes. Remove the foil and broil until the bread crumbs are lightly browned.

Let the lasagna rest for about 5 minutes. Serve with a large spoon.
Makes 12 servings.

**Tip:** Pesto Panko Bread Crumbs can also be used as a topping for baked chicken or fish.

## Spinach Ricotta Gnocchi
Campbell's

1 16-ounce package frozen dumpling-shaped pasta (gnocchi)

2 cups thawed and well-drained frozen cut leaf spinach

1 1/2 cups Prego* Heart Smart Traditional Italian Sauce

1/4 cup grated Parmesan Romano cheese

1/2 cup ricotta cheese

1 cup shredded mozzarella cheese (about 4 ounces)

Prepare pasta according to package directions in a 6-quart saucepot. Add spinach during the last 3 minutes of cooking. Drain the pasta mixture well in a colander. Return to the saucepot.

Stir Italian sauce, Parmesan Romano and ricotta into the pasta. Cook over medium heat until the mixture is hot and bubbling, stirring occasionally.

Top with mozzarella. Makes 6 servings.

*Brands may vary by region; substitute a similar product.*

## Four-Cheese Ravioli with Fresh Tomato Basil Cream Sauce
Kirkland Signature/Seviroli Foods

2 tablespoons olive oil

1 small yellow onion, diced

1 tablespoon thinly sliced garlic

Salt and pepper

6 fresh Roma (plum) tomatoes

1/4-1/2 cup heavy cream

1/4 cup coarsely chopped fresh basil

1 tablespoon butter

24 Kirkland Signature Four-Cheese Ravioli

Freshly grated Parmesan cheese (optional)

Heat olive oil in a 10- to 12-inch sauté pan over medium heat. Add onion and sauté until soft and translucent. Stir in garlic. Sprinkle with salt and pepper to taste.

Roughly chop tomatoes and add to the onions. Cook for about 5 minutes, then add 1/4 cup cream or more to lighten the sauce to taste. Turn up the heat to bring to a boil, then lower the heat and simmer until the sauce is reduced by about a third. When the sauce is nearly at your desired consistency, add basil and cook for a couple minutes longer. Add butter and stir until blended into the sauce.

Meanwhile, prepare ravioli according to package directions. Transfer to a serving bowl. Add 1/2-3/4 cup of the sauce and mix gently.

Add more sauce to each portion when serving. Top with grated Parmesan. Makes 4 servings.

## Polenta Pizza with Fontina and Red Grapes
Kirschenman

2 teaspoons active
  dry yeast
2 tablespoons olive oil
1 teaspoon kosher salt
1 1/2 cups all-purpose
  flour, plus more
  for dusting
3/4 cup fine-ground
  polenta
2 teaspoons unsalted
  butter, melted
4 ounces Fontina cheese,
  cut into thin slices
1 cup Kirschenman* red
  flame grapes (or other
  seedless red grapes),
  sliced in half
1/4 cup walnut
  pieces, toasted
2 teaspoons turbinado**
  sugar

Combine yeast with 1/4 cup warm water in a medium mixing bowl and let sit for 10 minutes. Stir in 5/8 cup warm water, olive oil and salt. Mix in flour and polenta. Knead for 7 minutes on a floured work surface.

Place dough in a large oiled bowl, cover and let rise in a warm place until doubled in size, about 1 1/2 hours. Punch down and pat or roll into a 10-inch circle; place on a pizza paddle, cover and let rise for 1 hour.

Preheat oven with a baking stone to 450°F.

Brush dough with melted butter and top with Fontina. Add grapes and walnuts, then sprinkle with sugar.

Bake for 12-15 minutes on the baking stone, or until the edges begin to turn golden.

Let cool for 5 minutes. Cut into 8 slices.
Makes 8 servings.

*Brands may vary by region; substitute a similar product.
** Turbinado sugar, commonly referred to as raw sugar, is coarser than granulated sugar.

## Croissant Welsh Rarebit
Kirkland Signature/Puratos

2 Kirkland Signature
  croissants
1 tablespoon butter
1 tablespoon flour
1 cup dark beer such
  as Guinness
1 teaspoon Dijon mustard
3 dashes Worcestershire sauce
Salt
Pepper
1 cup grated Gruyère
  cheese, plus
  4 tablespoons
  for topping
1 cup heavy cream
Chopped flat-leaf parsley,
  for garnish

Slice croissants in half lengthwise. Toast until crisp; set aside.

Melt butter in a saucepan over medium-low heat. Whisk in flour and cook until lightly browned. Add beer and whisk until smooth. Bring to a boil, then reduce to a simmer. Season with mustard, Worcestershire sauce and a pinch of salt and pepper.

Remove from the heat and add 1 cup cheese, then the cream. Let sit for 1 minute, then stir until smooth over low heat. Do not boil.

Preheat the broiler.

In a baking dish, arrange croissant halves in a single layer. Pour the cheese sauce over the croissants and sprinkle with the remaining cheese. Broil until the cheese is melted and golden brown, about 3 minutes.

Garnish with parsley. Makes 4-6 servings.

**Tip:** Serve with Guinness or a porter-style beer.

# Santa Fe Southwest Tostada Salad
## Kellogg's

3 MorningStar Farms* Chipotle Black Bean Burgers, Garden Veggie Patties or Gardenburger The Original, cooked and thinly sliced

2 cups shredded romaine lettuce

1 avocado, peeled and sliced

1/3 cup corn kernels

1 Roma tomato, cut in 1/4-inch dice

1/4 cup shredded pepper jack cheese

1/4 cup shredded Cheddar cheese

3 corn tostada shells

1 tablespoon roasted tomato salsa

1 tablespoon bias-cut green onions

### CILANTRO LIME SOUR CREAM DRESSING

4 ounces sour cream

1 1/2 tablespoons freshly squeezed lime juice

2 tablespoons minced fresh cilantro

1/2 teaspoon *each* ground cumin, chili powder, cayenne pepper, salt and black pepper

In a bowl, combine veggie burgers, romaine, avocado, corn, tomato and cheeses. Toss gently to mix.

Layer a tostada with a third of the veggie burger mixture. Repeat with 2 remaining shells. Garnish with salsa and green onions.

To prepare the dressing, combine all ingredients and mix well. Serve with the salad to taste. Makes 3 servings.

*Brands may vary by region; substitute a similar product.*

Desserts

## Apple Harvest Bread
L&M Companies

2 cups flour

$^1/_2$ cup packed light
brown sugar

$^1/_2$ teaspoon salt

1 teaspoon baking soda

$^1/_2$ teaspoon baking powder

1 teaspoon ground nutmeg

1 teaspoon ground cinnamon

$^1/_2$ teaspoon ground cloves

1 $^1/_2$ cups sugar

$^3/_4$ cup butter, softened

2 eggs

1 pound pumpkin,
cooked and mashed
(or 15-ounce can)

1 teaspoon vanilla extract

3-4 First Fruits* Granny
Smith apples, peeled and
diced (or shredded)

$^1/_2$ cup raisins (optional)

$^1/_2$ cup walnuts (optional)

*TOPPING*

2 teaspoons white sugar

2 teaspoons light
brown sugar

1 teaspoon ground cinnamon

Preheat oven to 350°F. Grease 3 small loaf pans.

Combine flour, brown sugar, salt, baking soda, baking powder and spices in a bowl.

In another bowl, cream sugar and butter. Beat in eggs, pumpkin and vanilla. Add the flour mixture, stirring until just moistened. Stir in apples, raisins and walnuts. Spoon the batter into the prepared pans.

Bake the loaves for 45-50 minutes, or until a toothpick inserted in the center comes out clean.

Meanwhile, place all the topping ingredients in a small bowl and stir to blend. Set aside.

When the bread comes out of the oven, sprinkle with the topping.

Let sit for 15 minutes, then remove from the pans and let cool on a wire rack. Makes 12 servings.

**Tip:** This recipe will also make 24 muffins. Bake for 20-25 minutes.

*\* Brands may vary by region; substitute a similar product.*

## Lemon Bread
AMC Direct

1 $^1/_2$ cups all-purpose
flour

$^1/_2$ teaspoon salt

1 teaspoon baking powder

6 tablespoons butter,
softened

1 cup sugar

2 eggs

$^1/_2$ cup milk

Grated peel and juice
of 1 lemon

$^1/_4$ cup poppy seeds
(or chopped walnuts)

$^1/_2$ cup confectioners'
sugar

Preheat oven to 350°F. Grease and flour a 9-by-5-inch loaf pan.

Whisk together flour, salt and baking powder.

In a large bowl, cream butter, sugar and eggs together until light and fluffy. Add milk alternately with the flour mixture in 2 parts; mix well. Stir in grated lemon peel and poppy seeds.

Pour the batter into the prepared loaf pan. Bake for 60 minutes, or until a toothpick inserted in the center comes out clean. Let the bread cool in the pan for 5 minutes.

Mix together lemon juice and confectioners' sugar to make a glaze. Remove the bread from the pan. Pour the glaze over the warm bread (poking holes in the bread first will make it absorb more of the glaze). Makes 10 servings.

**AMC** DIRECT
PART OF THE AMC GROUP

# "All-American" Chocolate Cake with Strawberry Whipped Cream and Strawberries
## Best Brands Corp.

1 Kirkland Signature fresh bakery "All-American" chocolate cake

1 cup seedless strawberry jam (not jelly)

1 quart whipping cream

2 quarts fresh strawberries

Cut cake into serving pieces. It is easier to cut the cake accurately and without distorting the frosting by using dental floss. Using taut floss (about 24 inches with ends wrapped around fingers), cut the cake in half, then each half in half again. Repeat cuts in the opposite direction. This will yield 16 wedges.

In a mixing bowl, combine jam and cream. With an electric mixer, whip ingredients until very stiff. This can be made 4 hours in advance. (If you're not serving the entire cake, the ratio is 1 cup whipping cream to $1/4$ cup jam.)

Rinse strawberries and pat dry. Trim and cut vertically into halves or quarters.

To serve, place a piece of chocolate cake on each plate. Top with strawberry whipped cream and fresh strawberries. Makes 16 servings.

**Tip:** After making a downward cut through the cake, slide one end of floss out through the side instead of pulling upward so that the frosting is minimally disturbed (think "cut, slide").

Best Brands Corp.

## Chocolate Cake with Berries
### Kirkland Signature

**Kirkland Signature
filled chocolate cake
with buttercream icing**

**2 tablespoons raspberry
dessert sauce**

**11 fresh blueberries**

**Whipped cream**

Cut a 2-by-6-inch wedge from the cake.

Garnish with raspberry sauce, blueberries and a dollop of whipped cream. Makes 1 serving.

## Mocha Chocolate Cake with Butter Mocha Frosting
### Folgers

**Crisco Original No-Stick
Cooking Spray**

**1 18.25-ounce package
Pillsbury Devil's
Food Cake mix**

**1 1/4 cups strong brewed
Folgers Classic Roast
Coffee, cooled to room
temperature**

**1/2 cup Crisco Pure
Vegetable Oil**

**3 large eggs**

**BUTTER MOCHA
FROSTING**

**1 1-pound package
confectioners' sugar
(about 3 3/4 cups)**

**1/4 cup unsweetened
cocoa powder**

**1/4 teaspoon salt**

**1/4 cup butter, softened**

**1/4 cup strong brewed
Folgers Classic Roast
Coffee, cooled to room
temperature**

**1 teaspoon vanilla extract**

**3-4 teaspoons milk**

Preheat oven to 350°F. Coat two 9-inch round cake pans with cooking spray.

Combine cake mix, 1 1/4 cups brewed coffee, oil and eggs in a large bowl with an electric mixer until moistened. Beat for 2 minutes on medium speed. Pour into the prepared pans.

Bake for 29-33 minutes, or until a toothpick inserted in the center comes out clean. Let cool for 10 minutes. Remove from the pans and place on a rack to cool completely.

To prepare the frosting, combine confectioners' sugar, cocoa and salt in a large bowl. Beat in butter with an electric mixer on low speed. Gradually add coffee, vanilla and enough milk to make a smooth and spreadable frosting.

Spread the frosting between the cake layers and on the top and sides. Makes 12 servings.

# Fuyu Persimmon Bundt Cake
## Regatta Tropicals Ltd.

2 teaspoons baking soda

3 cups chopped firm Regatta Tropicals* Fuyu persimmons

1/2 cup butter, softened

1 2/3 cups sugar

2 eggs

2 teaspoons lemon juice

2 teaspoons vanilla extract

2 cups flour

1 teaspoon baking powder

1 teaspoon salt

1 teaspoon ground cloves

1 teaspoon ground cinnamon

1/2 teaspoon grated nutmeg

1 cup chopped walnuts

3/4 cup raisins

Preheat oven to 350°F. Grease and flour a 10-inch Bundt pan.

Blend baking soda into chopped persimmons. Set aside.

In a large bowl, beat butter with sugar. Add eggs, lemon juice and vanilla and beat until fluffy. Stir in persimmons.

Sift together flour, baking powder, salt and spices. Stir into the persimmon mixture just until blended. Add walnuts and raisins.

Pour into the prepared pan. Bake for 55-60 minutes, or until a toothpick inserted in the center tests clean.

Let cool in the pan for 15 minutes, then turn onto a rack. Makes 8 servings.

*Brands may vary by region; substitute a similar product.*

# Oatmeal Apple Sauce Cake with Cream Cheese Frosting
## Tree Top

1 1/2 cups all-purpose flour

1 1/2 cups oatmeal (uncooked)

1/2 teaspoon salt

1 1/2 teaspoons ground cinnamon

3/4 teaspoon ground cloves

1 teaspoon baking powder

3/4 cup butter, softened

1 1/2 cups sugar

4 eggs

1 cup Tree Top* apple sauce

3/4 cup milk

1 1/2 cups raisins

### CREAM CHEESE FROSTING

1/2 cup butter, softened

8 ounces cream cheese, softened

2 pounds confectioners' sugar

1 teaspoon vanilla extract

Preheat oven to 350°F. Grease and flour two 9-inch round cake pans.

In a bowl, mix together flour, oatmeal, salt, cinnamon, cloves and baking powder.

In a large bowl, cream butter with sugar. Add eggs, apple sauce and milk; beat until well blended. Add the dry ingredients and mix well. Stir in raisins. Pour into the prepared pans.

Bake for 30-35 minutes, or until a cake tester inserted in the center comes out clean. Let sit for 5 minutes, then remove from the pans and cool on wire racks.

To prepare the frosting, place butter and cream cheese in a mixing bowl and beat until smooth. Gradually add confectioners' sugar, beating until smooth. Add vanilla and blend well.

Frost the cake when it is completely cool. Store in the refrigerator. Makes 8-10 servings.

*Brands may vary by region; substitute a similar product.*

# Applesauce Cake
Chelan Fresh

1 1/2 cups golden raisins
3/4 cup shortening
2 cups sugar
3 eggs
2 1/2 cups sifted flour
3 tablespoons cocoa
2 teaspoons baking soda
3/4 teaspoon grated nutmeg
1/2 teaspoon salt

2 cups applesauce (recipe below)
1 cup chopped walnuts
Confectioners' sugar

### APPLESAUCE
3 pounds mixed Chelan Fresh* apples (Golden Delicious, Gala, Fuji or Jonagold), quartered and cored
1/2 cup water

To prepare the applesauce, combine apples and water in a large saucepan, bring to a boil and simmer for about 20 minutes, stirring occasionally. When the apples are tender and have the consistency of a chunky puree, pass through a food mill and return to the saucepan. Simmer for 5-10 minutes, or until slightly thickened. Let cool to room temperature.

Cover raisins with boiling water. Soak for 20 minutes; drain.

Preheat oven to 350°F. Grease and flour a 12-cup Bundt pan.

Cream shortening with sugar. Add eggs and beat well.

Sift together dry ingredients; add alternately with applesauce to the creamed mixture. Fold in drained raisins and walnuts.

Spoon batter into the prepared pan and bake for 55-60 minutes, or until a skewer comes out clean. Let cool in the pan for 10-15 minutes, then turn out on a wire rack or serving plate. When cool, dust lightly with confectioners' sugar or frost with your favorite white icing. Makes 10-12 servings.

*Brands may vary by region; substitute a similar product.*

## Cutie Pie
Sun Pacific

**4-5 Cuties California clementines (about 1 pound)**

**6 eggs**

**1 cup plus 2 tablespoons sugar**

**2 1/3 cups ground almonds**

**1 heaping teaspoon baking powder**

Put clementines in a pot with cold water to cover and bring to a boil. Cover, lower the heat and simmer for 2 hours. Drain and let cool. Cut each clementine in half. Then finely chop the skins, pith and fruit in a food processor (or by hand).

Preheat oven to 375°F.

Butter an 8-inch springform pan and line the bottom with parchment paper.

In a bowl, beat eggs. Add sugar, almonds and baking powder. Add the chopped clementines, mixing well by hand.

Pour the cake mixture into the prepared pan and bake for 1 hour, or until a skewer inserted in the center comes out dry. Cover the cake with foil after about 40 minutes to prevent overbrowning. Remove from the oven and let cool in the pan on a rack.

When the cake is cold, remove it from the pan and serve. Makes 4-6 servings.

**Tip:** Serve with a dollop of crème fraîche and orange slices for a special presentation.

## Zesty Citrus Cake
Bravante Produce

**2 1/2 cups unbleached flour**

**1/4 teaspoon salt**

**1 cup butter, softened**

**1 1/4 cups granulated sugar**

**1 tablespoon grated lemon peel**

**1 tablespoon grated orange peel**

**5 tablespoons fresh lemon juice**

**1 teaspoon pure vanilla extract**

**5 large eggs**

**1/2 cup sliced red seedless grapes**

**1/2 cup sliced green seedless grapes**

**1 cup sliced strawberries**

*TOPPING*

**2 cups heavy cream**

**1 cup plain yogurt**

**2 tablespoons confectioners' sugar**

**1 tablespoon grated lemon peel**

**1 tablespoon grated orange peel**

**4 tablespoons fresh lemon juice**

Preheat oven to 325°F. Lightly grease a 9-by-5-inch pan.

Sift flour and salt into a small dish 3 times.

In a mixing bowl, blend butter and sugar on low speed until fluffy. Add grated peel, lemon juice and vanilla to the butter and beat until well blended. On low speed, add eggs and flour mixture alternately, blending after each addition until smooth. Pour into the prepared pan.

Bake for 1 hour, or until a toothpick inserted in the center comes out clean.

To prepare the topping, combine cream, yogurt, sugar, grated peel and lemon juice in a mixing bowl. Beat on medium speed until soft peaks form.

Serve slices of cake with the topping, grapes and strawberries. Makes 6-8 servings.

*Recipe developed by Fresh Start Café, Reedley, California.*

# Orange Polenta Almond Cake
## Booth Ranches/Fisher Capespan

1 1/2 quarts water

2 oranges

1 cup flour

2 tablespoons cornstarch

1 cup polenta

1 1/2 cups toasted blanched almonds

1 1/2 cups butter, softened

2 cups sugar

6 eggs

1 teaspoon vanilla extract

*MASCARPONE GRAND MARNIER CREAM*

16 ounces mascarpone cheese

4 tablespoons Grand Marnier

4 tablespoons confectioners' sugar

1 teaspoon grated orange peel

Preheat oven to 325°F. Butter two 8-inch cake pans.

Bring water to a boil in a large saucepan. Add whole oranges and simmer for 30 minutes. Drain and let cool.

In a mixing bowl, combine flour, cornstarch and polenta.

Grind almonds in a food processor until finely ground. Stir into the dry ingredients and set aside.

Puree the oranges in a food processor.

Cream together butter and sugar. With the mixer running, add eggs one at a time. Add orange puree and vanilla. Add dry ingredients and mix until combined.

Pour into the prepared cake pans and bake for about 40 minutes, or until a toothpick inserted in the center comes out clean.

To prepare the Mascarpone Grand Marnier Cream, combine all ingredients and blend until smooth. Serve with the cake. Makes 12 servings.

# Mini Upside-Down Pineapple Cakes
## Dole

Nonstick vegetable cooking spray

2 20-ounce cans Dole pineapple chunks

1/3 cup butter or margarine, melted

2/3 cup packed light brown sugar

12-13 maraschino cherries, cut in half

1 18 1/4-ounce package yellow or pineapple-flavored cake mix

Preheat oven to 350°F. Coat 24-26 muffin cups with cooking spray.

Drain pineapple; reserve the juice.

Stir together melted butter and brown sugar. Evenly divide the mixture among the muffin cups. In each cup, arrange 3 drained pineapple chunks over the sugar mixture and place a cherry in the center, sliced side up.

Prepare cake mix according to package directions, replacing the water with an equal amount of reserved pineapple juice. Pour the batter evenly into the muffin cups, about 1/4 cup in each.

Bake for 20-25 minutes, or until a toothpick inserted in the center comes out clean.

Let cool for 5 minutes. Loosen the edges and invert onto cookie sheets. Makes 24-26 servings.

## Lynette's Favorite Cherry-Almond Cake
Morada Produce

1 cup blanched almonds

1 cup all-purpose flour

1 teaspoon baking powder

1/4 teaspoon kosher salt

1/2 cup (1 stick) butter, softened

3/4 cup sugar, plus 1 teaspoon for topping

3 eggs

1/4 teaspoon almond extract

1/2 teaspoon vanilla extract

1 pound fresh Morada Produce Bing cherries, pitted

Confectioners' sugar, for dusting

Preheat oven to 350°F. Butter a 9-inch springform pan and line the bottom with parchment. Dust the sides with flour.

Coarsely chop almonds. Reserve 1/4 cup almonds. Place the remaining almonds in a food processor. Add flour, baking powder and salt. Process until the almonds are finely ground.

In a mixing bowl, cream butter with 3/4 cup sugar. Then beat in eggs one at a time. Add almond and vanilla extracts.

Add the flour mixture gradually, mixing until smooth. Scrape into the prepared pan. Place cherries on top in a single layer.

Mix the reserved 1/4 cup almonds with 1 teaspoon sugar and sprinkle around the cake's edges. Bake for 45 minutes, or until a toothpick comes out clean.

Let cool in the pan for 10 minutes, then unmold and let cool completely on a wire rack. Transfer to a cake plate. Dust the top edges with confectioners' sugar. Makes 4-6 servings.

## Berry Crumb Cake
Kirkland Signature/Rader Farms

1/2 stick butter, softened

3/4 cup sugar

1 egg

1 teaspoon vanilla extract

2 cups plus 1 teaspoon flour, divided

1 teaspoon baking powder

1/2 cup milk

2 cups Kirkland Signature/ Rader Farms Nature's Three Berries (frozen raspberries, blueberries and blackberries)

### TOPPING

1/2 cup sugar

1/2 stick cold butter, cut into small pieces

1/2 cup flour

Preheat oven to 350°F. Grease a 9-by-9-inch square pan.

In a large mixing bowl, blend softened butter and sugar with a spoon. Add egg, vanilla, 2 cups flour, baking powder and milk. Mix until blended.

In a separate bowl, mix together frozen berries and 1 teaspoon flour. Add berries to the batter and mix gently. Pour into the prepared pan.

Combine the topping ingredients in a bowl and blend until crumbly. Spread evenly over the batter.

Bake on the middle oven rack for 50-55 minutes, or until a toothpick inserted in the center comes out clean. Makes 6 servings.

*Recipe developed by Lynn Alimo, pastry chef.*

# Peach Refrigerator Cake
## Kingsburg Orchards

1/2 **pound marshmallows, cut in quarters**
1/2 **cup orange juice**
1/2 **cup ginger ale**
1 **cup heavy cream, whipped**
8 **Kingsburg Orchards yellow peaches, divided**
1 **16- to 20-ounce package Vienna Fingers sandwich cookies, or ladyfingers**
1/2 **cup chopped crystallized ginger**

Place marshmallows and orange juice in the top of a double boiler. Set over hot water and stir until marshmallows are almost melted. Let cool slightly and stir in ginger ale. When slightly thickened, fold in 3/4 cup of the whipped cream. Refrigerate the remaining whipped cream.

Peel and slice 7 of the peaches.

Line the bottom of a springform pan with waxed paper. Arrange a layer of cookies in the pan. Top with a layer of half the sliced peaches, then a layer of half the marshmallow mixture. Repeat with another layer of cookies, peaches and marshmallow mixture. Top with a final layer of cookies. Chill in the refrigerator overnight.

Unmold the cake. Peel and slice the remaining peach. Top the cake with peach slices, whipped cream and crystallized ginger. Makes 8-10 servings.

# Roses Are Red Cupcake Bouquet
## Kirkland Signature/Jelly Belly

1 1/4 **cups vanilla frosting**
4 **standard vanilla cupcakes, unfrosted**
1/4 **cup Raspberry Kirkland Signature Jelly Belly beans**
1 **cup Very Cherry Kirkland Signature Jelly Belly beans**
1/2 **cup Kiwi Kirkland Signature Jelly Belly beans**
8 **mini vanilla cupcakes, unfrosted**

Spread frosting on the standard cupcakes. In the center of each cupcake place a raspberry jelly bean. Place 2 raspberry beans above and 2 cherry beans below the center bean.

Continue with another circle of beans, cherry above and raspberry below. Arrange a row of cherry beans, side by side, below the circle. Continue with another partial circle of beans, varying cherry and raspberry. Add kiwi beans for the base of the rose.

Spread frosting on the mini cupcakes.

Place the rose cupcakes on a serving platter and use the mini cupcakes for the stems. Use kiwi jelly beans to make rose stems and leaves.

Add a love note and serve. Makes 8 servings.

## Strawberry Cheesecake Parfait Goblets
BakeMark USA

1 Kirkland Signature
   Strawberry Cheesecake
1 15-ounce can real
   whipped cream

*STRAWBERRY GLAZE*

1 cup fresh strawberries,
   washed, hulled
   and diced
1 cup fresh strawberries,
   washed, hulled and
   mashed or blended in
   a food processor
1 cup sugar
1/4 cup cornstarch
1/4 cup orange-
   flavored liqueur

To prepare the glaze, combine diced and mashed strawberries, sugar and cornstarch in a saucepan. Cook over medium heat until thickened, stirring constantly.

Remove from the heat and stir in liqueur. Cover and chill.

Cut cheesecake into squares.

In the bottom of each goblet, place 2 tablespoons glaze. Place a cheesecake square on top of the glaze, add a layer of whipped cream, and top with 2 tablespoons glaze. Makes 8 servings.

Authentic Taste.. We Deliver.'

## Impossibly Easy Cheesecake
General Mills

3/4 cup milk
2 teaspoons
   vanilla extract
2 eggs
1 cup sugar
1/2 cup Original
   Bisquick mix
2 8-ounce packages
   cream cheese, cut
   into 1/2-inch
   cubes, softened

*TOPPING (optional)*

1 cup sour cream
2 tablespoons sugar
2 teaspoons
   vanilla extract
Fresh fruit

Preheat oven to 350°F. Grease a 9-inch glass pie plate with shortening or cooking spray.

Combine milk, vanilla, eggs, sugar and Bisquick in a blender. Cover and blend on high speed for 15 seconds. Add cream cheese, cover and blend for 2 minutes longer, or until smooth. Pour into the pie plate.

Bake for 40-45 minutes, or until a knife inserted in the center comes out clean. Cool at room temperature for 1 hour. Refrigerate until chilled, at least 2 hours.

To prepare the topping, combine sour cream, sugar and vanilla in a small bowl and stir until blended. Spread on top of the completely cooled cheesecake. Serve with fruit, if desired. Store, covered, in the refrigerator. Makes 8 servings.

General
Mills

## Lemon Lime Cheesecake
### Bee Sweet Citrus/Market Source

**CRUST**

**1 cup graham cracker crumbs**

**3 tablespoons sugar**

**1/2 teaspoon ground cinnamon**

**3 tablespoons butter, melted**

**1 large fresh lemon**

**2 fresh limes**

**3 8-ounce packages cream cheese, softened**

**1 1/8 cups plus 2 tablespoons sugar, divided**

**5 large eggs**

**1/4 teaspoon salt**

**1 1/2 cups sour cream**

**1/2 teaspoon vanilla extract**

To prepare the crust, grease a 9-inch springform pan. Mix graham cracker crumbs, sugar, cinnamon and butter. Press onto the bottom and about 2 inches up the sides of the pan.

Preheat oven to 350°F.

Grate 1 teaspoon of lemon peel. Grate 1 teaspoon of lime peel. Place in a bowl with cream cheese and beat at medium speed until creamy. Add 1 1/8 cups sugar, eggs and salt. Beat at medium speed for 10 minutes. Pour batter into the pan and bake for 45 minutes, or until set. Let cool in the pan for 20 minutes.

Beat sour cream with 2 tablespoons sugar and vanilla for 1 minute, or until sugar is dissolved. Pour over the cheesecake and spread evenly over the top. Bake for an additional 15 minutes.

Let cool in the pan for 30 minutes, then refrigerate until chilled.

Remove cake from the pan and top with fruit and whipped cream, if desired. Makes 10 servings.

## Pistachio Tart
### Kirkland Signature/Paramount Farms

**1 refrigerated ready-made piecrust**

**3 cups Kirkland Signature pistachio kernels, divided**

**1 cup sliced almonds**

**5 tablespoons butter**

**3/4 cup light or dark brown sugar**

**1/3 cup dark corn syrup**

**2 tablespoons half-and-half**

**1/2 teaspoon vanilla extract**

**1/4 cup chocolate chips, melted**

Preheat oven according to piecrust package directions.

Line a 9-inch tart shell with piecrust. Bake as instructed for a single-crust pie until golden.

Pour 2 cups pistachio kernels and the sliced almonds over the crust in a single layer. Chop the remaining cup of pistachios; set aside.

Preheat oven to 350°F.

In a heavy saucepan over medium heat, melt butter with brown sugar, corn syrup, half-and-half and vanilla. Bring to a boil, stirring constantly. Pour the hot mixture over the pistachios and almonds.

Bake for 10 minutes, or until bubbly and golden. Let cool on a rack.

When cool, drizzle with melted chocolate and garnish with chopped pistachios. Makes 12 servings.

# Triple Berry Cheesecake Tart
Kraft

1 1/4 cups finely crushed Nilla
   Wafers* (about 45 wafers)

1/4 cup (1/2 stick) butter, melted

1 8-ounce package Philadelphia
   cream cheese, softened

1/4 cup sugar

1 cup thawed Cool Whip
   whipped topping

2 cups mixed fresh berries
   (raspberries, sliced strawberries
   and blueberries)

1 package (4-serving size) Jell-O
   lemon-flavor gelatin

3/4 cup boiling water

1 cup ice cubes

Mix wafer crumbs and butter in a small bowl until well blended. Press onto the bottom and up the sides of a 9-inch tart pan. Place in the freezer while preparing the filling.

Beat cream cheese and sugar in a large bowl with an electric mixer on medium speed until well blended. Gently stir in whipped topping. Spoon into the crust.

Arrange berries over the cream cheese filling. Cover and refrigerate.

Place dry gelatin mix in a medium bowl, add boiling water and stir for 2 minutes, until completely dissolved. Add ice cubes and stir until completely melted. Refrigerate for about 15 minutes, or until slightly thickened (consistency of unbeaten egg whites). Spoon gelatin over the berries in the pan. Refrigerate for 3 hours. Makes 10 servings.

* Brands may vary by region; substitute a similar product.

## Dulce de Leche Layered Brownies with Crème Fraîche and Berry Caviar
### Sugar Bowl Bakery

**16 Sugar Bowl Bakery\* brownie bites**

**1 cup dulce de leche**

**1 cup crème fraîche**

**1 pint fresh raspberries, crushed lightly to resemble caviar**

Place each brownie bite upside down on a plate. Use a thin knife to slice in half horizontally.

Carefully lift off the top layer. Spread with about 1 tablespoon dulce de leche. Replace the top layer.

Top each brownie bite with a dollop of crème fraîche and garnish with crushed raspberries. Makes 16 servings.

*\* Brands may vary by region; substitute a similar product.*

## Summertime Shortcake
### Pride Packing Co./Blossom Hill Packing Co.

**1 cup firmly packed light brown sugar**

**1/2 cup water**

**2 tablespoons almond- or orange-flavored liqueur**

**4 large fresh, ripe Mary's Pride\* peaches**

**4 fresh, ripe Mary's Pride\* nectarines**

**4 fresh, ripe Blossom Hill\* apricots**

**1 tablespoon lemon juice**

**2 cups cold heavy whipping cream**

**1/2 cup orange blossom or clover honey**

**8 shortcake biscuits, purchased or homemade**

Combine sugar and water in a saucepan and bring to a boil over medium-high heat. Boil for 1 minute, then remove from heat. Once cool, add liqueur. Cover tightly and refrigerate.

Remove skins from fruit by peeling or blanching. Slice fruit. To prevent browning, drop cut fruit into a bowl containing 1 quart ice-cold water and 1 tablespoon lemon juice for 3 minutes. Drain fruit and place in a clean bowl. Pour the chilled syrup over the fruit, cover tightly and marinate for 30 minutes.

Prechill a large mixing bowl and beaters. Whip cream on medium speed until it begins to thicken. With the mixer running, pour honey in a thin stream into the cream. Beat until soft peaks form. Cover and refrigerate until ready to serve.

Slice shortcakes in half horizontally, layer with fruit and top with whipped cream. Makes 8 servings.

*\* Brands may vary by region; substitute a similar product.*

# Blueberry Shortcakes with Blueberry Sauce
## Townsend Farms

### BLUEBERRY SAUCE
1/3 cup water

2/3 cup sugar

8 teaspoons cornstarch

1 teaspoon vanilla extract

Pinch of salt

Pinch of ground cinnamon

5 cups Townsend Farms* frozen blueberries, slightly thawed (or fresh)

### BISCUITS
4 cups flour

4 tablespoons sugar

2 tablespoons baking powder

1-2 teaspoons salt

2/3 cup butter, softened

1 1/2 cups milk or buttermilk

1 cup Townsend Farms* frozen or fresh blueberries

Whipped cream, for serving

For the sauce, combine 1/3 cup water (1 cup with fresh berries), sugar, cornstarch, vanilla, salt and cinnamon in a saucepan. Bring to a boil over medium-high heat, stirring constantly; boil for 1 minute. Stir in berries and cook until glazed, 30 seconds. Transfer to a bowl and let cool. Cover and refrigerate for 1 hour or overnight.

Preheat oven to 450°F.

For the biscuits, combine flour, sugar, baking powder and salt in a bowl. Cut butter into the flour mixture until it resembles small peas. Stir in milk, then berries.

On a lightly floured surface, pat or roll dough to 1/2-inch thickness. Cut out 8 biscuits with a 2 1/2-inch round biscuit cutter. Place on an ungreased cookie sheet 1 inch apart. Bake until golden, 12-15 minutes. Let cool on a wire rack.

Pour the sauce over sliced biscuits and top with whipped cream. Makes 8 servings.

*Brands may vary by region; substitute a similar product.*

# Triple Berry Shortcake
## Dawn Food Products

**2 tablespoons blueberries**
**2 tablespoons raspberries**
**1 Kirkland Signature blueberry muffin**
**Sweetened whipped cream**
**2 fresh strawberries, sliced**
**Confectioners' sugar**

In a small bowl, combine blueberries and raspberries. Stir gently to mix.

Slice muffin horizontally into 3 sections.

Pipe whipped cream onto the bottom muffin layer. Add half of the berry mixture. Repeat with another layer.

Add the muffin top, a dollop of whipped cream and strawberries. Dust with confectioners' sugar. Makes 2 servings.

# Nonni's Cherry Crisp
## Delta Packing

**2 cups pitted Delta Fresh\* cherries**
**1/2-1 cup sugar**
**Ground cinnamon to taste**
**6 tablespoons butter**

**TOPPING**
**2 eggs, well beaten**
**3/4 cup sugar**
**1 cup flour**
**1/2 cup shortening**
**2 tablespoons butter, softened**

Preheat oven to 300°F.

Combine cherries and sugar to taste. Spread evenly in an 8-inch square baking dish. Sprinkle with cinnamon and dot with butter.

To prepare the topping, combine and mix all ingredients. Pour over the cherries.

Bake for 1 hour, or until the top is golden brown.

Serve warm. Makes 8-10 servings.

*\* Brands may vary by region; substitute a similar product.*

# Peach Blueberry Crisp with Pumpkin Flax Granola Topping
## Nature's Path Organic Foods

- 1 pound (3 cups) fresh or frozen sliced peeled peaches
- 12 ounces (2 1/2 cups) fresh or frozen blueberries
- 1 cup Millet Rice Flakes
- 1 1/2 cups Nature's Path Pumpkin Flax Plus Granola* Organic
- 1/2 cup chopped walnuts
- 2 tablespoons cold butter, cut into bits
- 2 tablespoons brown sugar
- Coconut sorbet, for serving (optional)

Position rack in the middle of the oven and preheat to 375°F.

Place peaches and blueberries in a 9-inch square baking pan. Crush Millet Rice Flakes with your fingers and toss with the fruit.

Cover the pan tightly with foil. Bake until the fruit is soft, 20-30 minutes.

Remove the foil. Distribute granola, walnuts, butter and brown sugar evenly over the top. Bake, uncovered, until the top is browned and the fruit is bubbly, about 10 minutes.

Serve warm, with a scoop of coconut sorbet on top, if desired. Makes 6 servings.

*Brands may vary by region; substitute a similar product*

# Double Berry Cobbler
## Alpine Fresh

- 2 1/2 cups Alpine Fresh* blackberries, divided
- 2 1/2 cups Alpine Fresh* blueberries, divided
- 1/3 cup flour
- 1 1/2 cups sugar, divided
- 3 cups biscuit mix
- 1/4 teaspoon ground nutmeg
- 1/8 teaspoon ground cardamom
- 1/4 cup melted butter or margarine
- 3/4 cup milk (or for richer dessert, use 1 cup cream)
- 2 large eggs, slightly beaten
- Whipped cream or vanilla ice cream, for serving
- 1/2 cup chopped pecans or hazelnuts (optional)

Preheat oven to 350°F.

Rinse and drain 2 cups of each of the berries and place in a large bowl. Combine flour and 1 cup sugar. Add to the berries and toss to coat.

In a separate bowl, combine biscuit mix, remaining 1/2 cup sugar and spices. Add melted butter, milk and beaten eggs. Stir until evenly moistened.

Place the coated berries in a greased 9-by-13-inch baking dish. Spread the batter evenly over the top.

Bake for 45-55 minutes, or until the crust is lightly browned.

To serve, top with whipped cream or ice cream, the chopped nuts and the reserved fresh berries. Makes 10-12 servings.

*Recipe developed by Christine W. Jackson, food stylist.*
*Brands may vary by region; substitute a similar product.*

# Black Velvet Apricot Cobbler
## Kingsburg Orchards

**1 stick (¹/₂ cup) butter**

**3-4 cups quartered Kingsburg Orchards Black Velvet apricots and their juices**

**1 cup sugar, plus more for sprinkling over apricots**

**2 teaspoons baking powder**

**1 cup unbleached all-purpose flour**

**1 cup milk**

**Vanilla ice cream, for serving (optional)**

Put the stick of butter in a deep casserole dish at least 9 by 9 inches in diameter and place in a cold oven. Heat the oven to 350°F.

Place apricots and their juices in a bowl and sprinkle lightly with sugar; set aside.

In another bowl, whisk together baking powder, flour and 1 cup sugar. Add milk and mix well. The mixture will be thin.

When the butter has melted and the oven is at 350°F, pour the batter all at once into the casserole, then pour the fruit and its juices into the center of the batter.

Bake for 50-60 minutes, or until the batter is cooked and the top is golden brown.

Serve hot, warm or at room temperature. Great with ice cream.

Makes 8 servings.

# Mini Cherry Empanadas
## M&R Company

1 egg
2 tablespoons milk
2 ready-made piecrusts
Sugar

### FILLING

1 1/2 cups M&R* cherries, pitted and halved (1/2 pound)
1/3 cup sugar, plus more to sprinkle on dough
Dash of cinnamon
1/3 cup water, plus 1/4 cup water
2 tablespoons cornstarch
1/4 teaspoon almond extract (optional)

Preheat oven to 350°F.

Whisk egg with milk until frothy to make an egg wash; set aside.

To prepare the filling, mix cherries, sugar and cinnamon with 1/3 cup water in a small saucepan. Stir and bring to a boil. Mix cornstarch with 1/4 cup cold water in a small bowl. Stir into the hot cherry mixture. Cook until it thickens. Stir in almond extract. Let cool.

Unroll/unfold the piecrusts and cut out 4-inch-diameter rounds. Roll out the scraps and cut out additional circles. Brush the outside edges of the circles with the egg wash.

Place a spoonful of filling in the center of each round. Fold the dough in half over the filling. Crimp the edges with a fork to seal. Cut small slits in the top. Brush with egg wash. Sprinkle with sugar.

Place the empanadas on a greased or parchment-lined baking sheet and bake for 20-35 minutes, or until lightly browned. Makes 8-12 empanadas.

**Tip:** You can add 1/2 cup chopped hazelnuts or chocolate chips to the cooled cherry filling.

*Recipe developed by Christine W. Jackson, food stylist.*
*\* Brands may vary by region; substitute a similar product.*

# Blueberry and White Chocolate Mascarpone Strata
## Kirkland Signature/Puratos

4 Kirkland Signature croissants
Butter, softened
7 large eggs
1 cup heavy whipping cream
1/2 cup whole milk
3/4 cup sugar, divided
1 teaspoon vanilla extract
Pinch of ground cinnamon
Pinch of ground cardamom
Pinch of grated nutmeg
1 teaspoon salt
12 ounces fresh or frozen wild Maine blueberries
8 ounces white chocolate chips or chunks
4 ounces mascarpone cheese
Ice cream or gelato, for serving

Preheat oven to 325°F.

Cut croissants into cubes. Spread in an even layer on a sheet pan. Bake for about 10 minutes, or until lightly toasted and crisp.

Generously butter a 13-by-9-by-2-inch pan. Spread the croissant cubes in the pan.

In a bowl, combine eggs, cream, milk, 1/4 cup sugar, vanilla, cinnamon, cardamom, nutmeg and salt. Whisk until smooth.

Pour the egg mixture over the croissant cubes in the pan. Press lightly on the croissants to cover thoroughly with the custard.

Sprinkle blueberries and chocolate evenly over the strata. Distribute mascarpone in small pinches. Sprinkle the remaining 1/2 cup sugar over all.

Let soak for at least 30 minutes in the refrigerator before baking.

Preheat oven to 350°F.

Bake for about 1 hour, or until the center is set but still jiggles slightly when moved. Serve warm with ice cream or gelato. Makes 6-8 servings.

# Macarooned Fruit
## Fowler Packing

1 bunch table grapes

4 plums

4 nectarines

4 peaches

1 tablespoon lemon juice

1 cup water

12-18  6-inch bamboo
  skewers

*MACAROON FRUIT DIP*

6 coconut macaroon cookies

8 ounces mascarpone
  (Italian soft
  cream cheese)

8 ounces sour cream

3-4 tablespoons
  brown sugar

2 teaspoons vanilla extract

Rinse and separate grapes. Wash, pit and cut plums and nectarines into chunks. Scald and peel peaches. Remove pits and cut into chunks. Combine lemon juice with water. Dip the peaches and nectarines in the lemon water to prevent browning.

Thread the fruit onto the skewers.

To prepare the fruit dip, place cookies in a food processor and pulse until crumbled (or crumble in a zip-top bag with a rolling pin). Add the other ingredients in order and mix until well blended.

Serve the fruit and dip together. Makes 6-8 servings.

*Recipe developed by Christine W. Jackson, food stylist.*

FOWLER
PACKING
COMPANY

# Cantaloupe Fruit Bowls
## Nature's Partner

1/2 cup Nature's Partner*
  red or green seedless
  grapes, washed and
  sliced into halves

1/2 cup Nature's Partner*
  blueberries, washed

1/2 cup Nature's Partner*
  kiwifruit, peeled and
  chopped

1 Nature's Partner* peach,
  washed and chopped

1 Nature's Partner* apple,
  washed and chopped

1 Nature's Partner*
  cantaloupe, sliced
  in half, with seeds
  scooped out

Mint, for garnish (optional)

*LOW-FAT CUSTARD
  SAUCE*

2 cups fat-free milk

1/4 cup sugar substitute
  (such as Splenda)

1 tablespoon cornstarch

1 large egg

1 teaspoon vanilla extract

To prepare the custard sauce, heat milk in a double boiler over medium-low heat until it is simmering. In the meantime, whisk sugar and cornstarch together in a bowl. Add egg and whisk until there are no lumps. Stir in vanilla. Gradually stir the hot milk into the egg mixture, making sure there are no lumps.

Return the mixture to the double boiler. Cook over medium heat, stirring constantly, until thickened. Let cool to room temperature.

In a bowl, combine grapes, blueberries, kiwifruit, peach and apple; toss gently to blend. Ladle into the cantaloupe "bowls."

Garnish the melon bowls as desired with custard sauce and mint. Makes 2 servings.

*\* Brands may vary by region; substitute a similar product.*

NATURE'S ❦ PARTNER

## Vanilla Bean Poached Pears
### Kirkland Signature/Rodelle Vanilla

6 cups water

2 cups sugar

2-3 strips lemon peel

1 Kirkland Signature Rodelle vanilla bean, split lengthwise

1 whole star anise

4 Bartlett or Anjou pears, ripe but firm

1 pint vanilla ice cream

In a deep straight-sided, nonreactive saucepan, combine water, sugar, lemon peel, vanilla bean pod and seeds, and star anise. Bring to a boil over high heat, stirring until the sugar is completely dissolved.

Meanwhile, peel pears, leaving the stem intact. Cut just enough off the bottom of each pear to make it flat, creating a stable base.

Reduce the heat under the poaching liquid to a simmer and add the pears. It is okay to lay them on their sides. Cook the pears, gently turning occasionally, until just tender when pierced with a knife, about 6-9 minutes.

Let pears cool completely in the poaching liquid. Remove from the pan and stand each pear upright in a dessert glass.

Return the poaching liquid to the stovetop, bring to a boil and reduce until it coats the back of a spoon. Strain the sauce and set aside.

Add a scoop of ice cream to each pear and drizzle the sauce over the top. Serve immediately. Makes 4 servings.

## Fig Rolls with Honeydew Glaze
### Stellar Distributing/Mas Melons & Grapes

2/3 cup chopped fresh figs

1/2 cup chopped pecans

2 tablespoons brown sugar

2 tablespoons unsalted butter, softened

12 sheets frozen phyllo dough, thawed

4 tablespoons unsalted butter, melted

1 cup water

1/4 cup sugar

1 cup finely chopped honeydew melon

Preheat oven to 350°F.

In a bowl, combine figs, pecans, brown sugar and softened butter.

Cut phyllo sheets into thirds. For each roll, take one third of each phyllo sheet, brush with melted butter, place another on top, brush with butter, and place another on top and brush with butter. Place about 1 tablespoon of filling on one side, fold in the edges and roll. Brush with melted butter.

Place on a greased baking sheet and bake for about 20 minutes, or until golden brown.

In a saucepan, combine water, sugar and honeydew. Bring to a boil, then simmer until the melon has softened and the mixture has thickened. Lightly brush the warm glaze on the rolls and spoon on top. Makes 4 servings.

# Quick Apple Dumplings
Yakima Fresh

2 medium Yakima Fresh* Granny
   Smith apples
1 (8 count) package refrigerated
   crescent roll dough
1/2-1 teaspoon ground cinnamon
1/2 cup butter

1 cup sugar
1 cup orange juice
1 teaspoon vanilla extract
1/2 cup very finely chopped pecans
Ice cream or whipped cream,
   for serving

Preheat oven to 350°F. Butter an 8-inch square baking dish.

Peel and core apples. Cut each apple into quarters.

Unroll and separate crescent roll dough.

Wrap each apple section in a crescent roll. Place in the pan and sprinkle with cinnamon.

Combine butter, sugar and orange juice in a medium saucepan. Bring to a boil. Remove from the heat and stir in vanilla. Pour over the dumplings. Sprinkle pecans over the top.

Bake for 30 minutes, or until the crust is golden and beginning to bubble and the apples are just tender when pierced with a fork.

To serve, spoon some of the syrup from the baking dish over the dumplings. Serve with ice cream or whipped cream. Makes 8 servings.

*Brands may vary by region; substitute a similar product.*

## Tropical Mandarin Trifle
Festival

1 cup sweetened coconut

1 pint whipping cream

4 11-ounce cans Festival* mandarin oranges in light syrup, drained, syrup reserved

1 teaspoon vanilla extract

1/2 teaspoon ground cinnamon

1/4 cup plus 2 tablespoons granulated sugar

2 20-ounce cans Festival* golden pineapple chunks in syrup, drained, syrup reserved

1 tablespoon light rum (optional)

1 loaf Kirkland Signature pound cake, cut into 1/2-inch cubes

1/3 cup coarsely chopped macadamia nuts

1/3 cup coarsely chopped Kirkland Signature salted Marcona almonds

Preheat oven to 400°F. Spread coconut in a pan and toast for about 3-5 minutes; let cool.

Place cream, 1 2/3 cups mandarin syrup, vanilla, cinnamon and sugar in a mixing bowl. Beat until stiff peaks form.

In a separate bowl, stir together 1/2 cup mandarin syrup, 1/2 cup pineapple syrup and rum.

Layer a third of the cake cubes in a 3-quart dish and moisten with a third of the fruit syrup mixture. Lay a third of the fruit over the cake. Spread with a third of the whipped cream. Sprinkle with a third of the nuts and a third of the coconut. Repeat with 2 more layers.

Chill for at least 1 hour. Makes 12 servings.

*Recipe developed by Chef Tyler Hefford-Anderson.*
*\* Brands may vary by region; substitute a similar product.*

## Strawberries and Cream Trifle
Eagle Brand/Smucker's

1 14-ounce can Eagle Brand* sweetened condensed milk

1 1/2 cups cold water

1 4-serving size package instant vanilla-flavor pudding and pie filling mix

1 8-ounce container frozen whipped topping, thawed

4 cups sliced fresh strawberries, plus more for garnish

1 cup Smucker's* Special Recipe Strawberry Preserves

1 large (9-inch) prepared angel food cake, cut into 3/4-inch cubes (about 8 cups)

2 tablespoons sliced almonds, for garnish (optional)

Whisk sweetened condensed milk and water in a large bowl. Add pudding mix and whisk for 2 minutes, until well blended. Refrigerate for 5 minutes. Fold in whipped topping.

Stir together sliced strawberries and strawberry preserves.

Spoon 2 cups of the pudding mixture into the bottom of a 4-quart clear glass trifle bowl or round glass serving bowl. Top with half the cake cubes, half the strawberries and half the remaining pudding mix. Repeat the layers, ending with pudding.

Refrigerate for 3-4 hours, or until set. Garnish with sliced strawberries and almonds just before serving. Makes 10-12 servings.

*\* Brands may vary by region; substitute a similar product.*

# Nostalgic Apple Pie
## Splenda

**Pastry dough for 2-crust 9-inch pie**

**7 cups cored, peeled, thinly sliced baking apples**

**1 cup Splenda No Calorie Sweetener, granulated**

**3 tablespoons cornstarch**

**3/4 teaspoon ground cinnamon**

**1/4 teaspoon grated nutmeg**

**1/8 teaspoon salt**

Preheat oven to 425°F.

Place 1 crust in a 9-inch pie pan.

Place sliced apples in a large mixing bowl and set aside.

Combine Splenda, cornstarch, cinnamon, nutmeg and salt in a small bowl. Sprinkle over the apples and toss. Spoon the apple mixture into the piecrust.

Place the second crust over the filling. Seal the edges, trim and flute. Cut small openings in the top crust.

Bake until the top crust is light brown, about 15 minutes. Reduce heat to 375°F and finish baking for 30-40 minutes. Serve warm or chilled. Makes 8 servings.

**Nutritional information:** Each serving has 300 calories, 3 g protein, 40 g carbohydrates, 15 g fat, 4 g saturated fat, 0 mg cholesterol, 5 g fiber, 270 mg sodium, 14 g sugar.

# Margaret's Special Grape Pie
## Stevco

**Pastry dough for 2-crust 9-inch pie**

**5 cups halved Stevco* black seedless grapes**

**1/2 cup sugar**

**4 tablespoons cornstarch**

**1/2 teaspoon ground cinnamon**

**1/2 teaspoon salt**

**1 tablespoon fresh lemon juice**

**2 tablespoons butter**

Preheat oven to 425°F.

Roll out half of pastry dough and line a 9-inch pie pan.

In a medium bowl, stir together grapes, sugar, cornstarch, cinnamon and salt. Pour into the pie shell. Sprinkle with lemon juice and dot with butter.

Roll out the remaining pastry and place over the filling. Press to seal and flute the edges. Cut vents in the top of the pie.

Bake for 10 minutes, then reduce the heat to 350°F and cook for 30-35 minutes longer, or until the filling in the center is bubbly. Makes 8 servings.

*\* Brands may vary by region; substitute a similar product.*

## Rustic Apple and Dried Cherry Galette
Columbia Marketing International

**PASTRY DOUGH**

1 1/2 cups flour

1/2 teaspoon salt

1/2 cup unsalted butter, chilled and cut into 1/2-inch pieces

4 tablespoons ice water

1 1/2 pounds CMI* Granny Smith apples

1 tablespoon unsalted butter

4 tablespoons sugar, divided

1/3 cup dried cherries

1/4 teaspoon ground cinnamon

To prepare the pastry dough, mix flour and salt in a food processor. Add butter and pulse until crumbly. Add 2 tablespoons ice water and process until moist clumps form, adding more ice water as needed. Form the dough into a ball and pat into a disk shape. Wrap in plastic wrap and refrigerate.

Peel and core apples and cut each into 8 pieces.

Melt butter in a skillet over medium heat. Add apples and sprinkle with 3 tablespoons sugar. Sauté, stirring, for 5-10 minutes, or until the apples begin to soften. Add cherries and cinnamon and stir to blend. Remove from the heat and let cool.

Preheat oven to 350°F.

On a floured surface, roll out the pastry dough into a 12-inch circle and place on a baking sheet. Arrange the filling on top of the dough, leaving about an inch of dough exposed at the edges. Pinch up the dough edges to form a shallow rim. Sprinkle the filling and dough with the remaining 1 tablespoon of sugar.

Bake for 15 minutes. Increase the temperature to 375°F and bake for an additional 30 minutes, or until the crust is golden. Remove from the oven and let cool for about 15 minutes. Makes 6 servings.

**Tip:** Serve with warm caramel sauce and fresh whipped cream, if desired.

*Recipe courtesy of Chef David Toal of Ravenous Catering, Wenatchee, Washington.*
*\* Brands may vary by region; substitute a similar product.*

## Spiced Mango Galette
Alpine Fresh

1 refrigerated piecrust, softened

3 Alpine Fresh* whole mangoes, peeled and cut into small cubes, or 2 cups Alpine Fresh* fresh cut mangoes, cut into small cubes

1 tablespoon cornstarch

1 tablespoon butter

2 tablespoons brown sugar

2 teaspoons light rum

1 teaspoon vanilla extract

1/4 teaspoon ground cinnamon

1/4 teaspoon grated nutmeg

1/4 cup Alpine Fresh* blueberries

Preheat oven to 350°F.

Unroll softened piecrust onto a greased rimmed baking sheet. Set aside.

Combine mango and cornstarch in a medium bowl. Toss to coat evenly.

Melt butter in a small saucepan over low heat. Add brown sugar, rum, vanilla, cinnamon and nutmeg. Cook and stir for 1 minute. Pour over the mango and mix well.

Pour the filling onto the center of the piecrust, leaving a 2-inch border. Sprinkle blueberries over the filling. Fold the piecrust edges over the fruit. Bake for 30-35 minutes, or until lightly browned. Let cool for 15 minutes before cutting.

Serve warm. Makes 6 servings.

*Recipe developed by Kati Neville.*
*\* Brands may vary by region; substitute a similar product.*

# Chocolate Almond Brownie Pie
## Kirkland Signature/Kerry

3 eggs
1 cup light corn syrup
1 cup packed brown sugar
1/2 cup butter, melted
3 cups Kirkland Signature chocolate-covered almonds, finely ground

1 9-inch deep-dish unbaked piecrust (store bought or homemade)
Whipped cream, for serving (optional)
1 cup Kirkland Signature chocolate-covered almonds, chopped into thirds, for garnish (optional)

Preheat oven to 350°F.

In a bowl, combine eggs, corn syrup, brown sugar and melted butter. Add ground chocolate-covered almonds and mix by hand until blended.

Bake piecrust for about 5 minutes. Pour the filling into the hot crust. Bake for about 60-70 minutes, or until the filling quivers just a little in the center when the pan is gently shaken. Cover the edges with foil if they start to get too brown.

Let the pie cool completely. Serve with whipped cream and chopped almonds. Makes 8 servings.

# Caramel Chocolate Chunk Brioche Bread Pudding

Barry Callebaut

1 pound brioche bread, cut into 1-inch cubes

2 ounces butter, melted

1 ¹/₃ cups heavy whipping cream

4 eggs

2 egg yolks

¹/₄ cup sugar

2 teaspoons dark rum

1 teaspoon vanilla extract

3 ¹/₂ ounces Callebaut Dark Chocolate Chunks

3 ¹/₂ ounces prepared caramel sauce

Preheat oven to 350°F. Butter a 9-by-5-inch loaf pan.

In a mixing bowl, combine brioche and melted butter. Spread cubes on a baking sheet and place in the oven until toasted, about 6-10 minutes. Remove from the oven and let cool.

In a mixing bowl, combine cream, eggs, egg yolks, sugar, rum and vanilla. Mix until well blended. Stir in the bread cubes and let soak for 5 minutes. Fold in the chocolate chunks.

Layer the bread and caramel sauce in the prepared pan. Bake until the custard is set, about 20-30 minutes. Makes 6-8 servings.

# Rugala Crème Brûlée

Countryside Baking

8 pieces Kirkland Signature Rugala

4 egg yolks

1 whole egg

¹/₄ cup sugar

¹/₂ teaspoon ground cinnamon

2 ¹/₂ cups heavy cream, scalded

2 tablespoons light brown sugar

Preheat oven to 325°F.

Cut each rugala into 6 pieces. Divide the pieces evenly among 6 ramekins.

In a bowl, mix egg yolks, whole egg, sugar and cinnamon.

Gradually pour the hot cream into the egg mixture, stirring to combine. Pour into the ramekins.

Set the ramekins in a baking pan. Pour in hot water to come halfway up the sides of the ramekins. Bake for 45 minutes, or until a knife inserted near the center comes out clean. Remove from the water bath and let cool. Chill.

Preheat the broiler.

Sprinkle the brown sugar evenly over the chilled ramekins. Broil approximately 6 inches from the heat until the topping is bubbly and browned. Makes 6 servings.

# Grape Juice Pudding
Kirkland Signature/Newman's Own

4 tablespoons sugar

2 tablespoons cornstarch

3 tablespoons water

2 cups Kirkland Signature/ Newman's Own 100% Grape Juice

Whipped cream, for serving

Combine sugar, cornstarch and water in a bowl and stir until a smooth paste forms.

Heat grape juice in a saucepan over low heat until it simmers. Stirring constantly, slowly add the cornstarch paste. When the mixture is clear and thickened, remove from the heat.

Pour into individual bowls and chill.

Serve with whipped cream. Makes 4-6 servings.

**Tip:** Cubed fresh fruit can be stirred into the pudding after it is removed from the heat, or served on top of the chilled pudding.

# Crepes with Mascarpone Cream and Roasted Blueberries/Cherries
Grower Direct/Western Sweet Cherry Group

### CREPES

1 cup all-purpose flour

1 egg

1 1/2 cups whole milk

1/4 cup sugar

Pinch of salt

Butter

### MASCARPONE CREAM

8 ounces heavy whipping cream

8 ounces mascarpone cheese

5 tablespoons sugar

1 teaspoon vanilla extract

### TOPPING

2 cups Grower Direct Marketing* blueberries

2 cups Grower Direct Marketing* or Western Sweet Cherry Group* cherries, halved and pitted

3/4 cup sugar

To prepare the crepes, combine flour, egg, milk, sugar and salt in a bowl; mix until well blended. Melt a dab of butter in a 7-inch crepe pan over medium heat. Add 1/4 cup batter and cook for about 2 minutes on each side. Remove from the pan and stack between sheets of waxed paper. Let the crepes cool before filling. Otherwise the filling will melt too quickly.

To prepare the mascarpone cream, combine all ingredients and beat until well blended.

To prepare the topping, preheat oven to 400°F. Combine blueberries, cherries and sugar in a bowl and mix gently to blend. Spread on a rimmed sheet pan and roast for 10 minutes.

To assemble, lay the crepes flat. Put 1/4 cup of mascarpone cream on each one and fold in half. Top with the hot roasted fruit. Makes 8 servings.

* Brands may vary by region; substitute a similar product.

# Sautéed Pineapple and Bananas with Honey
## Del Monte Fresh Produce

Vanilla low-fat frozen yogurt
1/4 cup butter (1/2 stick)
1/4 cup honey
1 teaspoon vanilla extract
1 teaspoon ground cinnamon

4 cups Del Monte Gold Extra Sweet
  fresh-cut pineapple chunks
2 Del Monte bananas, cut in half
  lengthwise and then cut
  into quarters

Spoon frozen yogurt into individual serving bowls and keep in the freezer until the fruit mixture is ready.

Melt butter in a large saucepan over medium heat. Mix in honey, vanilla and cinnamon. Add pineapple and simmer for 2 minutes, stirring occasionally. Add bananas and stir until evenly coated and bananas are cooked through and soft.

Serve immediately over frozen yogurt. Makes 8 servings.

## Tropical Fruit Saronno
Dole

3 small, firm Dole
   bananas, peeled
2 tablespoons lemon juice
1/2 cup packed light
   brown sugar
1/4 cup butter or
   margarine
1 cup fresh Dole Tropical
   Gold Pineapple cut
   into chunks
1/2 teaspoon ground
   cinnamon
2 tablespoons
   amaretto liqueur
2 tablespoons brandy
Vanilla ice cream,
   for serving
Slivered almonds,
   for garnish
Fresh mint sprigs,
   for garnish

Cut bananas in half lengthwise, then crosswise into quarters. Drizzle with lemon juice.

Heat brown sugar and butter in a 10-inch nonstick skillet over medium heat until the sugar is melted and caramelized. Add bananas and pineapple chunks; cook slowly for 1-2 minutes, until heated and glazed, stirring gently. Sprinkle with cinnamon.

In a large metal spoon or ladle, carefully ignite the liqueur and brandy. Pour over the fruit mixture in the skillet and heat for a few minutes.

Serve warm over ice cream. Garnish with almonds and fresh mint, if desired. Makes 4 servings.

## Nectarine Ice Cream
WesPak

6-8 WesPak nectarines
   (7 cups pureed)
Juice of 1 lemon
3 cups sugar, divided
1/3 cup light corn syrup
4 eggs
1/4 teaspoon salt
1 tablespoon peach
   brandy (optional)
3 cups whipping cream
2 tablespoons
   vanilla extract
1/4 teaspoon
   almond extract
1-2 cups whole milk

Peel nectarines and cut into chunks. Puree with lemon juice in a food processor.

Pour into a large bowl and stir in 1 cup sugar and corn syrup. Refrigerate.

Place eggs in a mixing bowl and beat until thick (5 minutes). Gradually add 2 cups sugar, salt, peach brandy and cream. Beat well.

Transfer the mixture to a saucepan and cook over low heat, stirring constantly, for about 10-12 minutes, until slightly thickened (190°F). Add vanilla and almond extracts. Strain into a clean bowl.

Add nectarine puree to the egg mixture, beating (with clean beaters) on low until blended. Pour into the container of an ice cream machine. Add enough milk to fill to the suggested level. Chill overnight.

Freeze according to ice cream maker instructions. Makes 1 gallon.

**WESPAK.**

# Strawberry-Blueberry Buttermilk Ice Cream

Andrew & Williamson/SunnyRidge/
Curry & Company

### FRUIT PUREE

3 cups sliced fresh strawberries

3 cups fresh blueberries

3/4 cup sugar

1 teaspoon vanilla extract

1 1/2 tablespoons fresh lemon juice

### ICE CREAM

2 1/4 cups heavy cream, divided

1 1/2 cups buttermilk

1 1/2 cups sugar

6 large egg yolks

3/4 cup sour cream

1/8 teaspoon salt

To prepare the fruit puree, combine all ingredients in a medium saucepan. Bring to a boil, then simmer for 7-9 minutes, or until the mixture begins to thicken, skimming off any scum that rises to the surface. Remove from the heat and let cool. In a blender, puree the mixture in 2 batches. If desired, strain through a fine-meshed sieve. Let cool.

To prepare the ice cream, whisk together 1 1/2 cups cream, buttermilk, sugar and egg yolks in a heavy 4-quart saucepan. Cook over low heat, whisking constantly, for 12-15 minutes, or until the custard coats a metal spoon. Remove from the heat and let cool.

In a small bowl, whisk together 3/4 cup cream, sour cream and salt. Stir into the custard. Pour into a large bowl and set in a bowl of ice to cool. Blend in the fruit puree.

Freeze the mixture in an ice-cream maker according to the manufacturer's directions. Makes 10-12 servings (2 quarts).

Andrew Williamson FRESH PRODUCE  SUNNYRIDGE  CURRY & COMPANY

## Grape and Caramel Parfait
Pandol Bros., Inc.

4 Lorna Doone (or similar shortbread) cookies

2-4 scoops vanilla ice cream

1/2 cup Pandol red and green seedless grapes, sliced

Dollop of whipped cream

1 tablespoon sliced almonds

Caramel syrup

Break 2 cookies into small pieces and line the bottom of a parfait dish.

Add layers of ice cream, sliced grapes and the remaining cookies, broken into small pieces. Top with whipped cream.

Sprinkle sliced almonds on top and drizzle with caramel syrup to taste. Makes 1 serving.

*Recipe developed by Patricia Davis, employee of Pandol Bros., Inc.*

Where Fresh Gets Going.

## Red Grapefruit Baskets
Greene River Marketing/Tropicana

6 Tropicana* red grapefruits

Vanilla ice cream or frozen yogurt

4 teaspoons finely chopped peeled ginger

1/3 cup firmly packed light brown sugar

Fresh mint leaves, for garnish (optional)

Cut grapefruits in half horizontally. Cut all around the inside edges and between the membranes to release the segments. Place the segments in a bowl and cut into bite-size pieces.

Remove all the membrane from 6 of the grapefruit halves; discard the remaining halves.

Place a large scoop of ice cream in each hollowed-out grapefruit half. Cover and set in the freezer until ready to use.

Add ginger and sugar to the grapefruit in the bowl and toss gently. Cover and refrigerate.

To serve, spoon some grapefruit mixture over the ice cream in each grapefruit basket. Garnish with mint. Makes 6 servings.

*\* Brands may vary by region; substitute a similar product.*

# Chocolate Croissant Shell
## Vie de France

½ cup chocolate chips
1 Vie de France butter croissant
¾ cup raspberry ice cream

**OPTIONAL GARNISH**
¼ cup whipped cream
Raspberries

Melt chocolate chips in the microwave or over low heat in a saucepan.

Meanwhile, place a cooling rack on top of a cookie sheet. Slice croissant in half and place the halves side by side on the rack.

Pour the melted chocolate over the croissant halves, coating the entire surface. Let sit for about 15 minutes, or until the chocolate is firm.

Fill the bottom half of the croissant with ice cream and place the other half on top. If desired, serve with whipped cream and raspberries. Makes 1 serving.

# Café Ladyfinger Dessert
## Starbucks Coffee

2 3-ounce packages ladyfingers, split

1 cup strong brewed Starbucks coffee (any variety), cooled, divided

1 8-ounce package Philadelphia cream cheese, softened

2 cups cold milk

2 1.5-ounce packages Jell-O vanilla-flavor instant pudding

1 8-ounce tub Cool Whip whipped topping, thawed, divided

Brush the cut-sides of ladyfingers evenly with ¼ cup coffee. Arrange on the bottom and up the sides of a 2-quart serving bowl.

Place cream cheese and remaining coffee in a large bowl and beat with a whisk until blended. Gradually beat in milk until smooth. Add dry pudding mixes and beat for 2 minutes. Stir in half of Cool Whip. Spoon the mixture into the prepared bowl.

Refrigerate for 1 hour. Top with the remaining Cool Whip just before serving. Makes 12 servings.

# Chocolate Peanut Butter Passion Bars
## Ghirardelli

1/3 cup vegetable oil
2 eggs
1 pouch Ghirardelli* Triple Chocolate Brownie Mix
1 cup peanuts, chopped

**PEANUT BUTTER FILLING**
1 1/4 cups (14-ounce can) sweetened condensed milk
1/2 cup peanut butter

Preheat oven to 350°F. Lightly grease a 13-by-9-by-2-inch pan.

In a medium bowl, stir together oil and eggs. Add brownie mix and peanuts; stir until moistened. Press half of the brownie mixture into the pan, reserving the remainder for topping.

To make the filling, stir sweetened condensed milk and peanut butter in a medium bowl until smooth. Spread evenly over the brownie layer in the pan.

Drop rounded teaspoonfuls of the reserved brownie mixture over the peanut butter layer.

Bake for 25-30 minutes, or until the top is set. Cool thoroughly before cutting. Makes 24 bars.

*\* Brands may vary by region; substitute a similar product.*

GHIRARDELLI
CHOCOLATE
MOMENTS OF TIMELESS PLEASURE®

# Chocolate Chip Paisley Blondies
## The Hershey Company

3/4 cup (1 1/2 sticks) butter or margarine, softened

3/4 cup granulated sugar

3/4 cup packed light brown sugar

3 eggs

1 teaspoon vanilla extract

2 cups all-purpose flour

2 teaspoons baking powder

1/4 teaspoon salt

2 cups (12 ounces) semi-sweet chocolate chips

1/2 cup chopped nuts

1/2 cup Hershey's Syrup*

Preheat oven to 350°F. Grease a 13-by-9-by-2-inch baking pan.

Beat butter, granulated sugar and brown sugar until well blended. Add eggs one at a time, beating well after each addition. Stir in vanilla.

Stir together flour, baking powder and salt; beat into the butter mixture. Stir in chocolate chips and nuts.

Spread half of the batter (about 2 1/2 cups) in the prepared pan. Spoon syrup over the top; evenly spread over the surface to within 1/2 inch of the edges. Drop teaspoonfuls of the remaining batter over the syrup so the surface is almost completely covered. (As the blondies bake, the syrup showing in the spaces between the batter will form a paisley effect.)

Bake for 35-40 minutes, or until lightly browned. Cool completely in the pan on a wire rack. Cut into bars. Makes about 36 bars.

*Brands may vary by region; substitute a similar product.*

# Classic Raisin Oatmeal Cookies
## Sun-Maid Growers

3/4 cup butter or margarine, softened

1 cup brown sugar, packed

1/2 cup sugar

1/4 cup milk

1 large egg

1 teaspoon vanilla extract

1 cup all-purpose flour

1 teaspoon ground cinnamon

1/2 teaspoon baking soda

1/4 teaspoon salt

3 cups quick or old-fashioned oats

1 cup Sun-Maid raisins

1 cup coarsely chopped nuts (optional)

Preheat oven to 350°F.

Beat butter, sugars, milk, egg and vanilla in a large bowl until light and fluffy.

In a separate bowl, combine flour, cinnamon, baking soda and salt. Gradually add to the butter mixture, mixing well.

Stir in oats, raisins and nuts.

Drop the dough by tablespoonfuls onto ungreased cookie sheets. Bake for 12-15 minutes. For a softer cookie, bake until the edges are golden brown and the tops just set. For a crisper cookie, bake until the tops are golden brown.

Remove from the cookie sheets and let cool on wire racks. Makes 3 dozen cookies.

# Banana Nut Cookie Sandwich
## J&J Snack Foods

2 Kirkland Signature
   oatmeal cookies

1/2 cup marshmallow fluff and/or
   chocolate-hazelnut spread

1/2 banana, diced into
   1/4-inch pieces

1/2 cup of your favorite
   chopped nuts

Place 1 cookie flat side up on a dessert plate.

Spread half of the marshmallow fluff or chocolate-hazelnut spread on the cookie.

Top with diced banana and sprinkle with chopped nuts.

Spread remaining marshmallow fluff or chocolate-hazelnut spread on the second cookie and place on top. Makes 1 serving.

## Holiday Caramel Chex Mix
### General Mills

**4 cups** popped popcorn

**2 cups** *each* of Corn Chex and Rice Chex (these are found in Triple Chex cereal)

**1 cup** Kirkland Signature mixed nuts

**1/2 cup** butter or margarine, cut up

**3/4 cup** packed brown sugar

**1/4 cup** light corn syrup

**1/2 cup** white vanilla baking chips

**1/2 cup** sweetened dried cranberries

Preheat oven to 250°F.

Remove and discard any unpopped kernels from the popped popcorn.

In an ungreased large roasting pan, mix popcorn, cereal and nuts; set aside.

In a 1 1/2-quart saucepan, heat butter, brown sugar and corn syrup to boiling over medium heat, stirring frequently. Pour over the cereal mixture, stirring until evenly coated.

Bake for 1 hour, stirring every 15 minutes. Spread on waxed paper or foil to cool, about 15 minutes, stirring occasionally to break up.

In a 1-quart saucepan, heat baking chips over low heat, stirring frequently, until melted and smooth. Add 3 cups of the cooled cereal mixture to the melted chips; toss gently until evenly coated. Spread on waxed paper or foil. Cool for about 30 minutes, or until set.

In a serving bowl, mix both cereal mixtures and cranberries. Store in an airtight container. Makes 18 servings (1/2 cup each).

**Nutritional information:** Each serving has 230 calories, 2 g protein, 28 g carbohydrates, 12 g fat, 5 g saturated fat, 15 mg cholesterol, 1 g fiber, 140 mg sodium.

## Pumpkin Pecan Spice Streusel Muffins
### Kirkland Signature/Kerry

**1** 15-ounce can pumpkin

**1/2 cup** applesauce

**1 cup** water

**1** 16-ounce box angel food cake mix (add-water-only variety)

**2 tablespoons** pumpkin pie spice

**2 cups** Kirkland Signature Spiced Pecan cereal

***STREUSEL***

**1 cup** Kirkland Signature Pecan Spice cereal

**1 cup** flour

**1 cup** granulated sugar

**2 teaspoons** pumpkin pie spice

**1/2 cup** melted butter

Preheat oven to 350°F.

Combine all streusel ingredients in a bowl and mix until blended; set aside.

Place pumpkin, applesauce and water in a bowl and stir until blended.

In another bowl, combine cake mix, pumpkin pie spice and cereal. Stir into the pumpkin mixture.

Scoop the muffin batter into 24 greased muffin cups. Sprinkle the top of each muffin with streusel mix.

Bake for 35-45 minutes, or until the tops spring back when touched with gentle pressure. Makes 24 muffins.

# Churros Spanish-Style (Churros con Chocolate)

## J&J Snack Foods

Take home some delicious Double Twisted Churros from Costco's Food Court, or prepare J&J Snack Foods' Gourmet Double Twisted Churros (available in the freezer case at some Costcos) following the directions on the package. To serve in the traditional Spanish style, roll churros in granulated sugar. (For a flavorful twist, mix some cinnamon in with the sugar.*) While the churros are warming, prepare this delicious authentic chocolate dip to dunk them in.

**CHOCOLATE DIP**

4 ounces dark chocolate

2 cups milk, divided

1 tablespoon cornstarch

4 tablespoons sugar

Place chocolate and 1 cup milk in a saucepan over medium heat. Stir until the chocolate melts.

Dissolve cornstarch in the remaining milk. Using a whisk, slowly add to the melted chocolate mixture.

Whisk in sugar.

Reduce the heat to low and cook, whisking constantly, until it thickens, about 5 minutes. Remove from the heat and continue to whisk until smooth.

Serve the warm chocolate dip in a coffee cup. Dunk the churros into the chocolate dip to enjoy as the Spanish do! Makes 2 servings.

*\* Cinnamon sugar mix is included in the Gourmet Double Twisted Churro package.*

Beverages

## Iced Coffee
### Kirkland Signature

**4 ounces Kirkland Signature coffee, brewed double strength**

**Sugar or sweetener to taste (optional)**

**1-2 ounces half-and-half or milk (optional)**

**Ice**

Let coffee cool for at least 5 minutes. Then pour into a tall glass, or into a blender if blending with ice.

Add sugar and half-and-half.

Add ice to the glass or blend with ice. Makes 1 serving.

**Note:** For iced coffee, make the coffee double strength, unless you are using espresso, which is strong enough. You will be pouring it over ice, which will dilute it.

**Coffee:** Start with fresh Kirkland Signature or San Francisco Bay* gourmet whole-bean coffee, available in 3-pound bags.

**Grind:** Make sure the coffee is ground properly for your chosen coffeemaker. Drip filter coffee should be ground to the rough consistency of sand. Percolator should be coarser, espresso much finer. Use a burr grinder with the proper setting for your coffeemaker. You can also use a blade grinder for 8-15 seconds.

**Water:** It is important to use fresh, cold water. If the tap water in your area is not very good, use bottled water. Never use distilled or soft water. Never use hot tap water, which has gone through your hot-water heater.

**Amount:** Use approximately 3 rounded tablespoons of ground coffee for every 4 ounces of water (twice the normal strength). Adjust to taste. If making espresso, you do not need to make the coffee double strength.

**Method:** Best methods are drip filter, vacuum, French press and espresso.

*\* Brands may vary by region; substitute a similar product.*

## Chocolate and Chocolate-Raspberry Iced Coffee
### Kirkland Signature

***CHOCOLATE ICED COFFEE***

**4 ounces Kirkland Signature coffee, brewed double strength**

**Sugar or sweetener to taste (optional)**

**1-2 ounces half-and-half or milk (optional)**

**1-2 tablespoons chocolate syrup**

**Ice**

Let coffee cool for at least 5 minutes. Then pour into a tall glass or blender.

Add sugar, half-and-half and chocolate syrup and stir well.

Add ice to the glass or blend with ice. Makes 1 serving.

***CHOCOLATE-RASPBERRY ICED COFFEE***

**1 pint fresh or frozen raspberries**

**2 tablespoons sugar**

**2 tablespoons water**

**Chocolate Iced Coffee**

Combine raspberries, sugar and water in a saucepan and cook over low heat until the raspberries break down, about 10 minutes. Continue cooking for a few minutes to thicken, if necessary. Let cool. Strain through cheesecloth to remove the seeds. Store, covered, in the refrigerator.

To make the iced coffee, add 1-2 tablespoons raspberry syrup to Chocolate Iced Coffee and stir well before adding ice. Makes 1 serving.

**Tip:** Experiment! Only you know how you like your coffee.

## Brazilian Berry Smoothie
Kirkland Signature/Bolthouse Farms

1 ¼ cups Kirkland
   Signature Bom Dia
   Açaí Berry with
   Blueberry Juice
½ cup vanilla yogurt
1 banana, sliced
4 strawberries, trimmed
1 cup ice

Combine all ingredients in a blender and blend until smooth. Makes 2 servings.

## Tropical Fruit Smoothie
Ready Pac Foods, Inc.

1  4-pound Ready Pac*
   Gourmet Fruit Bowl
½ cup plain yogurt
2 tablespoons honey
2-3 tablespoons
   orange juice
1 tablespoon flax seeds
½ teaspoon
   vanilla extract
2-4 bamboo skewers
Fresh mint sprigs
   (optional)

Place 3 cups of chilled fruit in a heavy-duty blender jar. Add yogurt, honey, orange juice, flax seeds and vanilla. Secure the lid and blend until smooth, about 2-3 minutes.

Pour into two 16-ounce or four 8-ounce glasses.

Place 3 chunks of fruit on each bamboo skewer. Reserve the remaining fruit, covered, in the refrigerator for another use.

Garnish the smoothies with fruit kabobs and mint sprigs. Makes 2-4 servings.

*Brands may vary by region; substitute a similar product.*

## Ruby Red Tropical Smoothie
### Apple & Eve

**2 cups sliced bananas**

**1 cup trimmed strawberries, fresh or frozen**

**1 cup Apple & Eve\* Ruby Red Grapefruit Juice Cocktail, chilled**

**1 cup pineapple juice, chilled**

**1 cup crushed ice**

**Fresh fruit, for garnish (optional)**

In a blender, combine bananas, strawberries, juices and ice. Blend until smooth.

Pour into glasses and garnish with fresh fruit. Makes 4 servings.

*\* Brands may vary by region; substitute a similar product.*

## Grape and Kiwi Smoothie
### Trucco/Castle Rock Vineyards

**$^3/_4$ cup sugar-free lemonade**

**$^1/_2$ cup whole milk**

**3 Trucco Italian kiwis, peeled and diced**

**$^1/_2$ cup Castle Rock Vineyards red or green seedless grapes**

Combine lemonade, milk and kiwis in a blender. Blend on high speed until the mixture is smooth.

Add grapes and blend on high speed again until smooth. Serve immediately. Makes 2 servings.

**Tip:** Substitute any sugar-free drink for lemonade in this recipe.

# Berry Chocolate Smoothie
## Kirkland Signature/Cliffstar

2 cups Kirkland Signature Cranberry Juice Cocktail, chilled

2 1/2 cups frozen strawberries

1 cup strawberry yogurt

2 tablespoons confectioners' sugar

1/4 cup chocolate chips

Put juice, strawberries, yogurt and sugar in a food processor and spin on the highest setting until smooth.

Add chocolate chips and pulse until the desired consistency is reached.

Pour into glasses. Serve immediately. Makes 3-4 servings.

# Citrus Berry Cooler
## Tropicana

1 1/2 cups Tropicana Pure Premium Orange Juice

1 1/2 cups lemon sorbet

1/2 cup raspberry sorbet

Raspberries, for garnish

Mint leaves, for garnish

Place juice and lemon sorbet in a blender. Cover and blend until smooth.

Drop 2 small spoonfuls of raspberry sorbet into each glass. Top each serving with a quarter of the orange juice mixture. Divide spoonfuls of the remaining sorbet evenly between the glasses. Top with the remaining orange juice mixture.

Garnish with raspberries and mint. Serve immediately. Makes 2 servings.

**Nutritional information:** Each serving has 350 calories, 1 g protein, 86 g carbohydrates, 0 g fat, 0 mg cholesterol, 0 g fiber, 30 mg sodium.

**Tips:** Chill the glasses in the freezer for up to 2 hours before using. Substitute strawberry, peach or mango sorbet for the raspberry sorbet, if desired.

**Tropicana**

# Index

# Supplier Listing

**ACH Foods, Inc /Mazola Oils**, 115
www.mazola.com
1-866-4MAZOLA

**Acme Food Sales**, 198
www.acmefood.com
206-762-5150

**Aconex**, 31, 112
www.aconex.cl
011-56-2-9413312

**AJ Trucco, Inc.**, 219
www.truccodirect.com
866-AJTRUCC

**Alaska Glacier Seafoods**, 155
www.alaskaglacierseafoods.com
907-790-3590

**Alpine Fresh, Inc.**, 46, 64, 73, 192, 201
www.alpinefresh.com
800-292-8777

**Alsum Produce**, 82
www.alsum.com
800-236-5127

**AMC Direct Inc.**, 177
www.amcdirect.net

**American Fish & Seafood Co.**, 155
www.americanfish.com
213-612-0350

**American Pride Seafoods**, 165
www.americanprideseafoods.com
508-997-0031

**Andrew & Williamson Fresh Produce**, 207
www.andrew-williamson.com
619-661-6000

**Ann's House of Nuts**, 171
800-466-2667

**Anthony Vineyards, Inc.**, 48, 49
www.anthonyvineyards.com
661-858-6211

**Apio, Inc.**, 73
www.apioinc.com
800-454-1355

**Apple & Eve**, 219
www.appleandeve.com
800-969-8018

**Aquachile**, 147
www aquachile.com
877-522-8420

**Aquamericas/Fresh Tilapia Fillets**, 160
www.aquamericas.com
800-569-8323

**Atlantic Cape Fisheries**, 166
www.atlanticcapes.com
508-990-9040

**Atlantic Veal & Lamb, Inc**, 40, 130, 131, 132
800-222-VEAL

**Australian Lamb Company**, 96, 97, 98
www.australianlamb.com

**Bakemark USA**, 186
www.yourbakemark.com
866-232-8575

**Bard Valley Medjool Date Growers**, 52
www.bardmedjool.com
928-726-9191

**Barry Callebaut**, 203
www.barry-callebaut.com
802-524-9711

**BC Hot House Foods, Inc.**, 140
www.bchothouse.com
800-663-1889

**Bee Stweet Citrus**, 187
www.beecitrus.com
559-834-5345

**Best Brands Corp.**, 116, 178
www.bestbrandscorp.com
800-866-3300

**Bimbo Bakeries USA**, 20
wwwBimbobakeriesusa.com
877-224-7374

**Blossom Hill**, 189
www.blossomhillapricots.com
209-892-6500

**Booth Ranches, LLC.**, 183
www.boothranches.com
559-626-7653

**Borton & Sons, Inc.**, 111
www.bortonfruit.com
509-966-3905

**Boskovich Farms, Inc.**, 141
www.boskovichfarms.com
805-487-2299

**Bravante Produce**, 182
www.bravanteproduce.com

**Bybee Foods, LLC.**, 42, 74
www.bybeefoods.com
509-542-0018

**Calavo Growers**, 119
www.calavo.com
805-525-1245

**California Avocado Commission**, 119
www.californiaavocado.com

**California Pear Advisory Board**, 27
www.calpear.com
916-441-0432

**California Walnut Board**, 138
www.walnuts.org
916-932-7070

**Cal-Maine Foods**, 21
www.calmainefoods.com
601-948-6813

**Camanchaca Inc.**, 148
www.camanchacainc.com
800-335-7553

**Campbells**, 137, 173
www.campbellsoup.com
800-257-8443

**Cardile Bros. Mushroom, Inc.**, 34, 35
www.cardilebrothersmushrooms.com
610-268-2470

**Castlerock Vineyards**, 219
www.castlerockvineyards.com
661-721-8717

**Cecelia Packing Corporation**, 52
www.ceceliapack.com
559-626-5000

**Cedar Key Aquaculture Farm**, 167
www.cedarkeyclams.com

**Chelan Fresh**, 181
www.chelanfresh.com
509-682-3854

**Chestnut Hill Farms**, 170
www.chfusa.com
305-592-6969

**Chicken of the Sea**, 66, 67
www.chickenofthesea.com

**Chilean Avocado Importers Assoc.**, 42
www.chileanavocado.org
831-689-0962

**Christopher Ranch**, 128
www.christopherranch.com
408-847-1100

**Citterio USA**, 61
www.citterio.com
800-435-8888

**Clear Springs Foods**, 164
www.clearsprings.com
800-635-8211

**CM Holtzinger Fruit Co.**, 39
www.holtzingerfruit.com
509-249-4232

**Columbia Marketing International**, 200, 201
www.cmiapples.com
509-663-1955

**ConAgra Foods**, 68
www.conagrafoods.com
813-241-1500

**Consolidated Catfish Products**, 153
800-CAT-FISH